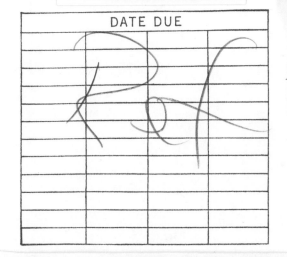

DATE DUE			

Baseball's All-Star Game

**Ted Williams (left) and Joe DiMaggio exchange laughs
prior to the 1946 midsummer classic.**

Baseball's All-Star Game: A Game-by-Game Guide

by
Jeff Lenburg

McFarland & Company, Inc., Publishers
Jefferson, North Carolina, and London

NI

Other books by Jeff Lenburg

Steve Martin: The Unauthorized Biography
(with Randy Skretvedt and Greg Lenburg)
The Encyclopedia of Animated Cartoon Series
The Three Stooges Scrapbook
(with Joan Howard Maurer and Greg Lenburg)
Dustin Hoffman: Hollywood's Antihero
Dudley Moore: An Informal Biography
Peekaboo: The Story of Veronica Lake
The Great Cartoon Directors
Not Just a Stooge
(with Joe Besser and Greg Lenburg)

Library of Congress Cataloguing-in-Publication Data

Lenburg, Jeff.
Baseball's All-Star Game.

Includes index.
1. All-Star Baseball Game — History.
2. Baseball — United States — History.
3. Baseball — United States — Records.
I. Title.
GV878.L46   1986   796.357'78409   86-2708

ISBN 0-89950-231-8 (acid-free natural paper)

Printed in the United States of America.

McFarland   Box 611   Jefferson NC 28640

To Steve Koza, a genius
in his own right,
and his lovely wife, Jo

Table of Contents

All Star Review   1

1933	5
1934	8
1935	11
1936	14
1937	17
1938	21
1939	24
1940	27
1941	30
1942	33
1943	36
1944	39
1946	42
1947	46
1948	49
1949	53
1950	57
1951	61
1952	64
1953	67
1954	71
1955	75
1956	79
1957	82
1958	86
1959 (Game One)	89
1959 (Game Two)	93
1960 (Game One)	96
1960 (Game Two)	100

1961 (Game One)   104
1961 (Game Two)   108
1962 (Game One)   111
1962 (Game Two)   114
1963   117
1964   120
1965   123
1966   126
1967   129
1968   133
1969   136
1970   140
1971   144
1972   147
1973   150
1974   154
1975   158
1976   161
1977   164
1978   167
1979   171
1980   175
1981   178
1982   182
1983   185
1984   189
1985   192
1986   195

Appendix I. Team Statistics   199
Appendix II. Individual Records   201
Appendix III. Most Valuable Players   205

Index   207

**Lou Gehrig (left), Jimmie Foxx, and Babe Ruth
before the 1935 All-Star game.**

Roger Maris (left), Willie Mays, and Mickey Mantle.

All-Star Review

Baseball's "dream game," better known as the All-Star game, has been a favorite now of baseball fans for more than fifty glorious years. Originally intended as "a one-game promotion" to pit players from both leagues in a mid-season exhibition, perhaps nobody ever dreamed it would turn into such an annual spectacle.

The All-Star Game was the brainchild of a gentleman by the name of F.C. Lane, who, in 1914, first proposed the idea of sponsoring an interleague contest. Until now, Lane has never received appropriate credit for his actions, but his entire plan was made public in an article he penned for *Baseball Magazine* in 1915.

Lane's concept varied slightly from the one being utilized today, however. His dream was for the players from both leagues — the National and the American — to team up against each other in a series of seven consecutive games, à la the World Series, to crown a champion of this annual competition. Unfortunately, Lane's unique proposal was way ahead of its time and was shot down by the commissioner and baseball owners, who feared that players' salaries were much too high then to make the games profitable.

While Lane regrettably abandoned his dream game, in 1933, Arch Ward, sports editor of the *Chicago Tribune,* made the game a reality. With salaries now severely trimmed back after the great Depression, the owners found Ward's revamped proposal more to their liking. The contest would be held to one game — billed as "The Game of the Century" — and would be scheduled as a special event in conjunction with the Chicago Century of Progress Exposition which Ward had been organizing to celebrate the city's 100th anniversary.

Ward did have his share of obstacles to hurdle in pushing through the idea, however. Commissioner Kenesaw Mountain Landis played an important role in breaking the stalemate that brought about the first midsummer contest. The owners wanted the *Tribune* to guarantee both leagues against any losses if, for some reason, the contest was postponed for rain or because of some unforseeable circumstance. Landis worked on the owners' behalf in negotiating such a clause with the *Tribune.*

Another catch-all which concerned the owners was whether such a contest would bring about a rash of injuries to key players and jeopardize pennant hopes for their teams. This time, Ward stepped in to make a counterproposal: The contest would be "a one-year spectacular" (he used the word long before it came into general use as a noun) and the gate receipts would be earmarked for a retired players fund.

Ward was in from then on, and Chicago's Comiskey Park became the site of the inaugural game on July 6, 1933. Players were selected to team rosters by fan voting (Babe Ruth polled just over 100,000 votes, a far cry from the million-plus votes some players receive today), while the choice of managers was almost automatic. (A number of Chicago newspapers published ballots for fans to mail in, with popular voting acting as an advisory to manager selections.) John McGraw, the recently retired manager of the New York Giants, and Connie Mack, still the manager of the Philadelphia Athletics, were named to pilot the two teams in their first interleague confrontation.

Even though the event was scheduled during the bottom of the Depression and four months after President Franklin D. Roosevelt took office, 47,595 screaming fans jammed inside Comiskey Park for this special interleague affair. The atmosphere was all that Ward had imagined, too. Fans gawked at "all the talent collected on the field," and the excitement of the day helped spread baseball fever throughout the Windy City that much more.

Babe Ruth headed the list of noted All-Stars, and his clutch home run—the first in All-Star game history—led the Americans to a 4–2 victory over the Nationals. This seemingly uneventful game created so much interest among the baseball communities of America—and, surprisingly, the owners—that it became an annual fixture. Each year the commissioner's office alternated between American and National league ballparks to offer fans in various cities a chance to cheer on their favorites.

Year by year, the games have been dramatic and eventful. Who can forget Carl Hubbell's phenomenal five consecutive strikeouts in the 1934 game? Or Ted Williams blasting a blooper pitch by Rip Sewell to win the 1946? Or Dizzy Dean taking a carom off the bat of Earl Averill to end his career? Or Yogi Berra's home run over the Los Angeles Coliseum's "impossible" right-centerfield fence—where Dodger Wally Moon made famous his "Moonshots"—to beat Don Drysdale? Or Reggie Jackson's record 520-foot blast at Briggs Stadium? Or Steve Garvey's heroic MVP performance as a write-in candidate following a glandular infection in the 1974 contest?

Fan voting has played an important and often controversial role since the method was revised in 1934. Also, the size of each team has increased throughout the years, from 20 players in 1934 to 25 in 1939 to 30 in 1982. From 1935 through 1946, managers from each league selected players from both All-Star squads and used their own discretion, of course. New York Yankees manager Joe McCarthy still holds the record for having most opportunities to pick starting lineups; he piloted a record *seven* American League teams.

All-Star voting also went through another major overhaul from 1947 through 1957, when fans again elected the star players with the Associated

Press tabulating the results. But when Cincinnati fans overzealously stuffed the ballot boxes in 1957, Commissioner Ford Frick returned the voting chores back to the players, managers, and coaches the following year. This method of voter polling was finally changed in 1969 — using the same process fans use today — when Commissioner Bowie Kuhn returned voting to the fans. Since then, over 71 million fans participate annually in All-Star voting, which is a far cry from 1960 when only two million votes were counted.

Ward's midsummer classic experienced only two other interruptions. In 1945, during World War II, President Roosevelt ordered that no game be played, and from 1959 through 1962 the event was expanded to two contests a year for the purpose of raising more money for the players' retirement fund. In 1963 the extra game was abolished when it was agreed that one interleague match a year was enough.

Today, however, baseball fans just can't seem to get enough.

July 6, 1933

Comiskey Park

Chicago's Comiskey Park, one of the oldest ball parks in the majors, was the site of the first All-Star game. It was billed as "baseball's dream game" and "the game of the century" and never before had so much talent been brought together on one field. Led by the mighty war club of 38-year-old slugger Babe Ruth, the American League made it a memorable "first" by beating the National League 4–2 before 47,595 screaming fans.

The game proved to be a jubilant affair, but mostly for American League supporters. Yankee hurler Vernon "Lefty" Gomez, a two-time 20-game winner, dueled St. Louis Cardinals' southpaw Bill Hallahan. Hallahan was the ace of the Cardinals' staff and had notched two victories in the 1931 World Series.

The American Leaguers sported their regular home uniforms, while the National League squad, at the urging of the league president John Heydler, wore special uniforms for the occasion. These outfits were steel gray with the words "National League" emblazoned in blue letters across the front of their shirts.

But Ruth's third-inning home-run dramatics put the American League on the scoreboard first and proved to be the margin of victory. It was the type of clutch situation long associated with his career. Ruth had reached the age where he could no longer make sparkling plays in the field, but could he hit! And hit he did.

Still upset over his strikeout from his first plate appearance, Ruth rode Bill Hallahan's two-strike pitch over the right field wall, scoring Charley Gehringer, to make the score 3–0. The Bambino, his pet name, enjoyed being in the spotlight, it brought the best out of him. He had led the Yankees almost single-handedly to several World Series championships with his powerful bat. Thus, it was fitting that such an All-Star classic had arrived. After all, what would it have been like without Babe Ruth?

Ruth turned from hero to goat in the sixth inning, however, when he misplayed pitcher Lonnie Warneke's liner into a triple. The official scorer ruled it a hit, but everyone in the stadium knew otherwise. Ruth got part of the webbing of his glove on the ball but dropped it. As a result, Warneke later

The 1933 All-Star Game

National League	AB	R	H	PO	A	E
Martin (Cardinals) 3b	4	0	0	0	3	0
Frisch (Cardinals) 2b	4	1	2	5	3	0
Klein (Phillies) rf	4	0	1	3	0	0
P. Waner (Reds) rf	0	0	0	0	0	0
Hafey (Reds) lf	4	0	1	0	0	0
Terry (Giants) 1b	4	0	2	7	2	0
Berger (Braves) cf	4	0	0	4	0	0
Bartell (Phillies) ss	2	0	0	0	3	0
Traynor (Pirates) ph	1	0	1	0	0	0
Hubbell (Giants) p	0	0	0	0	0	0
Cuccinello (Dodgers) ph	1	0	0	0	0	0
Wilson (Cardinals) c	1	0	0	2	0	0
O'Doul (Giants) ph	1	0	0	0	0	0
Hartnett (Cubs) c	1	0	0	2	0	0
Hallahan (Cardinals) p	1	0	0	1	0	0
Warneke (Cubs) p	1	1	1	0	0	0
English (Cubs) ss	1	0	0	0	0	0
Totals	34	2	8	24	8	0

American League	AB	R	H	PO	A	E
Chapman (Yankees) lf–cf	5	0	1	1	0	0
Gehringer (Tigers) 2b	3	1	0	1	3	0
Ruth (Yankees) rf	4	1	2	1	0	0
West (Browns) cf	0	0	0	0	0	0
Gehrig (Yankees) 1b	2	0	0	12	0	1
Simmons (White Sox) cf–lf	4	0	1	4	0	0
Dykes (White Sox) 1b	3	1	2	2	4	0
Cronin (Senators) ss	3	1	1	2	4	0
R. Ferrell (Red Sox) c	3	0	0	4	0	0
Gomez (Yankees) p	1	0	1	0	0	0
Crowder (Senators) p	1	0	0	0	0	0
Averill (Indians) ph	1	0	1	0	0	0
Grove (Athletics) p	1	0	0	0	0	0
Totals	31	4	9	27	11	1

```
National League ........................ 0 0 0 0 0 2 0 0 0 – 2
American League........................ 0 1 2 0 0 1 0 0 x – 4
```

DP—Americans 1, Nationals 1. LOB—Americans 10, Nationals 5. 2B—Traynor. 3B—Warneke. HR—Ruth, Frisch. SB—Gehringer. RBIs—Martin, Frisch, Ruth (2), Gomez, Averill.

National League	IP	H	R	ER	BB	SO
Hallahan (L)	2	2	3	3	5	1
Warneke	4	6	1	1	0	2
Hubbell	2	1	0	0	1	1

American League	IP	H	R	ER	BB	SO
Gomez (W)	3	2	0	0	0	1
Crowder	3	3	2	2	0	0
Grove	3	3	0	0	0	3

---

scored on third baseman Pepper Martin's scorching single to left, followed by an even bigger blow off the bat of slugging sensation Frankie Frisch. With the announcement of Frisch, Gomez departed and manager Connie Mack brought in Washington Senator hurler Alvin Crowder, affectionately known as "The General," to pitch. The move proved fatal as Frisch, matching Ruth muscle for muscle, lost the battle. Frisch powered Crowder's second pitch into the right field seats to even the score at two.

Not to be outscored, the American League came roaring back in the bottom half of the sixth to take the lead 4-2. Third baseman Jimmie Dykes got things rolling when he scored on a single by Cleveland Indians' Earl Averill, who was batting for Crowder.

For Ruth the boos turned back to cheers in the eighth when he made a spectacular leaping catch in right to thwart a serious scoring drive by the National League. With the Americans leading by two runs, the Nationals had a runner on first with two outs when Cincinnati outfielder and N.L. batting champion, Chick Hafey, stepped up to the plate. Facing Lefty Grove, now hurling for the Americans, Hafey took one of Lefty's high-strike fastballs deep to the wall in right. The crowd stood silently as the drive seemed destined to clear the wall for a home run. Ruth saved the game with a split-second, ballerina-type catch which robbed Hafey of a home run.

Besides a heavy hitting attack, the American League's staff of hurlers managed to keep the National League hitters at bay for most of the afternoon. Gomez pitched a strong three innings of scoreless ball before he gave way to Crowder, who pitched three-hit ball during his three innings but allowed two costly runs. Philadelphia Athletics' Lefty Grove then took over for Crowder and hurled a perfect seventh, with New York Giants veteran Carl Hubbell yielding only one hit in the final two innings of relief.

Ruth's batting mate, Lou Gehrig, another member of the famous Bronx Bombers, went hitless in his first All-Star game appearance. In addition, there were several other players on the field who eventually gained entry into baseball's Hall of Fame. They included Al Simmons, Charley Gehringer, Joe Cronin, Earl Averill, Bill Terry, Paul Waner, Frankie Frisch, Gabby Hartnett, and Pie Traynor.

Two other masters of baseball were also present: manager John McGraw, aged 60, lured out of retirement to pilot the first all-star National League squad, and the stately 71-year-old Connie Mack, the American League's skipper.

Yet, in the end, the hero was Babe Ruth.

July 10, 1934

Polo Grounds

Carl Hubbell mystified the opposition during the second All-Star clash by striking out a record six batters — five in succession — in three innings. Since then, his six-strikeouts feat has been equaled by only a handful of players, but not his five consecutive strikeouts string.

Hubbell was appointed the starter by manager Bill Terry, who firmly believed the left-hander's screwball would baffle American League hitters. Hubbell, en route to a 21–12 season with a league-leading 2.30 earned run average, did just that. He held the Americans scoreless, even though his team lost 9–7 at New York's famous Polo Grounds.

"King Carl," Hubbell's moniker, started off a bit shaky in the early part of the proceedings, but settled down after Charley Gehringer singled to open the first inning. Gehringer took an extra base when Wally Berger bobbled the ball. Heinie Manush then walked to set the stage for Babe Ruth. The King of Swat worked the count to one ball and two strikes, and then stood puzzled as Hubbell sneaked a screwball that just nipped the outside corner for a called third strike. Ruth didn't argue, but walked away wondering where Hubbell's pitch came from.

Lou Gehrig was Hubbell's next concern. Hub took six pitches to strike Gehrig out, with Lou swinging on the last pitch. Gehringer and Manush then pulled a double steal, following Hubbell's first pitch to Jimmie Foxx, the fifth batter of the inning. The crowd of 48,363 gasped in horror as it appeared as if the Americans were going to score. But Hubbell kept up his shield of resistance by striking out Foxx, swinging, to end the inning.

Frankie Frisch gave Hubbell room to breath in the bottom of the first by belting a homer to left to stake the Nationals to a quick 1–0 lead. That was Frisch's second homer in as many All-Star games, one left-handed and one right-handed.

In the second inning, Hubbell continued his mastery over the opposition. His magic screwball did the trick, whiffing Al Simmons, two-time A.L. batting champion, on four pitches, and Joe Cronin, one of baseball's most dependable hitters and former MVP. Cronin also whiffed on four pitches, notching Hubbell's fifth strikeout of the game and fifth in succession.

The 1934 All-Star Game

American League	AB	R	H	PO	A	E
Gehringer (Tigers) 2b	3	0	2	2	1	0
Manush (Senators) lf	2	0	0	0	0	0
Ruffing (Yankees) p	1	0	1	0	0	0
Harder (Indians) p	2	0	0	1	0	0
Ruth (Yankees) lf	2	1	0	0	0	0
Chapman (Yankees) rf	2	0	1	0	0	0
Gehrig (Yankees) 1b	4	1	0	11	1	1
Foxx (Athletics) 3b	5	1	2	1	2	0
Simmons (White Sox) cf–lf	5	3	3	3	0	0
Cronin (Senators) ss	5	1	2	2	8	0
Dickey (Yankees) c	2	1	1	4	0	0
Cochrane (Tigers) c	1	0	0	1	1	0
Gomez (Yankees) p	1	0	0	0	0	0
Averill (Indians) ph–rf	4	1	2	1	0	0
West (Browns) cf	0	0	0	1	0	0
Totals	39	9	14	27	13	1

National League	AB	R	H	PO	A	E
Frisch (Cardinals) 2b	3	3	2	0	1	0
Herman (Cubs) ph–2b	2	0	1	0	1	0
Traynor (Pirates) 3b	5	2	2	1	0	0
Medwick (Cardinals) lf	2	1	1	0	0	0
Klein (Cubs) ph–lf	3	0	1	1	0	0
Cuyler (Cubs) rf	2	0	0	2	0	0
Ott (Giants) ph–rf	2	0	0	0	1	0
Berger (Braves) cf	2	0	0	0	0	1
P. Waner (Pirates) ph–cf	2	0	0	1	0	0
Terry (Giants) 1b	3	0	1	4	0	0
Jackson (Giants) ss	2	0	0	0	1	0
Vaughan (Pirates) ss	2	0	0	4	0	0
Hartnett (Cubs) c	2	0	0	9	0	0
Lopez (Dodgers) c	2	0	0	5	1	0
Hubbell (Giants) p	0	0	0	0	0	0
Warneke (Cubs) p	0	0	0	0	0	0
Mungo (Dodgers) p	0	0	0	0	0	0
Martin (Cardinals) ph	0	1	0	0	0	0
Dean (Cardinals) p	1	0	0	0	0	0
Frankhouse (Braves) p	1	0	0	0	0	0
Totals	36	7	8	27	5	1

American League.......................... 0 0 0 2 6 1 0 0 0 – 9
National League .... 1 0 3 0 3 0 0 0 0 – 7

DP–Nationals 1. LOB–Americans 12, Nationals 5. 2B–Foxx, Simmons (2), Cronin, Averill, Herman. 3B–Chapman, Averill. HR–Frisch, Medwick. RBIs– Frisch, Medwick (3), Cronin (2), Averill (3), Foxx, Simmons, Ruffing (2), Traynor, Klein. SB–Gehringer, Manush, Traynor, Ott.

American League	IP	H	R	ER	BB	SO
Gomez	3	3	4	4	1	3
Ruffing	1	4	3	3	1	0
Harder (W)	5	1	0	0	0	0

National League	IP	H	R	ER	BB	SO
Hubbell	3	2	0	0	2	6
Warneke	1	3	4	4	3	1
Mungo (L)	1	4	4	4	2	1
Dean	3	5	1	1	1	4
Frankhouse	1	0	0	0	1	0

Umpires — Pfirman and Stark (N.L.), Owens and Moriarty (A.L.). Time — 2:44. Attendance — 48,363.

His string was finally broken by Bill Dickey, the hard-hitting Yankee catcher, who singled. But Lefty Gomez became strikeout victim number six to finish the inning and turn the Americans away from another scoring opportunity.

Lefty Gomez, Joe Cronin's choice to oppose Hubbell, left for the showers earlier than Hubbell. Joe Medwick blasted a Gomez fastball in the bottom of the third — a three-run shot — to put the Nationals in front 4-0. Hubbell would have gained the victory if his team hadn't lost their comfortable lead — and the game.

Without King Carl, the Nationals were ineffective. Hubbell's mound successors, Lon Warneke and Van Lingle Mungo, were ferociously mauled for eight runs in the fourth and fifth innings. The A.L.'s six runs also remains an All-Star high for runs scored in a single inning. Most of these runs were delivered on key hits by Earl Averill of Cleveland: a ringing triple in the fourth and a two-run double in the fifth.

But Bill Terry's team never gave up. In their half of the fifth, they drove across three runs and knocked Red Ruffing out of the box before he could retire a single batter. Mel Harder, Ruffing's replacement, closed the door on the Nationals by using a mixture of breaking curves and wicked fastballs to hold them scoreless during his five innings on the hill. Unlike later interleague exhibitions, a relief pitcher could go more than three innings, if necessary.

The Americans scored one more run in the sixth, and eventually won the game 9-7, overshadowing Hubbell's six-strikeout performance, but not people's memories of it.

July 8, 1935

Cleveland Municipal Stadium

The largest crowd in All-Star game history, some 69,812 spectators, jammed Cleveland Municipal Stadium on the banks of Lake Erie to watch the American League out–Foxx the National League 4–1.

The score was one run better than the winning margins of the first two All-Star contests, thanks to a clutch home run off the bat of Philadelphia Athletics slugger Jimmie Foxx. Foxx received some help from the Americans' starting pitcher, Lefty Gomez of the New York Yankees, whose performance alone sent the National League reeling to its third consecutive interleague defeat.

Gomez, sporting good stuff, started the game and held the opposition to three hits over six innings. It was – and still remains – the longest stint of any starter in All-Star game history, and for good reason. Managers Frankie Frisch of the National League and Mickey Cochrane of the American League, together the game's first player-managers, agreed that pitchers could go more than three innings if necessary. Cleveland Indians ace Mel (Chief) Harder, replacing Gomez and pitching before the hometown crowd, silenced the National League with one-hit ball over the final three innings of play to preserve the victory.

Starting for the National League was left-hander Bill Walker, a teammate of Frisch's on the St. Louis Cardinals, who posted a 13–8 record that season. Several other qualified hurlers were waiting in the wings, namely Hal Schumacher, who was not scheduled to start until the last minute, and pitching great Dizzy Dean. Unfortunately, Dean wasn't brought in until the final inning when the game was out of reach.

The American League hitters, headed by Jimmie Foxx, got to Walker early in the first inning. Foxx, who had two hits in three at bats, clubbed a two-run home run to put the American League ahead. Lou Gehrig, safe on a force play, scored. It was 2–0 American League.

Schumacher came in to replace Walker and went on to strike out five batters in four innings of work. His only trouble came in the second inning when Rollie Hemsley of the St. Louis Browns, playing for injured Yankee catcher Bill Dickey, tripled by a diving Joe Medwick in left. The Boston Red Sox's

The 1935 All-Star Game

National League	AB	R	H	PO	A	E
Martin (Cardinals) 3b	4	0	1	0	0	1
Vaughan (Pirates) ss	3	1	1	2	2	0
Ott (Giants) rf	4	0	0	1	0	0
Medwick (Cardinals) lf	3	0	0	0	0	0
Terry (Giants) 1b	3	0	1	5	1	0
Collins (Cardinals) 1b	1	0	0	2	0	0
Berger (Braves) cf	2	0	0	1	0	0
Moore (Giants) cf	2	0	0	1	0	0
Herman (Cubs) 2b	3	0	0	1	4	0
Wilson (Phillies) c	3	0	1	8	0	0
Whitehead (Cardinals) pr	0	0	0	0	0	0
Hartnett (Cubs) c	0	0	0	3	0	0
Walker (Cardinals) p	0	0	0	0	0	0
Mancuso (Giants) ph	1	0	0	0	0	0
Schumacher (Giants) p	1	0	0	0	1	0
P. Waner (Pirates) ph	1	0	0	0	0	0
Derringer (Reds) p	0	0	0	0	0	0
Dean (Cardinals) p	0	0	0	0	0	0
Totals	31	1	4	24	8	1

American League	AB	R	H	PO	A	E
Vosmik (Indians) rf	4	1	1	1	0	0
Gehringer (Tigers) 2b	3	0	2	1	3	0
Gehrig (Yankees) 1b	3	1	0	12	0	0
Foxx (Athletics) 3b	3	1	2	0	0	0
Bluege (Senators) 3b	0	0	0	0	0	0
Johnson (Athletics) lf	4	0	0	4	0	0
Chapman (Yankees) lf	0	0	0	0	0	0
Simmons (White Sox) cf	4	0	2	2	0	0
Cramer (Athletics) cf	0	0	0	0	0	0
Hemsley (Browns) c	4	1	1	6	0	0
Cronin (Red Sox) ss	4	0	0	1	4	0
Gomez (Yankees) p	2	0	0	0	2	0
Harder (Indians) p	1	0	0	0	1	0
Totals	32	4	8	27	10	0

National League .... 0 0 0 1 0 0 0 0 0 – 1
American League......................... 2 1 0 0 1 0 0 0 x – 4

DP – none. LOB – Americans 7, Nationals 5. 2B – Vaughan, Wilson, Gehringer, Simmons. 3B – Hemsley. HR – Foxx. RBIs – Foxx (3), Cronin, Terry.

National League	IP	H	R	ER	BB	SO
Walker (L)	2	3	3	3	1	2
Schumacher	4	4	1	1	1	5
Derringer	1	1	0	0	0	1
Dean	1	1	0	0	1	1

American League	IP	H	R	ER	BB	SO
Gomez (W)	6	3	1	1	2	4
Harder	3	1	1	0	0	1

Umpires — Ormsby and Geisel (A.L.), Magerkurth and Sears (N.L.). Time — 2:06. Attendance — 69,831.

———————————————

Joe Cronin followed with a towering fly ball to center, which was deep enough to score Hemsley from third. The American League now led 3-0.

The Americans' final tally came in the fifth when Foxx delivered again, this time a single scoring Cleveland Indians' slugger Joe Vosmik, a native Clevelander, who started his career playing in local sandlot ball. The score: American League 4, National League 0.

In order to avoid a shutout, the National League squad scored a run in the top of the fourth when Pittsburgh Pirates' shortstop Arky Vaughan doubled and scored the Nationals' only run of the game on Bill Terry's single.

The American League won 4-1.

Leading the eight-hit attack was Jimmie Foxx, Charley Gehringer, and Al Simmons, all with two hits apiece. Lou Gehrig failed to join the hit parade; he was hitless in his third All-Star game.

But the outcome might have been different without a ballplayer named Jimmie Foxx.

July 7, 1936

Fenway Park

A notorious hitters haven with its alluring Green Monster in left, Fenway Park proved to be just that as the National League posted its first victory, snapping a three-game losing streak 4–3.

Behind the airtight pitching of Dizzy Dean, throwing in his first All-Star game as a starter, the National League collected nine hits, with four members of the Chicago Cubs doing most of the damage. The game also featured Joe DiMaggio, who was hitting a crisp .358 with 60 RBIs and 11 home runs. DiMaggio, 20, with just three months of major league experience, became the first rookie to win a starting berth in All-Star competition. It was also his least memorable.

Dean, a member of the renowned St. Louis Cardinals "Gashouse Gang" and a 30-game winner, was the real story here. With a blazing fastball and dipping curveball, the crafty southpaw faced a minimum of nine batters in three innings, striking out three — two in succession (Michael "Pinky" Higgins and Lefty Grove) — in the third. Catcher Rick Ferrell was Dean's first victim, but outfielder Raymond Radcliff walked to break up Dean's chance of striking out three in a row.

New York Yankees' manager Joe McCarthy, who managed a record seven A.L. All-Star teams, was selected to pilot his first when Tiger manager Mickey Cochrane, the previously named skipper, suffered a nervous breakdown. McCarthy tabbed Lefty Grove, making his first All-Star start, to open the game for the Americans.

But the National League, piloted by Cub manager Charley Grimm, drew first blood in the second inning to make things definitely "Grimm" for the American League. Four of Grimm's Cub starters were involved in all the scoring. Outfielder Frank Demaree (Mel Ott replaced him in the eighth with his first All-Star appearance) and catcher Gabby Hartnett combined for the Nationals' first two runs. Then, in the bottom of the fifth, Augie Galan and Billy Herman added two more runs when Galan homered off the flagpole in right and Herman singled, scoring later on Joe Medwick's single to right, to make the score 4–0 Nationals.

Meanwhile, Carl Hubbell, relieving for Dean, baffled American League

The 1936 All-Star Game

American League	AB	R	H	PO	A	E
Appling (White Sox) ss	4	0	1	2	2	0
Gehringer (Tigers) 2b	3	0	2	2	1	0
DiMaggio (Yankees) rf	5	0	0	1	0	1
Gehrig (Yankees) 1b	2	1	1	7	0	0
Averill (Indians) cf	3	0	0	3	1	0
Chapman (Senators) cf	1	0	0	0	0	0
Ferrell (Red Sox) c	2	0	0	4	0	0
Dickey (Yankees) c	2	0	0	2	0	0
Radcliff (White Sox) lf	2	0	1	2	0	0
Goslin (Tigers) lf	1	1	1	1	0	0
Higgins (Athletics) 3b	2	0	0	0	1	0
Foxx (Red Sox) 3b	2	1	1	0	1	0
Grove (Red Sox) p	1	0	0	0	0	0
Rowe (Tigers) p	1	0	0	0	0	0
Selkirk (Yankees) ph	0	0	0	0	0	0
Harder (Indians) p	0	0	0	0	1	0
Crosetti (Yankees) ph	1	0	0	0	0	0
Totals	32	3	7	24	7	1

National League	AB	R	H	PO	A	E
Galan (Cubs) cf	4	1	1	1	0	0
Herman (Cubs) 2b	3	1	2	3	4	0
Collins (Cardinals) 1b	2	0	0	9	1	0
Medwick (Cardinals) lf	4	0	1	0	0	0
Demaree (Cubs) rf	3	1	1	1	0	0
Ott (Giants) rf	1	0	1	0	0	0
Hartnett (Cubs) c	4	1	1	7	0	0
Whitney (Phillies) 3b	3	0	1	0	2	0
Riggs (Reds) 3b	1	0	0	0	0	0
Durocher (Cardinals) ss	3	0	1	4	0	0
J. Dean (Cardinals) p	1	0	0	0	2	0
Hubbell (Giants) p	1	0	0	2	1	0
Davis (Cubs) p	0	0	0	0	1	0
Warneke (Cubs) p	1	0	0	0	0	0
Totals	31	4	9	27	11	0

```
American League.........................  0 0 0 0 0 0 3 0 0 – 3
National League .........................  0 2 0 0 2 0 0 0 x – 4
```

DP—Americans 1, Nationals 1. LOB—Americans 9, Nationals 7. 2B—Gehringer. 3B—Hartnett. HR—Galan, Gehrig. RBIs—Hartnett, Whitney, Medwick, Galan, Appling (2), Gehrig. WP—Hubbell.

American League	IP	H	R	ER	BB	SO
Grove (L)	3	3	2	2	2	2
Rowe	3	4	2	1	1	2
Harder	2	2	2	0	0	2

National League	IP	H	R	ER	BB	SO
J. Dean (W)	3	0	0	0	2	3
Hubbell	3	2	0	0	1	2
Davis	⅔	4	3	3	1	0
Warneke	2⅓	1	0	0	3	2

Umpires—Reardon and Stewart (N.L.), Summers and Kills (A.L.). Time—2:00. Attendance—25,556.

---

hitters for two innings until the roof almost caved in. Cub pitcher Curt Davis saw action in the sixth, but his ineffectiveness resulted in the Americans first scoring drive of the afternoon. Lou Gehrig, hitless in his last three All-Star games, picked up his first hit: a towering home run that sailed high into the right field bleacher section. Wasting little time, manager Charley Grimm took Davis out and handed the ball to relief pitching ace Lonnie Warneke.

But Warneke didn't have his usual good stuff either. In the top of the seventh inning, the American League mounted its most potent attack of the day. Shortstop Luke Appling got the American Leaguers another run with a single to right, scoring Leon Goslin, to narrow the score to 4–3. Warneke walked the next batter, second baseman Charley Gehringer, which put runners on first and second with two out and brought Joe DiMaggio to the plate.

The 25,556 fans still hadn't forgotten DiMaggio's misplay of Gabby Hartnett's triple in the second inning. DiMaggio overran the ball and watched it trickle under his glove to the wall in right. With the boo-birds in force, this was a golden opportunity for the Yankee Clipper, a name he later earned, to redeem himself. DiMaggio dug in against Lonnie Warneke. But with two strikes on him, Joe lined out hard to shortstop Leo Durocher to end the inning, and inevitably the game. It was the Americans' last major scoring threat.

After the game, a dejected Joe DiMaggio remembered that caught drive, "If the ball had been a foot higher, or even a couple of inches to the left or right of Durocher, I might have hit one for extra bases. I couldn't have hit the ball any harder..."

The winning pitcher was Dizzy Dean, his first victory in All-Star play. Lefty Grove, in his third All-Star game, took the defeat.

On his performance, Dean told reporters after the game, "You'd have seen something if I was feeling really good. I had all my speed, but I just wasn't feeling my best."

In this case, Dean's "worst" was clearly enough in a game that will be best remembered as the one DiMaggio let slip away.

July 7, 1937

Griffith Stadium

The 1937 game was one of firsts.

All-Star managers Joe McCarthy of the Yankees and Bill Terry of the Giants, in an unusual move, were able to choose their entire All-Star rosters for the first time and not through fan voting. The first U.S. dignitary to throw out the customary first ball was also in attendance: President Franklin D. Roosevelt. And, in sweltering 90-degree heat in Washington, D.C., our nation's capital, Lou Gehrig blasted his second All-Star game home run to lead the American League to its fourth interleague victory 8–3. The loss went to N.L. starter Dizzy Dean, his first defeat in this midsummer classic.

The game was a pitching duel from the start, which matched Yankee hurler Lefty Gomez with Dean, while 31,391 interested spectators looked on. Gomez was one of five Yankees named to the American League squad. Given carte blanche, McCarthy stockpiled his team with four other Yankees: Lou Gehrig, Bill Dickey, Joe DiMaggio, and Red Rolfe.

Gomez was impressive in his three frames of work; he pitched two shutout innings before he left in the third. Dean, making his second consecutive All-Star start, also kept the Americans scoreless during his first two frames.

Then lightning finally struck in the third when Yankee Lou Gehrig strode to the plate. Joe DiMaggio was safe on first after a line single to right, his first All-Star hit. Gehrig came into the game batting .351 with 149 RBIs, a season best for him. Dean had the count three-and-two when he tried fogging one past Gehrig, who promptly clobbered the ball over the right field seats — a blast topping 450 feet — to stake the Americans to an early 2–0 lead. It was a lead the Americans never relinquished.

That same inning, still miffed at himself, Dean tried rifling a pitch past Earl Averill, but Averill's line drive back to the box struck Dean on the right foot and trickled by the mound. Dean went after the ball, picked it up, and threw out Averill on a close play. Dizzy limped to the clubhouse and, after a thorough examination of the injury, it was discovered he had a broken toe. Dean tried to pitch too soon after the injury by putting an unnatural strain on his right arm, and ruined his career. Later, when he was traded to the

The 1937 All-Star Game

National League	AB	R	H	PO	A	E
P. Waner (Pirates) rf	5	0	0	0	0	0
Herman (Cubs) 2b	5	1	2	1	4	0
Vaughan (Pirates) 3b	5	0	2	3	0	0
Medwick (Cardinals) lf	5	1	4	1	0	0
Demaree (Cubs) cf	5	0	1	3	1	0
Mize (Cardinals) 1b	4	0	0	7	0	0
Hartnett (Cubs) c	3	1	1	6	0	0
Whitehead (Giants) pr	0	0	0	0	0	0
Mancuso (Giants) c	1	0	0	1	0	0
Bartell (Giants) ss	4	0	1	2	3	0
J. Dean (Cardinals) p	1	0	0	0	1	0
Hubbell (Giants) p	0	0	0	0	0	0
Blanton (Pirates) p	0	0	0	0	0	0
Ott (Giants) ph	1	0	1	0	0	0
Grissom (Reds) p	0	0	0	0	0	0
Collins (Cubs) ph	1	0	1	0	0	0
Mungo (Dodgers) p	0	0	0	0	1	0
Moore (Giants) ph	1	0	0	0	0	0
Walters (Phillies) p	0	0	0	0	1	0
Totals	41	3	13	24	11	0

American League	AB	R	H	PO	A	E
Rolfe (Yankees) 3b	4	2	2	0	1	2
Gehringer (Tigers) 2b	5	1	3	2	5	0
DiMaggio (Yankees) rf	4	1	1	1	1	0
Gehrig (Yankees) 1b	4	1	2	10	1	0
Averill (Indians) cf	3	0	1	2	0	0
Cronin (Red Sox) ss	4	1	1	4	3	0
Dickey (Yankees) c	3	1	2	2	0	0
West (Browns) lf	4	1	1	5	0	0
Gomez (Yankees) p	1	0	0	0	0	0
Bridges (Tigers) p	1	0	0	0	1	0
Foxx (Red Sox) ph	1	0	0	0	0	0
Harder (Indians) p	1	0	0	1	1	0
Totals	35	8	13	27	13	2

National League .... 0 0 0 1 1 1 0 0 0 – 3
American League......................... 0 0 2 3 1 2 0 0 x – 8

DP—Nationals 1. LOB—Nationals 11, Americans 7. 2B—Gehrig, Dickey, Cronin, Ott, Medwick (2). 3B—Rolfe. HR—Gehrig. RBIs—Gehrig (4), Rolfe (2), Gehringer, Dickey, P. Waner, Medwick, Mize.

National League	IP	H	R	ER	BB	SO
J. Dean (L)	3	4	2	2	1	2
Hubbell	⅔	3	3	3	1	1
Blanton	⅓	0	0	0	0	1
Grissom	1	2	1	1	0	2
Mungo	2	2	2	2	2	1
Walters	1	2	0	0	0	0

American League	IP	H	R	ER	BB	SO
Gomez (W)	3	1	0	0	0	0
Bridges	3	7	3	3	0	0
Harder	3	5	0	0	0	0

Umpires—McGowan and Quinn (A.L.), Barr and Pinelli (N.L.). Time—2:30. Attendance—31,391.

Cubs, Dean developed a pitch he called "the dipsy doodle," but he was never the same pitcher.

In the fourth inning, with Dean gone, Carl Hubbell came in to pitch for the Nationals, but the results were the same. Hubbell had posted eight scoreless innings against the Americans over a span of three All-Star games. His streak came to a thundering halt as the Americans blasted three more runs across home plate. It started with Bill Dickey walking and taking third on Sammy West's crisp single to center. Bridges struck out for the second out. Then, the Yankees' Red Rolfe belted a triple off the scoreboard in right to score Dickey and West. Gehringer ensued with a sharp single off the glove of first baseman Johnny Mize, scoring Rolfe and ending Hubbell's domination over the American League. Hubbell was quickly replaced by Cy Blanton, a fireballing right-hander of the Pittsburgh Pirates, who struck out DiMaggio to end the inning.

But the game clearly belonged to Gehrig. In the fifth, the Americans scraped up a single run against Reds pitcher Lee Grissom and finished their scoring ways in the sixth with a pair of runs off the Dodger's Van Mungo. The crushing blow that inning, however, was Lou Gehrig's towering double, which scored two more runners and gave Gehrig four RBIs on the day.

All told Gehrig and his Yankee teammates accounted for seven of the eight American League runs.

The Nationals' only scoring drive came at the expense of the Detroit Tigers' Tommy Bridges, who pitched the middle three innings. Bridges was rocked for three runs, with outfielder Joe "Ducky" Medwick leading the attack. Medwick, the only .400 hitter in either league, banged out four straight hits on the afternoon, including two doubles and two singles. Ducky thus became the first player in All-Star history to reach the four-hit plateau. In 1946, hitting star Ted Williams tied the record with a four-for-five afternoon of his own.

After Bridges exited the game, Mel Harder held the enemy scoreless over the final three innings to clinch the victory. Gomez was credited with the victory after he had held the Nationals to a solitary single and no runs in three frames of play. It was Lefty's third triumph in All-Star competition and the fourth victory of the Americans in five midsummer classics.

Even though the National League matched the Americans in total hit production with 13, they couldn't take advantage of numerous scoring opportunities. Eleven base runners were stranded by the Nationals, with several key players missing in the clutch. Pirate shortstop Arky Vaughan failed twice. Cub outfielder Frank Demaree couldn't clean the bases in the fourth, seventh, or ninth. And Johnny Mize, up twice with runners in scoring position, produced nothing more than a long fly ball.

The Americans didn't waste their opportunities, thanks to their man of the hour, Lou Gehrig.

July 6, 1938

Crosley Field

Leo Durocher's "bunt home run" turned National League manager Bill Terry into a full-fledged psychic as his team rolled past the American League 4–1 before a crowd of 26,067 pro–National League fans in Cincinnati.

Terry had promised sports writers before the game that he would pull all stops to insure a victory for his underdog National League squad. Ironically, his strategic maneuvering paid off in the seventh when he signaled Durocher to bunt after Frank McCormick singled to right. Durocher laid a sacrifice bunt down the third base line and it appeared as if nobody would be able to field it. But Jimmie Foxx, inserted at third, grabbed the ball perfectly and fired it to first where second baseman Charley Gehringer failed to cover. Foxx's accurate throw sailed down the right field line and was fielded by Joe DiMaggio, who tried nailing McCormick at the plate but his throw bounced over Bill Dickey's head into the National League dugout, which accounted for the second error on the play. Meanwhile, Durocher steamed around the bases to score the Nationals' fourth and decisive run.

The game took on even greater importance earlier when Reds pitching sensation Johnny Vander Meer started on the mound for the Nationals. National Leaguers were extremely confident that "the kid" spelled an easy victory. He had recently become the first pitcher to throw back-to-back no-hitters and was the first rookie pitcher to start an All-Star game. His first pitch of the game was a strike, and he was simply unhittable from then on. Vander Meer kept the American League batters handcuffed with his blazing fastball, which was clocked at over 90 miles per hour. In three innings, the Cincinnati flamethrower made short work of the opposition; he needed only 31 pitches as he faced just ten men, one over the minimum, and gave up just one single.

Cub pitcher Bill Lee, an ace right-hander on his way to a 22–9 record, kept the Americans in check for three innings, too. It wasn't until the sixth inning that Lee gave up his first and only hit in relief, a fluke double by catcher Bill Dickey which shortstop Leo Durocher lost in the sun. Fortunately, Durocher made up for his mistake in the following inning, or he might have been that day's goat instead of hero.

The 1938 All-Star Game

American League	AB	R	H	PO	A	E
Kreevich (White Sox) lf	2	0	0	1	0	0
Cramer (Red Sox) lf	2	0	0	0	0	0
Gehringer (Tigers) 2b	3	0	1	2	2	0
Averill (Indians) cf	4	0	0	5	0	0
Foxx (Red Sox) 1b-3b	4	0	1	5	1	1
DiMaggio (Yankees) rf	4	1	1	2	0	1
Dickey (Yankees) c	4	0	1	8	0	1
Cronin (Red Sox) ss	3	0	2	0	2	1
Lewis (Senators) 3b	1	0	0	0	1	0
Gehrig (Yankees) 1b	3	0	1	1	0	0
Gomez (Yankees) p	1	0	0	0	0	0
Allen (Indians) p	1	0	0	0	0	0
York (Tigers) ph	1	0	0	0	0	0
Grove (Red Sox) p	0	0	0	0	0	0
Johnson (Athletics) ph	1	0	0	0	0	0
Totals	34	1	7	24	6	4

National League	AB	R	H	PO	A	E
Hack (Cubs) 3b	4	1	1	1	2	0
Herman (Cubs) 2b	4	0	1	3	4	0
Goodman (Reds) rf	3	0	0	2	0	0
Medwick (Cardinals) lf	4	0	1	2	0	0
Ott (Giants) cf	4	1	1	3	0	0
Lombardi (Reds) c	4	0	2	5	0	0
McCormick (Reds) 1b	4	1	1	11	0	0
Durocher (Dodgers) ss	3	1	1	0	3	0
Vander Meer (Reds) p	0	0	0	0	3	0
Leiber (Giants) ph	1	0	0	0	0	0
Lee (Cubs) p	1	0	0	0	0	0
Brown (Pirates) p	1	0	0	0	1	0
Totals	33	4	8	27	13	0

```
American League....................... 0 0 0 0 0 0 0 0 1 – 1
National League ...................... 1 0 0 1 0 0 2 0 x – 4
```

DP—none. LOB—Americans 8, Nationals 6. 2B—Dickey, Cronin. 3B—Ott. RBIs—Medwick, Lombardi, Cronin. SB—Goodman, DiMaggio. HBP—By Allen (Goodman).

American League	IP	H	R	ER	BB	SO
Gomez (L)	3	2	1	0	0	1
Allen	3	2	1	1	0	3
Grove	2	4	2	0	0	3

National League	IP	H	R	ER	BB	SO
Vander Meer (W)	3	1	0	0	0	1
Lee	3	1	0	0	1	2
Brown	3	5	1	1	1	2

Umpires—Ballanfant and Klem (N.L.), Basil and Geisel (A.L.). Time—1:58. Attendance—27,067.

A.L. starter Lefty Gomez, in his fifth All-Star start, was equally dominating. He pitched a solid three innings and yielded only one run in his first inning on a booted grounder by shortstop Joe Cronin. This wasn't a day for shortstops!

Manager Joe McCarthy, piloting his third straight American League squad, followed with Cleveland Indians right-hander Johnny Allen. He lasted the fourth, but not without Mel Ott lashing the day's longest drive, a 387-foot triple off the center field wall. Ott came around to score on Ernie Lombardi's single. With Allen ineffective, McCarthy next called on Lefty Grove, 38 years old and now a member of the Boston Red Sox, to pitch the seventh. That inning Durocher and company became his undoing.

Pittsburgh Pirate ace Mace Brown pitched the last three innings for the N.L. club and struck out Detroit's murderous home run king, Rudy York.

Vander Meer was credited with his first All-Star victory, and Gomez with his first loss in four All-Star appearances.

And Bill Terry—he was baseball's newest prophet.

July 11, 1939

Yankee Stadium

Six New York Yankees, piloted by A.L. manager Joe McCarthy, made life miserable for the National League with a 3–1 victory at Yankee Stadium before 62,892, the second largest crowd in All-Star history.

McCarthy's starting nine were headed by Red Ruffing and Bill Dickey as the pitching-and-catching battery, Joe DiMaggio in center, George Selkirk in left, Joe Gordon at second, and Red Rolfe at third. An all-Yankee show, Ruffing, in his first All-Star start, faced another relative newcomer, Cincinnati Reds ace Paul Derringer.

While McCarthy had six Yankees on his squad, N.L. manager Gabby Hartnett of the Chicago Cubs countered with five members of the Cincinnati Reds on his team. Besides Derringer, Hartnett named to his starting lineup second baseman Lonnie Frey, outfielder Ival Goodman, first baseman Frank McCormick, and catcher Ernie Lombardi.

Derringer kept the Yankee-loaded Americans honest during his first innings of dueling; he allowed only two hits and no runs. The National League, ironically, broke on top first in the third when they strung together three hits for their only run of the game. Lonnie Frey's double scored Arky Vaughan.

But the game was all Yankees. The boys from the Bronx struck up an uprising of their own in the fourth off Cub pitcher Bill Lee, who was the unfortunate victim of most of the American League's blows. George Selkirk's single brought in the first run, scoring Bill Dickey. Hank Greenberg, who singled after Dickey walked, crossed the plate with the second run of the inning on Joe Gordon's booted grounder by shortstop Arky Vaughan. Greenberg's run posted the Americans to a 2–1 lead.

Joe DiMaggio, playing before the hometown crowd, padded the lead with his first home run in All-Star competition, a shot that traveled 450 feet into the left field seats. The score was now 3–1, Americans.

Ruffing left the game in the third when he gave way to Detroit Tigers hurler Tommy Bridges, the A.L.'s previous All-Star goat. This time Bridges came through to keep the National League batters in check until McCarthy called on Bob Feller to finish the game. Feller, a 20-year-old fireballing phenom from the Cleveland Indians, mowed down National League hitters

The 1939 All-Star Game

National League	AB	R	H	PO	A	E
Hack (Cubs) 3b	4	0	1	1	1	0
Frey (Reds) rf	4	0	1	0	4	0
Goodman (Reds) rf	1	0	0	0	0	0
Herman (Cubs) ph	1	0	0	0	0	0
Moore (Cardinals) cf	1	0	0	0	0	0
McCormick (Reds) 1b	4	0	0	7	1	0
Lombardi (Reds) c	4	0	2	6	0	0
Medwick (Cardinals) lf	4	0	0	1	0	0
Ott (Giants) cf–rf	4	0	2	4	0	0
Vaughan (Pirates) ss	3	1	1	4	1	1
Derringer (Reds) p	1	0	0	0	0	0
Camilli (Dodgers) ph	1	0	0	0	0	0
Lee (Cubs) p	0	0	0	0	0	0
Phelps (Dodgers) ph	1	0	0	0	0	0
Fette (Braves) p	0	0	0	1	0	0
Mize (Cardinals) ph	1	0	0	0	0	0
Totals	34	1	7	24	7	1

American League	AB	R	H	PO	A	E
Cramer (Red Sox) rf	4	0	1	3	0	0
Rolfe (Yankees) 3b	4	0	1	1	0	0
DiMaggio (Yankees) cf	4	1	1	1	0	0
Dickey (Yankees) c	3	1	0	10	0	0
Greenberg (Tigers) 1b	3	1	1	7	1	0
Cronin (Red Sox) ss	4	0	1	2	3	1
Selkirk (Yankees) lf	2	0	1	0	0	0
Gordon (Yankees) 2b	4	0	0	2	5	0
Ruffing (Yankees) p	0	0	0	0	0	0
Hoag (Browns) ph	1	0	0	0	0	0
Bridges (Tigers) p	1	0	0	0	1	0
Feller (Indians) p	1	0	0	0	0	0
Totals	31	3	6	27	10	1

```
National League .......................... 0  0  1  0  0  0  0  0  0 – 1
American League.......................... 0  0  0  2  1  0  0  0  x – 3
```

DP—Americans 1. LOB—Nationals 9, Americans 8. 2B—Frey. HR—DiMaggio. RBIs—DiMaggio, Selkirk, Frey.

National League	IP	H	R	ER	BB	SO
Derringer	3	2	0	0	0	1
Lee (L)	3	3	3	2	3	4
Fette	2	1	0	0	1	1

American League	IP	H	R	ER	BB	SO
Ruffing	3	4	1	1	1	4
Bridges (W)	2⅓	2	0	0	1	3
Feller	3⅔	1	0	0	1	2

Umpires—Hubbard and Rommel (A.L.), Goetz and Magerkurth (N.L.). Time—1:55. Attendance—62,892.

with his blazing fastball, who managed only one hit off him. The Americans' final run, via DiMaggio's home run, came off Boston Bees thrower Lou Fette.

Following the victory, the American League clubhouse was jubilant. Players kept referring to the National League as "just another minor league after all." Manager Joe McCarthy made rounds to shake hands with his players, and then told reporters afterwards, "We got our share of breaks and capitalized on them." McCarthy added that Bob Feller's timely pitching kept the game close.

In the loser's clubhouse, N.L. manager Gabby Hartnett was naturally disappointed over the American League's dominance in this midsummer classic. It was as if the Nationals were getting used to being trimmed in All-Star competition. As Hartnett admitted, "I wanted that game and wanted it badly, but the breaks were against us. Feller may not have been his usual self, but he was good enough to stop our hitters cold."

With the Yankees' support, of course.

July 9, 1940

Sportsman Park

For some strange reason, the American League had so far mostly dominated the National League at each year's All-Star game. It was as if they had some sort of voodoo curse on National League players. No matter how good the Nationals' team was, it folded under pressure from the Americans.

The 1940 contest was different, however.

The American League office decided some changes were due. They replaced Joe McCarthy, who piloted five straight A.L. teams, with Red Sox player-manager Joe Cronin. Apparently, some people complained that McCarthy had been managing the team too long.

The A.L. may have regretted its decision because the National League shut out the American League 4–0 at St. Louis' Sportsman Park before 32,373 faithful onlookers. It took five pitchers and seven hits to send the Americans to only their third defeat in interleague play.

N.L. manager Bill McKechnie came to the park smelling a victory. His idea to alternate pitchers kept American League batters baffled, with his two top Cincinnati Red hurlers, Paul Derringer and Bucky Walters, showing the way. Cronin went with his own ace in the hole, the Yankees' 20-game winner, Red Ruffing, a standout in the 1939 All-Star game.

This time Ruffing found himself on the other end of the fence. He was roughed up in the very first inning when Arky Vaughan, "a goat" on the 1939 N.L. squad, led the assault with a scratch single over Joe Cronin's head. Chicago Cub slugger Billy Herman, on the verge of a three-hit game, pulled off a hit-and-run play by singling Vaughan to third. Then Boston Bees outfielder Max West got into the act. West was inserted in the lineup at the last minute. He replaced Giants' Hall of Famer Mel Ott, who was appearing in his seventh All-Star contest. McKechnie told reporters that he had "a hunch" this was going to be West's day. His hunch paid off as West poled a 360-foot four-bagger into the right field pavillion to score Vaughan and Herman.

The score: Nationals 3, Americans 0.

McKechnie kept pulling all the right strings by using his pitchers two innings at a time to keep the enemy off guard. He followed with Whitlow Wyatt of the Brooklyn Dodgers, Larry French of the Chicago Cubs, and Carl

The 1940 All-Star Game

American League	AB	R	H	PO	A	E
Travis (Senators) 3b	3	0	0	0	0	0
Keltner (Indians) 3b	1	0	0	2	1	0
Williams (Red Sox) lf	2	0	0	3	0	0
Finney (Red Sox) rf	0	0	0	0	0	0
Keller (Yankees) rf	2	0	0	4	0	0
Greenberg (Tigers) lf	2	0	0	0	0	0
DiMaggio (Yankees) cf	4	0	0	1	0	0
Foxx (Red Sox) 1b	3	0	0	4	2	0
Appling (White Sox) ss	3	0	2	0	0	0
Boudreau (Indians) ss	0	0	0	0	0	0
Dickey (Yankees) c	1	0	0	2	0	0
Hayes (Athletics) c	1	0	0	1	0	0
Hemsley (Indians) c	1	0	0	3	0	0
Gordon (Yankees) 2b	2	0	0	3	1	0
Mack (Indians) 2b	1	0	0	0	0	0
Ruffing (Yankees) p	1	0	0	0	0	0
Newsom (Tigers) p	1	0	1	0	0	0
Feller (Indians) p	1	0	0	1	0	0
Totals	29	0	3	24	4	1
National League	**AB**	**R**	**H**	**PO**	**A**	**E**
Vaughan (Pirates) ss	3	1	1	0	1	0
Miller (Braves) ss	1	0	0	2	1	0
Herman (Cubs) 2b	3	1	3	0	3	0
Coscarart (Dodgers) 2b	1	0	0	0	2	0
West (Braves) rf	1	1	1	0	0	0
Nicholson (Cubs) rf	2	0	0	1	0	0
Ott (Giants) rf	0	1	0	0	0	0
Mize (Cardinals) 1b	2	0	0	8	0	0
McCormick (Reds) 1b	1	0	0	2	0	0
Lombardi (Reds) c	2	0	1	3	0	0
Phelps (Dodgers) c	0	0	0	1	0	0
Danning (Giants) c	1	0	1	6	0	0
Medwick (Dodgers) lf	2	0	0	1	0	0
J. Moore (Giants) lf	2	0	0	1	0	0
Lavagetto (Dodgers) 3b	2	0	0	0	1	0
May (Phillies) 3b	1	0	0	0	0	0
T. Moore (Cardinals) cf	3	0	0	2	0	0
Derringer (Reds) p	1	0	0	0	1	0
Walters (Reds) p	0	0	0	0	1	0
Wyatt (Dodgers) p	1	0	0	0	0	0
French (Cubs) p	0	0	0	0	0	0
Hubbell (Giants) p	0	0	0	0	0	0
Totals	29	4	7	27	10	0

```
American League........................ 0  0  0  0  0  0  0  0  0 - 0
National League  ....................... 3  0  0  0  0  0  0  1  x - 4
```

DP—Nationals 1. LOB—Nationals 7, Americans 4. 2B—Appling. HR—West. SAC—F. McCormick, French. RBIs—West (3), Danning.

American League	IP	H	R	ER	BB	SO
Ruffing (L)	3	5	3	3	0	2
Newsom	3	1	0	0	1	1
Feller	2	1	1	1	2	3
National League	IP	H	R	ER	BB	SO
Derringer (W)	2	1	0	0	1	3
Walters	2	0	0	0	0	0
Wyatt	2	1	0	0	0	1
French	2	1	0	0	0	2
Hubbell	1	0	0	0	1	1

Umpires — Reardon and Stewart (N.L.), Pipgras and Basil (A.L.). Time — 1:53. Attendance — 32,373.

Hubbell, who was making his last All-Star appearance, to close out the competition. Hubbell, incidentally, didn't allow a run in one inning of work.

The Nationals did manage one more run in the eighth off Cleveland Indians fireballer Bob Feller, even though the three previous runs would have been enough. In one of his wild streaks, Feller walked Mel Ott on four straight balls and then watched Frank McCormick sacrifice Ott to second. Ott scored on Giant catcher Hank Danning's single to right.

Manager Joe Cronin took most of the flak for the Americans' defeat. He was heavily criticized for not using the league's top double-play combination, shortstop Lou Boudreau and second baseman Ray Mack, both of Cleveland, until the last inning. Of the A.L. starters, only Joe DiMaggio and Jimmie Foxx endured the full nine innings, with White Sox shortstop Luke Appling as the Americans' hitting star with two hits.

Yet, the game was tailored for McKechnie.

July 8, 1941

Briggs Stadium

Ted Williams was artistry in motion. Entering the 1941 All-Star break, Williams was batting a robust .405 for the Boston Red Sox. He still holds the distinction of being the last player to hit .400 in a single season. (George Brett came the closest to matching this feat, in 1980, when he batted .390 to win the batting crown.)

Fans from all over shoved their way into Detroit's Briggs Stadium to watch baseball's greatest hitter perform. Pro that he was, Williams didn't let anybody down.

Before 56,674, the third largest crowd in the game's nine-year history, Williams cranked a dramatic ninth-inning home run to power the Americans to a 7–5 comeback victory over the unlucky Nationals. It was the first All-Star game to be won in the final frame and the Americans' sixth victory against three defeats.

Williams' smash bounced against the football press box which overlooked the right field stands. As catcher Hank Danning watched the ball's flight, a crush of fans poured on to the field to mob the hero Williams as he crossed home plate. Williams recalled that hit, "I just shut my eyes and swung." The victim of his mighty blow was Cub hurler Claude Passeau, who kicked the ground in disgust.

Until his clout, the National League had been coasting with a 5–3 lead, thanks to two home runs by shortstop Arky Vaughan. Vaughan had also led the Nationals the year before in their 4–0 victory. This time, if the Nationals had held on, Vaughan would have been remembered as the game's hitting hero. He collected three hits in four at bats and cracked his home runs, each time with one aboard, on successive trips to the plate in the seventh and eighth innings. Both hits landed into the second tier of the right field seats.

In that famous come-from-behind ninth, the Americans had already scored one run before Williams' towering drive, shaving the Nationals lead to 5–4. Joe DiMaggio came up next with the bases loaded and one out, but grounded a perfect double-play ball to shortstop Eddie Miller, which should have ended the game. But Billy Herman made a bad throw in taking the relay, and one run scored. Then, Williams took his swipes. He fouled off Passeau's

The 1941 All-Star Game

National League	AB	R	H	PO	A	E
Hack (Cubs) 3b	2	0	1	3	0	0
Lavagetto (Dodgers) 3b	1	0	0	0	0	0
T. Moore (Cardinals) lf	5	0	0	0	0	0
Reiser (Dodgers) cf	4	0	0	6	0	2
Mize (Cardinals) 1b	4	1	1	5	0	0
McCormick (Reds) 1b	0	0	0	0	0	0
Nicholson (Cubs) rf	1	0	0	1	0	0
Elliot (Pirates) rf	1	0	0	0	0	0
Slaughter (Cardinals) rf	2	1	1	0	0	0
Vaughan (Pirates) ss	4	2	3	1	2	0
Miller (Braves) ss	0	0	0	0	1	0
Frey (Reds) 2b	1	0	1	1	3	0
Herman (Dodgers) 2b	3	0	2	3	0	0
Owen (Dodgers) c	1	0	0	0	0	0
Lopez (Pirates) c	1	0	0	3	0	0
Danning (Giants) c	1	0	0	3	0	0
Wyatt (Dodgers) p	0	0	0	0	0	0
Ott (Giants) ph	1	0	0	0	0	0
Derringer (Reds) p	0	0	0	0	1	0
Walters (Reds) p	1	1	1	0	0	0
Medwick (Dodgers) ph	1	0	0	0	0	0
Passeau (Cubs) p	1	0	0	0	0	0
Totals	35	5	10	26	7	2
American League	AB	R	H	PO	A	E
Doerr (Red Sox) 2b	3	0	0	0	0	0
Gordon (Yankees) 2b	2	1	1	2	0	0
Travis (Senators) 3b	4	1	1	1	2	0
J. DiMaggio (Yankees) cf	4	3	1	1	0	0
Williams (Red Sox) lf	4	1	2	3	0	1
Heath (Indians) rf	2	0	0	1	0	0
D. DiMaggio (Red Sox) rf	1	0	1	1	0	0
Cronin (Red Sox) ss	2	0	0	3	0	0
Boudreau (Indians) ss	2	0	2	0	1	0
York (Tigers) 1b	3	0	1	6	2	0
Foxx (Red Sox) 1b	1	0	0	2	2	0
Dickey (Yankees) c	3	0	1	4	2	0
Hayes (Athletics) c	1	0	0	2	0	0
Feller (Indians) p	0	0	0	0	1	0
Cullenbine (Browns) ph	1	0	0	0	0	0
Lee (White Sox) p	1	0	0	0	1	0
Hudson (Senators) p	0	0	0	0	0	0
Keller (Yankees) ph	1	0	0	0	0	0
Smith (White Sox) p	0	0	0	1	0	1
Keltner (Indians) ph	1	1	1	0	0	0
Totals	36	7	11	27	11	3

National League .... 0 0 0 0 0 1 2 2 0 – 5
American League........................ 0 0 0 1 0 1 0 1 4 – 7

DP—Americans 1, Nationals 1. LOB—Americans 7, Nationals 6. 2B—Travis, Williams, Walters, Herman, Mize, J. DiMaggio. HR — Vaughan (2), Williams, SAC — Hack, Lopez. RBIs — Williams (4), Moore, Boudreau, Vaughan (4), D. DiMaggio, J. DiMaggio.

National League	IP	H	R	ER	BB	SO
Wyatt	2	0	0	0	1	0
Derringer	2	2	1	0	0	1
Walters	2	3	1	1	2	2
Passeau (L)	2⅔	6	5	4	1	3
American League	IP	H	R	ER	BB	SO
Feller	3	1	0	0	0	4
Lee	3	4	1	1	0	0
Hudson	1	3	2	2	1	1
Smith (W)	2	2	2	2	0	2

Umpires — Summers and Grieve (A.L.), Jorda and Pinelli (N.L.). Time — 2:23. Attendance — 56,674.

---

initial offering, then, after drawing a ball, Williams rifled Passeau's next pitch over the boards. His homer chased Joe Gordon and DiMaggio around to score to win the game and spoil a strong showing by the underdog Nationals.

Unfortunately, Williams' hitting exploits overshadowed the performance of A.L. pitchers. A.L. manager Del Baker, piloting his first All-Star squad, recorded with Bob Feller. Feller started 27 victories the year before, and had won 16 up to the All-Star break. Known for his blazing fastball, Feller worked three innings, fanned four and faced the minimum nine batters.

His opponent was Whitlow Wyatt, a former American Leaguer traded to the Brooklyn Dodgers in the off-season. Wyatt, 32, also threw competitively. Under McKechnie's two-inning rule, he didn't give up a hit and walked only Williams, who was thrown out in a double play. McKechnie then tried keeping the game close with Paul Derringer and Bucky Walters in relief until Passeau took charge in the seventh, only to lose the game.

In the American League clubhouse afterwards, Williams had a flock of admirers swarming around him: Schoolboy Rowe of the Detroit Tigers, pitcher Tom Yawkey, and Red Sox owner Herb Pennock, along with a storm of reporters. On Williams' decisive home run, manager Del Baker chimed, "I couldn't ask for anything more than to win the way we did. Williams really polished that one off. It went a country mile, high and away."

Williams said he had a feeling that he might connect with a homer if he had a chance to bat again. Although he did admit he was "a little late" all afternoon in his swings, Williams was determined to get in front of one.

Savoring his game-winning hit, he said, "Ain't that just a great feeling to bang out a home run. I just wanted to beat the hell out of them National Leaguers. I'll bet my mother is the happiest woman in the world."

Not to mention the American League.

July 6, 1942

Polo Grounds

The Polo Grounds. The site of the tenth annual All-Star game, which was being played at a time when America was at war and President Franklin D. Roosevelt tried to bring the country closer together. Despite these distractions, the game went on as planned.

Baseball Commissioner Kenesaw E. Landis and American League president Will Harridge headed the list of dignitaries who cheered along with 34,178 brave souls in chilly, rainy weather.

Dodger manager Leo Durocher was selected to manage the N.L. club and Yankee manager Joe McCarthy was to pilot the A.L. squad. With the game starting almost three hours late, the delay didn't prevent the inevitable from happening: the American League scored another victory over the hapless National League 3-1, with Lou Boudreau and Rudy York as the stars.

Durocher was originally going to start Claude Passeau, last year's All-Star victim, but penciled in Mort Cooper of the St. Louis Cardinals to open the game. Cooper didn't fare much better, however. All the American League's scoring came at his expense in the first inning.

With fans growing restless, Lou Boudreau, at 24, the player-manager of the Cleveland Indians, led off the inning with a home run into the upper left field stands to put the American League in front early 1-0. The game picked right up where the Americans left off the previous year with Ted Williams' surprise ninth-inning home run. Cooper slowly settled down to stop Ted Williams and Joe DiMaggio on easy outs before he gave up two more decisive blows. Tommy Henrich of the Yankees doubled and scored when home run king Rudy York crushed one of Cooper's inside pitches into the right field stands for another homer. The Polo Grounds had short fences in left and right, which measured 300 feet, or, a little under the length of York's drive.

McCarthy, back after a year's absence from the All-Star game, couldn't have been happier. Besides timely hitting, Spud Chandler of his own team and Al Benton of the Detroit Tigers combined to keep the Nationals scoreless until the eighth. Then Mickey Owen cracked a pinch homer to score the Nationals' lone run of the game. It was also the Nationals' sixth hit.

The 1942 All-Star Game

American League	AP	R	H	PO	A	E
Boudreau (Indians) ss	4	1	1	4	5	0
Henrich (Yankees) rf	4	1	1	2	0	0
Williams (Red Sox) lf	4	0	1	0	0	0
DiMaggio (Yankees) cf	4	0	2	2	0	0
York (Tigers) 1b	4	1	1	11	3	0
Gordon (Yankees) 2b	4	0	0	1	4	0
Keltner (Indians) 3b	4	0	0	0	1	0
Tebbetts (Tigers) c	4	0	0	4	1	0
Chandler (Yankees) p	1	0	0	3	1	0
Johnson (Athletics) ph	1	0	1	0	0	0
Benton (Tigers) p	1	0	0	0	1	0
Totals	35	3	7	27	16	0

National League	AB	R	H	PO	A	E
Brown (Cardinals) 2b	2	0	0	1	0	1
Herman (Dodgers) 2b	1	0	0	0	0	0
Vaughan (Dodgers) 3b	2	0	0	1	2	0
Elliot (Pirates) 3b	1	0	1	1	2	0
Reiser (Dodgers) cf	3	0	1	3	0	0
Moore (Cardinals) cf	1	0	0	1	0	0
Mize (Giants) 1b	2	0	0	3	0	0
McCormick (Reds) 1b	2	0	0	3	0	0
Ott (Giants) rf	4	0	0	1	0	0
Medwick (Dodgers) lf	2	0	0	1	0	0
Slaughter (Cardinals) lf	2	0	1	1	0	0
W. Cooper (Cardinals) c	2	0	1	7	0	0
Lombardi (Braves) c	1	0	0	2	0	0
Miller (Braves) ss	2	0	0	2	1	0
Reese (Dodgers) ss	1	0	0	0	1	0
M. Cooper (Cardinals) p	0	0	0	0	0	0
Marshall (Giants) ph	1	0	0	0	0	0
Vander Meer (Reds) p	0	0	0	0	1	0
Litwhiler (Phillies) ph	1	0	1	0	0	0
Passeau (Cubs) p	0	0	0	0	0	0
Owen (Dodgers) ph	1	1	1	0	0	0
Walters (Reds) p	0	0	0	0	0	0
Totals	31	1	6	27	7	1

American League........................ 3 0 0 0 0 0 0 0 0 – 3
National League .... 0 0 0 0 0 0 0 1 0 – 1

DP – Americans 2. LOB – Nationals 6, Americans 5. 2B – Henrich. HR – Boudreau, York, Owen. RBIs – Boudreau, York (2), Owen. PB – Tebbetts.

American League	IP	H	R	ER	BB	SO
Chandler (W)	4	2	0	0	0	2
Benton	5	4	1	1	2	1

National League	IP	H	R	ER	BB	SO
M. Cooper (L)	3	4	3	3	0	2
Vander Meer	3	2	0	0	0	4
Passeau	2	1	0	0	0	1
Walters	1	0	0	0	0	1

Umpires — Ballanfant and Barlick (A.L.), Stewart and McGowan (N.L.). Time — 2:07. Attendance — 34,178.

But the opposition had nothing but praise for Boudreau, who set the game in motion for the Americans with his lead-off homer. As a somber Leo Durocher said, "Best guy on the American League club? That's easy, it was Boudreau. Batting and fielding, he was aces."

Boudreau might have agreed.

July 13, 1943

Shibe Park

Philadelphia may be known as the City of Brotherly Love, but Red Sox second baseman Bobby Doerr never took that into consideration. His three-run homer helped pace the American League past the National League 5–3 before a capacity crowd of 31,938. It was the first All-Star game held at night.

Doerr, a smooth, basically quiet infielder, let his bat do all the talking as he belted his game-winning homer in the second inning to decide the struggle between superpowers then and there.

Shibe Park fans had expected more fireworks from their National League favorites, but this wasn't to be the case. Their club banged out ten hits, but wasted many opportunities. In previous dream games, the A.L. clubs were lead by an almost all–Yankee lineup. As a result, manager Joe McCarthy was criticized for favoring his own players when others who were having more outstanding years deserved to play. Miffed by such criticism, McCarthy didn't employ any of his six Yankee starters in the game, which proved that they were not missed.

Doerr's three runs batted in came off of the rosy-cheeked St. Louis Cardinal hurler, Mort Cooper, one of five world champion Cardinals on the N.L. team. Cooper's inability to escape the game unscathed marked his fourth failure against American League sluggers; twice in the World Series and in the 1942 All-Star affair at the Polo Grounds.

Doubles by Ken Keltner and Dick Wakefield produced another run in the third.

Afterwards, Reds pitching ace Johnny Vander Meer almost held the Americans scoreless for two and two-thirds innings. N.L. manager Billy Southworth went to the fireballing strikeout leader in the third when Cooper got in trouble for the third time in as many innings. Showing remarkable poise, Vander Meer struck out Rudy York and Chet Laabs to end the inning. In all, Vander Meer struck out six (trying Carl Hubbell's record for most strikeouts in an All-Star game). Vander Meer surrendered just one run in the fifth when George Case, playing out a double steal, took home on Billy Herman's wild throw to the plate.

The 1943 All-Star Game

National League	AB	R	H	PO	A	E
Hack (Cubs) 3b	5	1	3	0	2	1
Herman (Dodgers) 2b	5	0	2	3	3	2
Musial (Cardinals) lf–rf	4	0	1	0	0	0
Nicholson (Cubs) rf	2	0	0	0	0	0
Galan (Dodgers) lf	1	0	0	1	0	0
Fletcher (Pirates) 1b	2	0	0	3	0	0
Dahlgren (Phillies) 1b	2	0	0	3	0	0
W. Cooper (Cardinals) c	2	0	1	7	1	0
Lombardi (Giants) c	2	0	0	3	0	0
H. Walker (Cardinals) cf	1	0	0	1	0	0
DiMaggio (Pirates) cf	3	2	3	1	0	0
Marion (Cardinals) ss	2	0	0	2	2	0
Ott (Giants) ph	1	0	0	0	0	0
Miller (Reds) ss	1	0	0	0	1	0
M. Cooper (Cardinals) p	1	0	0	0	1	0
Vander Meer (Reds) p	1	0	0	0	1	0
Sewell (Pirates) p	0	0	0	0	0	0
F. Walker (Dodgers) ph	1	0	0	0	0	0
Javery (Braves) p	0	0	0	0	0	0
Frey (Reds) ph	1	0	0	0	0	0
Totals	37	3	10	24	11	3

American League	AB	R	H	PO	A	E
Case (Senators) rf	2	1	0	0	0	0
Keltner (Indians) 3b	4	1	1	2	2	0
Wakefield (Tigers) lf	4	0	2	3	0	0
Johnson (Athletics) lf	0	0	0	1	0	0
Stephens (Browns) ss	3	0	1	1	3	1
Siebert (Athletics) 1b	1	0	0	3	1	0
York (Tigers) 1b	3	0	1	4	0	0
Laabs (Browns) cf	3	1	0	7	0	0
Early (Senators) c	2	1	0	3	0	0
Doerr (Red Sox) 2b	4	1	2	3	3	0
Leonard (Senators) p	1	0	1	0	1	0
Newhouser (Tigers) p	1	0	0	0	0	0
Heath (Indians) ph	1	0	0	0	0	0
Hughson (Red Sox) p	0	0	0	0	0	0
Totals	29	5	8	27	10	1

National League	1	0	0	0	0	0	1	0	1 – 3
American League	0	3	1	0	1	0	0	0	x – 5

DP – Nationals 3, Americans 1. LOB – Nationals 8, Americans 6. 2B – Musial, Keltner, Wakefield. 3B – DiMaggio. HR – Doerr, DiMaggio. RBIs – Musial, F. Walker, DiMaggio, Doerr (3), Wakefield. SAC – Stephens. HBP – By M. Cooper (Case).

National League	IP	H	E	ER	BB	SO
M. Cooper (L)	2 ⅓	4	4	4	2	1
Vander Meer	2 ⅔	2	1	0	1	6
Sewell	1	0	0	0	0	0
Javery	2	2	0	0	0	3

American League	IP	H	E	ER	BB	SO
Leonard (W)	3	2	1	1	0	0
Newhouser	3	3	0	0	1	1
Hughson	3	5	2	2	0	2

Umpires — Rommel and Rue (A.L.), Conian and Dunn (N.L.). Time — 2:07. Attendance — 31,938.

For a while, however, it looked as if the Nationals were going to finally break the Americans' consecutive and series win streak when they climbed on top in the very first inning. Emil (Dutch) Leonard, whose selection by manager Joe McCarthy was somewhat of a surprise, opened the game for the Americans. Leonard, a knuckleball specialist for the Washington Senators, was a little bit rusty in the first.

The N.L.'s first run crossed the plate when Stan Hack and Billy Herman combined for back-to-back singles, with a fly by Stan "The Man" Musial to bring Hack home. It was Musial's first All-Star game appearance. Otherwise, Leonard was in control and bottled up the Nationals until he gave way to Hal Newhouser of the Detroit Tigers. Newhouser, a regular in All-Star play, came in at the top of the fourth and bewildered the opposition for the remainder of the contest. Tex Hughson of the Red Sox also kept the National League batters in check for the final innings of the game.

Leonard was credited with the victory, and Cooper with the loss.

Vince DiMaggio was the N.L.'s hitting star. The eldest of the famous DiMaggio brothers, Vince pounded out a single, a triple and a home run. His homer accounted for the Nationals' last run in the ninth.

When the game was over, there was grinning, back-slapping, and mutual admiration in the Americans' dressing room. Led by Bobby Doerr, some players chanted, "We're the champions again!"

It was a feeling the Americans earned, thanks to Doerr.

July 11, 1944

Forbes Field

Bill Nicholson and Phil Cavarretta, both outfielders for the Chicago Cubs, were excited at being named to the National League All-Star team. They considered it an honor to be selected with other top-bracket players in the league. They also had the unenviable task of helping the Nationals dethrone the Americans. The result was a 7–1 whitewashing of the Americans that gave the senior league its fourth and most impressive victory of the series.

The heroes were Nicholson and Cavarretta, of course.

On the day, Cavarretta tripled, singled and walked three times, while Nicholson belted a double to score the tying run and raced home on Augie Galan's single to put the Nationals in front to stay.

A small crowd of 29,589 took in the game, being played under lights for the second straight year. Game promoters were expecting between 35,000 to 40,000 fans to show, but sweltering 90-degree heat kept most people home. It's too bad since they missed history in the making. How many times was it that the National League pounded the American League ... and won?

Especially when the war had had a detrimental effect on baseball by now. Some top players were either drafted or enlisted. Thank goodness such stars as Ted Williams, Bobby Doerr, Joe Gordon, Rudy York, Vern Stephens, Red Schoendienst, Stan Musial, Enos Slaughter, Johnny Mize, Dixie Walker, and Hal Newhouser were left untouched.

After the game, A.L. manager Joe McCarthy might have wished that Cavarretta and Nicholson had been drafted. They almost single-handedly led the National Leaguers on a 12-hit shellacking that sent four runs home in the fifth, two more in the seventh, and another in the eighth. The Americans scored their lone run in the second when Ken Keltner raced home from third on Hank Borowy's single for a short-lived lead.

Yankee hurler Hank Borowy, a slim right-hander, also got the nod to open the game for the Americans and pitched masterfully. He gave up just three hits and struck out none. Borowy entered the contest with 11 victories and four defeats.

N.L. skipper Billy Southworth asked Bucky Walters to handle the

The 1944 All-Star Game

American League	AB	R	H	PO	A	E
Tucker (White Sox) cf	4	0	0	4	0	0
Spence (Senators) rf	4	0	2	2	1	0
McQuinn (Browns) 1b	4	0	1	5	1	1
Stephens (Browns) ss	4	0	1	1	0	0
Johnson (Red Sox) lf	3	0	0	2	1	0
Keltner (Indians) 3b	4	1	1	0	4	0
Doerr (Red Sox) 2b	3	0	0	4	1	1
Hemsley (Yankees) c	2	0	0	2	0	0
Hayes (Athletics) c	1	0	0	3	0	1
Borowy (Yankees) p	1	0	1	0	0	0
Hughson (Red Sox) p	1	0	0	0	0	0
Muncrief (Browns) p	0	0	0	1	0	0
Higgins (Tigers) ph	1	0	0	0	0	0
Newhouse (Tigers) p	0	0	0	0	1	0
Newsom (Athletics) p	0	0	0	0	0	0
Totals	32	1	6	24	9	3

National League	AB	R	H	PO	A	E
Galan (Dodgers) lf	4	1	1	2	0	0
Cavarretta (Cubs) 1b	2	1	2	12	0	0
Musial (Cardinals) cf–rf	4	1	1	2	1	0
W. Cooper (Cardinals) c	5	1	2	5	2	0
Mueller (Reds) c	0	0	0	0	0	0
Walker (Dodgers) cf	4	0	2	0	0	0
DiMaggio (Pirates) cf	0	0	0	0	0	0
Elliot (Pirates) 3b	3	0	0	0	3	0
Kurowski (Cardinals) 3b	1	0	1	0	1	0
Ryan (Braves) 2b	4	1	2	4	4	0
Marion (Cardinals) ss	3	1	0	2	3	0
Walters (Reds) p	0	0	0	0	1	0
Ott (Giants) ph	1	0	0	0	0	0
Raffensberger (Phillies) p	0	0	0	0	0	0
Nicholson (Cubs) ph	1	1	1	0	0	0
Sewell (Pirates) p	1	0	0	0	0	0
Medwick (Giants) ph	0	0	0	0	0	0
Tobin (Braves) p	0	0	0	0	0	0
Totals	33	7	12	27	15	1

American League	0	1	0	0	0	0	0	0	0 – 1
National League	0	0	0	0	4	0	2	1	x – 7

DP – Nationals 1, Americans 1. LOB – Nationals 9, Americans 5. 2B – Nicholson, Kurowski. 3B – Cavarretta. RBIs – Kurowski (2), Nicholson, Galan, W. Cooper, Walker, Musial, Borowy. SB – Ryan. SAC – Marion, Musial, Medwick. WP – Muncrief.

American League	IP	H	R	ER	BB	SO
Borowy	3	3	0	0	1	0
Hughson (L)	1⅔	5	4	3	1	2
Muncrief	1⅓	1	0	0	0	1
Newhouser	1⅔	3	3	2	2	1
Newsom	⅓	0	0	0	0	0

National League	IP	H	R	ER	BB	SO
Walters	3	5	1	1	0	1
Raffensberger (W)	2	1	0	0	0	2
Sewell	3	0	0	0	1	2
Tobin	1	0	0	0	0	0

Umpires — Barr and Sears (N.L.), Berry and Hubbard (A.L.). Time — 2:11. Attendance — 29,589.

---

pitching chores for the Nationals. Walters, a lanky, powerful right-hander for the Cincinnati Reds, equaled Borowy's performance. He scattered five hits, struck out one, and allowed only one run in three innings of work.

For the Americans, however, the lights went out in Pittsburgh in the fourth when the Nationals made mincemeat of Borowy's successor, Red Sox sinker baller Tex Hughson. Hughson had posted a 14–3 record going into the All-Star break. But all records aside, he went to the mound in the fourth and skated past the first three batters he faced until he was pounded for four runs on five hits in the fifth. It resembled a Bunker Hill–type slaughter.

The fireworks exploded when Connie Ryan singled to center, stole second, and scored when pinch-hitter Nicholson powdered a single to right. The game was now tied at one.

But that wasn't it. Audie Galan of the Dodgers sent the Nationals ahead with a sharp single to drive Nicholson home. Then Phil Cavarretta walked and the league-leading hitter, Stan Musial, was safe on first baseman George McQuinn's error of Bobby Doerr's relay throw on Musial's grounder. Dixie Walker kept the inning going, singling to score Musial, with Bob Muncrief relieving Hughson to close out the inning.

Detroit's Hal Newhouser became the National's next victim in the seventh when Whitey Kurowski's bases clearing double scored Cavarretta and Walker Cooper. The lead was now 6–1, with the Nationals notching their final run in the eighth on Bob Johnson's scoring fly ball, which sent Marty Marion home from third.

Along with Bucky Walters, N.L. pitchers Ken Raffensberger, Rip Sewell, and Jim Tobin combined to blank the Americans over the final six hittings on just one hit.

Connie Ryan, who went 2 for 4, summed up the importance of the victory thusly: "The victory was a sweet one for the National League since we hadn't done too well in All-Star competition up to that point, and the writers kept saying that the Americans had a big edge over us. But we won this one decisively and looked good doing it."

So did Cavarretta and Nicholson.

July 9, 1946

Fenway Park

What better way to resume All-Star play than have the game at Fenway Park in Boston, with Ted Williams performing before the hometown crowd.

Baseball fever was soaring in the home of the bean and the cod. The Red Sox, thick in the pennant race, were having a banner year. With such stars as Ted Williams, Dom DiMaggio, Bobby Doerr, Johnny Pesky, and Ted Hughson, the Sox won the divisional crown by 12 games over the second-place Detroit Tigers, with a phenomenal 104–50 won-loss record.

Therefore, it couldn't have been more appropriate than to stage this grand encounter at Fenway. It was the second time the All-Star game was played in Boston, but the outcome was something nobody ever dreamed possible.

With Ted Williams smacking two home runs and having a perfect four-for-four day, the Americans soundly beat the powerless Nationals 12–0 with not a fan out of the 34,906 leaving and all the cheers going to Williams.

Charley Grimm, handed the thankless task of managing the N.L. All-Star squad, was presented with a somewhat undistinguished pitching staff. Cub hurler Claude Passeau, aged 37, led the delegation which included Rip Sewell of Pittsburgh and Howie Pollett of the Cardinals. These men were elected to carry out the heroic task of keeping the power-laden American League lineup under control.

Apparently, the job was too much to handle as the Americans rattled out 14 hits and three home runs, the third by Charley Keller. Bob Feller, the great Cleveland Indians star, combined with Hal Newhouser and Jack Kramer to pitch three innings each and limit the Nationals to just three hits. In Fenway, that's incredible!

Two of the hits off Feller were infield. The only solid blow was delivered by Peanuts Lowery in the sixth, a single past Hal Newhouser to center field. Feller struck out three to run his All-Star record total, in four games, to 12.

Claude Passeau, who opened for the National League, wasn't so fortunate. In the first inning, Keller blistered one of his pitches, with Williams

The 1946 All-Star Game

National League	AB	R	H	PO	A	E
Schoendienst (Cardinals) 2b	2	0	0	0	2	0
Gustine (Pirates) 2b	1	0	0	1	1	0
Musial (Cardinals) lf	2	0	0	0	0	0
Ennis (Phillies) lf	2	0	0	0	0	0
Hopp (Braves) cf	2	0	1	0	0	0
Lowrey (Cubs) cf	2	0	1	3	0	0
Walker (Dodgers) rf	3	0	0	1	0	0
Slaughter (Cardinals) rf	1	0	0	0	0	0
Kurowski (Cardinals) 3b	3	0	0	2	1	0
Verban (Phillies) ph	1	0	0	0	0	0
Mize (Giants) 1b	1	0	0	7	0	0
McCormick (Phillies) ph	1	0	0	1	1	0
Cavarretta (Cubs) 1b	1	0	0	1	0	0
Cooper (Giants) c	1	0	1	0	0	0
Masi (Braves) c	2	0	0	4	1	0
Marion (Cardinals) ss	3	0	0	4	6	0
Passeau (Cubs) p	1	0	0	0	1	0
Higbe (Dodgers) p	1	0	0	0	0	0
Blackwell (Reds) p	0	0	0	0	0	0
Lamanno (Reds) ph	1	0	0	0	0	0
Sewell (Pirates) p	0	0	0	0	0	0
Totals	31	0	3	24	13	0
American League	AB	R	H	PO	A	E
D. DiMaggio (Red Sox) cf	2	0	1	1	0	0
Spence (Senators) cf	0	1	0	1	0	0
Chapman (Athletics) cf	2	0	0	1	0	0
Pesky (Red Sox) ss	2	0	0	1	0	1
Stephens (Browns) ss	3	1	2	0	4	0
Williams (Red Sox) lf	4	4	4	1	0	0
Keller (Yankees) rf	4	2	1	1	0	0
Doerr (Red Sox) 2b	2	0	0	1	1	0
Gordon (Yankees) 2b	2	0	1	0	1	0
Vernon (Senators) 1b	2	0	0	2	1	0
York (Red Sox) 1b	2	0	1	5	0	0
Keltner (Indians) 3b	0	0	0	0	0	0
Stirnweiss (Yankees) 3b	3	1	1	0	0	0
Hayes (Indians) c	1	0	0	3	0	0
Rosar (Athletics) c	2	1	1	5	0	0
Wagner (R. Sox) c	1	0	0	4	0	0
Feller (Indians) p	0	0	0	0	0	0
Appling (White Sox) ph	1	0	0	0	0	0
Newhouser (Tigers) p	1	1	1	1	0	0
Dickey (Yankees) ph	1	0	0	0	0	0
Kramer (Browns) p	1	1	1	0	0	0
Totals	36	12	14	27	7	1

National League .... 0 0 0 0 0 0 0 0 0 – 0
American League........................ 2 0 0 1 3 0 2 4 x – 12

DP – Nationals 2. LOB – Nationals 5, Americans 4. 2B – Stephens, Gordon. HR – Williams (2), Keller. RBIs – Keller (2), Williams (5), Stephens (2), Gordon (2), Chapman. WP – Blackwell.

National League	IP	H	R	ER	BB	SO
Passeau (L)	3	2	2	2	2	0
Higbe	1⅓	5	4	4	1	2
Blackwell	2⅔	3	2	2	1	1
Sewell	1	4	4	4	0	0

American League	IP	H	R	ER	BB	SO
Feller (W)	3	2	0	0	0	3
Newhouser	3	1	0	0	0	4
Kramer	3	0	0	0	1	3

Umpires – Summers and Rommel (A.L.), Boggess and Goetz (N.L.). Time – 2:19. Attendance – 34,906.

---

on base, into the right field bull pen. The score was quickly 2–0, Americans.

Passeau settled down and retired the Americans during the last two innings he pitched. Kirby Higbe then took the mound in the fourth, but proceeded to give up a home run to Ted Williams, his first of the day. The blast landed 450 feet away in the center field bleachers. By the end of the afternoon, Ted appeared as if he owned National League pitching.

Three more runs crossed the plate in the fifth when Higbe surrendered successive singles by Buddy Rosar and Hal Newhouser. Stan Spence walked, and all three runners scored on a double by shortstop Vern Stephens and a single by Williams. This scoring drive alone blew the game wide open and sent Higbe to the showers early.

Ewell Blackwell, Higbe's replacement, might have been wary in following such a trouncing. He was also jarred for two more runs in the seventh when Williams singled, Keller walked, and Joe Gordon smacked a double off the short left field fence. The score read 8–0.

But Williams wasn't finished dazzling the Boston faithful. Enter Rip Sewell in the eighth. Sewell, known for his "blooper pitch," took the brunt of the Americans' day-long attack. His blooper pitch, which he called "an eephus," was thrown in a high arc and dropped straight down on home plate. But he didn't fool anybody this time around. He gave up a total of four runs in one inning of relief. The bulk of these runs were on Williams' second home run of the day, a three-run clout, which scored Vern Stephens and Jack Kramer. The pitch Williams hit: Sewell's famed blooper.

After the game, A.L. manager Steve O'Neill suggested that the Red Sox "lend their slugger to every other club for a week." He added, "That Williams is the greatest hitter of all time. And Feller never has been much better. He had all his stuff clicking perfectly."

With reporters crowding into the clubhouse, Williams was still laughing over his second home run off Sewell. Basking in his glory, Ted remarked, "I wished I had a slow motion film of that pitch. But I have to thank Bill Dickey for that one. He told me to step into it."

Ted stepped into it all right—right into the All-Star game record books.

July 8, 1947

Wrigley Field

What promised to be a slugfest turned into an all-out pitching war and one of the most dramatic clashes in All-Star game history.

The site: Wrigley Field, Chicago. The first All-Star classic to be held there. Long known as a hitters' paradise with its ivy-covered walls, Wrigley Field promoters were expecting a bombardment of extra-base hits and home runs to entertain its 41,123 paying customers.

Instead, because of pitcher Johnny Sain's throwing error, the Americans squeezed out a 2–1 victory over the Nationals to give the junior circuit a 10–4 edge in the series, which dated back to the first game at Comiskey Park in 1933.

The game featured a strong pitching matchup: Ewell Blackwell, Cincinnati's beanpole sidearmer, versus Detroit's Hal Newhouser. Blackwell, a 14–2 winner with 12 straight victories, won the starting berth over Harry (The Cat) Brecheen and George Munger, both members of the St. Louis Cardinals. Braves ace Warren Spahn and the Dodgers' Ralph Branca were also available, but neither expected to see action since they had both pitched regular season games prior to this contest.

It was manager Eddie Dyer's firm contention that Blackwell, because of his consecutive win streak and experience in All-Star wars, had the best chances in turning out a victory.

Whereas A.L. manager Joe Cronin, originally criticized for announcing plans to start Yankee hurler Spud Chandler, went with Hal Newhouser since he was also a veteran in these campaigns. Evidently, Cronin played his cards right. The Americans had more distance hitters in their lineup than the Nationals. The Nationals' only power trust was Johnny Mize and Walker Cooper.

In fact, Mize, the fence-busting New York Giants first baseman, put the Nationals on the scoreboard first in the fourth when he smashed a home run halfway up the right center field bleachers. His 380-foot blast came off rookie Frank "Spec" Shea, Newhouser's successor, which provided the N.L.'s only run of the game. Shea was the eventual winner of the contest after blanking the Nationals for the remainder of his stint.

The 1947 All-Star Game

American League	AB	R	H	PO	A	E
Kell (Tigers) 3b	4	0	0	0	0	0
Johnson (Yankees) 3b	0	0	0	0	0	0
Lewis (Senators) rf	2	0	0	1	0	0
Appling (White Sox) ph	1	1	1	0	0	0
Henrich (Yankees) rf	1	0	0	3	0	0
Williams (Red Sox) lf	4	0	2	3	0	0
DiMaggio (Yankees) cf	3	0	1	1	0	0
Boudreau (Indians) ss	4	0	1	4	4	0
McQuinn (Yankees) 1b	4	0	0	9	1	0
Gordon (Yankees) 2b	2	0	1	0	4	0
Doerr (Red Sox) 2b	2	1	1	0	2	0
Rosar (Athletics) c	4	0	0	6	0	0
Newhouser (Tigers) p	1	0	0	0	0	0
Shea (Yankees) p	1	0	0	0	0	0
Spence (Senators) ph	1	0	1	0	0	0
Masterson (Senators) p	0	0	0	0	0	0
Page (Yankees) p	0	0	0	0	0	0
Totals	34	2	8	27	11	0
National League	AB	R	H	PO	A	E
H. Walker (Phillies) cf	2	0	0	1	0	0
Pafko (Cubs) cf	2	0	1	2	0	0
F. Walker (Dodgers) rf	2	0	0	1	0	0
Marshall (Giants) rf	1	0	0	3	0	0
W. Cooper (Giants) c	3	0	0	6	0	0
Edwards (Dodgers) c	0	0	0	2	0	0
Cavarretta (Cubs) 1b	1	0	0	1	0	0
Mize (Giants) 1b	3	1	2	8	0	0
Masi (Braves) c	0	0	0	0	0	0
Slaughter (Cardinals) lf	3	0	0	1	0	0
Gustine (Pirates) 3b	2	0	0	0	2	0
Kurowski (Cardinals) 3b	2	0	0	0	1	0
Marion (Cardinals) ss	2	0	1	0	1	0
Reese (Dodgers) ss	1	0	0	0	2	0
Verban (Phillies) 2b	2	0	0	0	0	0
Stanky (Dodgers) 2b	2	0	0	2	2	0
Blackwell (Reds) p	0	0	0	0	0	0
Haas (Reds) ph	1	0	1	0	0	0
Brecheen (Cardinals) p	1	0	0	0	1	0
Sain (Braves) p	0	0	0	0	0	1
Musial (Cardinals) ph	1	0	0	0	0	0
Spahn (Braves) p	0	0	0	0	0	0
Rowe (Phillies) ph	1	0	0	0	0	0
Totals	32	1	5	27	9	1

American League	0	0	0	0	0	1	1	0	0	– 2
National League	0	0	0	1	0	0	0	0	0	– 1

DP—Nationals 1. LOB—Nationals 8, Americans 6. SB—Williams, Gordon. HR—Mize. RBIs—Mize, Spence, DiMaggio. SB—Doerr. WP—Blackwell. PB—W. Cooper.

American League	IP	H	R	ER	BB	SO
Newhouser	3	1	0	0	0	0
Shea (W)	3	3	1	1	2	2
Masterson	1⅔	0	0	0	1	2
Page	1⅓	1	0	0	1	0
National League	IP	H	R	ER	BB	SO
Blackwell	3	1	0	0	0	4
Brecheen	3	5	1	1	0	2
Sain (L)	1	2	1	1	0	1
Spahn	2	0	0	0	1	1

Umpires — Boyer and Passarella (A.L.), Conlan and Henline (N.L.). Time — 2:19. Attendance — 41,123.

Up until then, the scoreboard showed nothing but goose eggs. Newhouser and Blackwell each gave up single hits and, otherwise, they were just unhittable. Newhouser struck out two, and Blackwell whiffed four.

Blackwell was relieved in the fourth by Harry Brecheen, who blanked the Americans through the sixth. It was in that fateful inning that Luke Appling, batting for Buddy Lewis, stroked a single to left and advanced to third on Ted Williams' base hit to right. Joe DiMaggio then smacked Brecheen's first offering to shortstop Pee Wee Reese, who turned it into a 6–4–3 double play. Appling scored on the play, tying the game up 1–1.

Johnny Sain came in to pitch for the Nationals in the seventh, but it was his costly throwing error which lost his team the game. The play occurred after shortstop Bobby Doerr singled and stole second. Sain, trying to pick Doerr off, whirled around and in one sweeping motion fired the ball to Reese. The ball hit Doerr and caromed off into right center, and permitted Doerr to reach third. Doerr scored the winning run when Stan Spence, batting for Shea, drilled one of Sain's high fastballs to center for a base hit.

The loss had to be demoralizing for the underdog Nationals. They had gained a moral victory by holding their rivals to just a one-run margin, but that wasn't enough. In a postgame interview, manager Eddie Dyer blamed Sain for the defeat. He had told Sain before pitching to Spence, "Don't throw a high one." Sain didn't listen and tried sneaking one past Spence, but couldn't fool him.

With the Nationals' 10th loss in 14 games, National League president Ford Frick warned his managers and players that he would call for discontinuing the interleague game unless they took it more seriously.

That even applied to Sain.

July 13, 1948

Sportsman Park

It was a game of "the walking wounded." Joe DiMaggio and Ted Williams were both out of the starting lineup nursing nagging injuries. Williams was suffering from a torn cartilage and DiMaggio from a swollen left knee. Third baseman George Kell, also hobbled with a badly puffed knee, never saw action at all. Hal Newhouser, the Americans' top pitching ace, entered the game as a pinch runner since he developed bursitis in his pitching arm and couldn't play.

Yet, for the second straight year, the All-Star game was being played in a National League ball park, this time in St. Louis. Someone thought it would help the Nationals snap their interleague losing streak.

It didn't.

In spite of the Americans missing DiMaggio, Williams, Kell, and Newhouser, the Nationals failed to muster up a victory, losing for the 11th time in 15 games, 5–2.

The hero of the game was a virtual no-name. (That, of course, changed after the game.) His name was Vic Raschi, a strong, silent newcomer from the New York Yankees, who slugged and pitched the aching-back Americans to victory.

Raschi came on in the sixth to pitch three scoreless innings and pulled the Americans out of trouble by striking out rookie Richie Ashburn of the Phillies with the bases loaded.

As A.L. manager Bucky Harris told reporters before the contest, "Despite our injuries, we'll give the Nationals the best fight we can."

So they did.

Harris surprised everyone when he assigned Walt Masterson to start the game. Masterson, on his way toward fashioning an undistinguished 8–15 record for the Washington Senators, was the last person anyone expected to get the call. Harris had Joe Coleman (8–6) of the Philadelphia A's, Cleveland's Bob Lemon (13–7), and, of course, Vic Raschi (10–3), if Masterson got in a mess.

Harris took everyone's criticisms lightly. He handed the ball to Masterson and gave him a confident pat on the back before he went out to face the

The 1948 All-Star Game

National League	AB	R	H	PO	A	E
Ashburn (Phillies) cf	4	1	2	1	0	0
Kiner (Pirates) lf	1	0	0	1	0	0
Schoendienst (Cardinals) 2b	4	0	0	0	1	0
Rigney (Giants) 2b	0	0	0	2	0	0
Musial (Cardinals) lf-cf	4	1	2	3	0	0
Mize (Giants) 1b	4	0	1	4	1	0
Slaughter (Cardinals) rf	2	0	1	2	0	0
Holmes (Braves) rf	1	0	0	1	0	0
Pafko (Cubs) 3b	2	0	0	0	0	0
Elliot (Braves) 3b	2	0	1	0	0	0
Cooper (Braves) c	2	0	0	3	0	0
Masi (Braves) c	2	0	1	4	0	0
Reese (Dodgers) ss	2	0	0	2	2	0
Kerr (Giants) ss	2	0	0	1	0	0
Branca (Dodgers) p	1	0	0	0	0	0
Gustine (Pirates) ph	1	0	0	0	0	0
Schmitz (Cubs) p	0	0	0	0	0	0
Sain (Braves) p	0	0	0	0	0	0
Waitkus (Cubs) ph	0	0	0	0	0	0
Blackwell (Reds) p	0	0	0	0	0	0
Thomsom (Giants) ph	1	0	0	0	0	0
Totals	35	2	8	24	4	0

American League	AB	R	H	PO	A	E
Mullin (Tigers) rf	1	0	0	0	0	0
DiMaggio (Yankees) ph	1	0	0	0	0	0
Zarilla (Browns) rf	2	0	0	2	0	0
Henrich (Yankees) lf	3	0	0	1	0	0
Boudreau (Indians) ss	2	0	0	2	0	0
Stephens (Red Sox) ss	2	0	1	0	0	0
Gordon (Indians) 2b	2	0	0	1	2	0
Doerr (Red Sox) 2b	2	0	0	0	3	0
Evers (Tigers) cf	4	1	1	0	0	0
Keltner (Indians) 3b	3	1	1	0	6	0
McQuinn (Yankees) 1b	4	1	2	14	0	0
Rosar (Athletics) c	1	0	0	1	0	0
Tebbetts (Red Sox) c	1	1	0	5	1	0
Masterson (Senators) p	0	0	0	0	0	0
Vernon (Senators) ph	0	1	0	0	0	0
Raschi (Yankees) p	1	0	1	0	0	0
Williams (Red Sox) ph	0	0	0	0	0	0
Newhouser (Tigers) pr	0	0	0	0	0	0
Coleman (Athletics) p	0	0	0	0	1	0
Totals	29	5	6	26	13	0

National League .... 2 0 0 0 0 0 0 0 0 – 2
American League........................ 0 1 1 3 0 0 0 0 x – 5

DP – none. LOB – Nationals 10, Americans 8. HR – Musial, Evers. RBIs – Musial (2), Evers, Boudreau, Raschi (2), DiMaggio. SAC – Coleman. WP – Masterson.

National League	IP	H	R	ER	BB	SO
Branca	3	1	2	2	3	3
Schmitz (L)	⅓	3	3	3	1	0
Sain	1⅔	0	0	0	0	3
Blackwell	3	2	0	0	3	1
American League	IP	H	R	ER	BB	SO
Masterson	3	5	2	2	1	1
Raschi (W)	3	3	0	0	1	3
Coleman	3	0	0	0	2	3

Umpires — Berry and Paparella (A.L.), Reardon and Stewart (N.L.). Time — 2:27. Attendance — 34,009.

National Leaguers. In the first inning, Harris might have questioned his choice, as the Nationals jumped all over Masterson for two runs on Stan Musial's two-run home run which scored Richie Ashburn, who had singled. The homer landed on the right field pavillion roof over the 360-foot mark.

Once he overcame these early butterflies, Masterson settled down and took command. He didn't allow any additional scoring.

Brooklyn's Leo Durocher, the N.L. skipper, then had Ralph Branca take on the Americans, but Branca had an even rougher outing than Masterson. He gave up two runs, walked three, and struck out three, but, for the most part, he didn't throw a typical Branca game.

Slugger Hoot Evers picked on a Branca pitch for a home run to left field in the second to bring the Americans within one of the Nationals, 2–1.

Then, in the third, the Americans tied the score up at two when Mickey Vernon, pinch-hitting for Masterson, drew a walk. Vernon and Pat Mullin, the new right fielder, then executed a perfect double steal. Lou Boudreau, the scrappy Indians shortstop-manager, hit a long fly to Enos Slaughter, deep enough to score Vernon and knot the game at two all.

But in the fourth, the Americans launched ahead of the Nationals 5–2 by scoring three runs off two National League pitchers, Johnny Schmitz and Johnny Sain. Schmitz replaced Branca, but did little to help his teammates stay close. He lasted just a third of an inning. Singles by Ken Keltner and George McQuinn put runners at first and second, with one out. Then Birdie Tebbetts walked to fill the bases before Vic Raschi came to the plate. Not known for his hitting, Raschi promptly smacked a single to score Keltner and McQuinn, with Tebbetts stopping at third.

With the Americans now on top 5–2, Leo Durocher wasn't going to take any chances. He called on Johnny Sain to put out the fire; instead, Sain contributed to it. DiMaggio and Musial, both appearing as pinch hitters, came through with back-to-back singles to score Tebbetts and Raschi.

With the game clearly out of reach, Raschi blanked the Nationals for the middle three innings until Joe Coleman saved the game with perfect relief in the final three frames.

For a team beat up with injuries, Raschi was just what the doctor ordered.

July 12, 1949

Ebbetts Field

The All-Star wars resumed at Brooklyn's Ebbetts Field, where 32,577 squirmed through three hours and four minutes of sloppy baseball play, only for the Nationals to go down to their third straight defeat, 11–7. The victory boosted the Americans' game edge to 12–4 in what had become known for the Nationals as "an annual nightmare."

The game's batting star was Joe DiMaggio. DiMaggio, who missed 65 games of the regular season with a sore heel, was selected to the A.L. team by manager Lou Boudreau, even though his batting statistics at the midseason break didn't warrant it.

A born leader, Big Joe D led the way by driving in three big runs with a sixth-inning double and a first-inning single. Five errors by the National League, an All-Star game record, was the senior circuit's undoing along with some shoddy pitching. Of course, the Americans' staff of arms was nothing much to rave about either.

Both starting pitchers, Warren Spahn for the N.L. and Mel Parnell for the A.L., didn't last past the second inning. Spahn, the Milwaukee Braves' ace, was rocked for four runs on two hits and two errors in the very first inning. It was the type of game neither side really deserved to win.

George Kell, missing from the 1948 All-Star classic with a leg injury, got things rolling when he was safe at first on Eddie Kazak's throwing error. Kell stole second as Williams struck out. Eddie Joost followed with a walk, and then Joe DiMaggio singled to right to score Kell. Spahn continued to labor, but he didn't have good stuff as Eddie Robinson laced a single to right to score DiMaggio. Kell advanced to third. Pee Wee Reese then made the second error of the inning by juggling Cass Michaels' high-hopping grounder. Joost scored on the miscue, with Robinson moving to second. Birdie Tebbetts, a hitting star in the previous year's American League win, picked up where he left off with a sharp single to left to score Robinson. Michaels roared around to third, but was stranded when Mel Parnell struck out.

Then, in the home half of the first, the Nationals took their shots at Parnell. He lasted an inning and a third, giving up three earned runs on three hits. Jackie Robinson, who broke the color barrier with the Brooklyn

The 1949 All-Star Game

American League	AB	R	H	PO	A	E
D. DiMaggio (Red Sox) rf–cf	5	2	2	2	0	0
Raschi (Yankees) p	1	0	0	0	1	0
Kell (Tigers) 3b	3	2	2	0	1	0
Dillinger (Browns) 3b	1	2	1	0	2	0
Williams (Red Sox) lf	2	1	0	1	0	0
Mitchell (Indians) lf	1	0	1	1	0	1
J. DiMaggio (Yankees) cf	4	1	2	0	0	0
Doby (Indians) rf–cf	1	0	0	2	0	0
Joost (Athletics) ss	2	1	1	2	2	0
Stephens (Red Sox) ss	2	0	0	2	0	0
E. Robinson (Senators) 1b	5	1	1	8	0	0
Goodman (Red Sox) 1b	0	0	0	1	1	0
Michaels (White Sox) 2b	2	0	0	1	3	0
Gordon (Indians) 2b	2	1	1	3	3	0
Tebbetts (Red Sox) c	2	0	2	2	0	0
Berra (Yankees) c	3	0	0	2	1	0
Parnell (Red Sox) p	1	0	0	0	1	0
Trucks (Tigers) p	1	0	0	0	0	0
Brissie (Athletics) p	1	0	0	0	0	0
Wertz (Tigers) rf	2	0	0	0	0	0
Totals	41	11	13	27	15	1

National League	AB	R	H	PO	A	E
Reese (Dodgers) ss	5	0	0	3	3	1
Robinson (Dodgers) 2b	4	3	1	1	1	0
Musial (Cardinals) cf–rf	4	1	3	2	0	0
Kiner (Pirates) lf	5	1	1	3	0	0
Mize (Giants) 1b	2	0	1	1	0	1
Hodges (Dodgers) 1b	3	1	1	8	2	0
Marshall (Giants) rf	1	1	0	1	0	1
Bickford (Braves) p	0	0	0	0	0	0
Thomson (Giants) ph	1	0	0	0	0	0
Pollet (Cardinals) p	0	0	0	1	0	0
Blackwell (Reds) p	0	0	0	0	0	0
Slaughter (Cardinals) ph	1	0	0	0	0	0
Roe (Dodgers) p	0	0	0	0	0	0
Kazak (Cardinals) 3b	2	0	2	0	1	0
S. Gordon (Giants)	2	0	1	0	4	0
Seminick (Phillies) c	1	0	0	3	0	1
Campanella (Dodgers) c	2	0	0	2	0	1
Spahn (Braves) p	0	0	0	0	0	0
Newcombe (Dodgers) p	1	0	0	0	0	0
Schoendiesnt (Cardinals) ph	1	0	1	0	0	0
Munger (Cardinals) p	0	0	0	0	0	0
Pafko (Cubs) cf	2	1	1	2	0	0
Totals	37	7	12	27	11	5

```
American League........................ 4 0 0 2 0 2 3 0 0 – 11
National League ....................... 2 1 2 0 0 2 0 0 0 –  7
```

DP – Americans 2, Nationals 1. LOB – Nationals 12, Americans 8. 2B – J. Robinson, Tebbetts, S. Gordon, J. DiMaggio, D. DiMaggio, J. Gordon, Mitchell. HR – Musial, Kiner. SB – Kell. HBP – By Parnell (Seminick).

American League	IP	H	R	ER	BB	SO
Parnell	1	3	3	3	1	1
Trucks (W)	2	3	2	2	2	0
Brissie	3	5	2	2	2	1
Raschi	3	1	0	0	3	1

National League	IP	H	R	ER	BB	SO
Spahn	1⅓	4	4	0	2	3
Newcombe (L)	2⅔	3	2	2	1	0
Munger	1	0	0	0	1	0
Bickford	1	2	2	2	1	0
Pollet	1	4	3	3	0	0
Blackwell	1	0	0	0	0	2
Roe	1	0	0	0	0	0

Umpires – Barlick, Gore, and Ballanfant (A.L.), Hubbard, Summers, and Grieve (N.L.). Time – 3:04. Attendance – 32,577.

Dodgers, was playing in his first All-Star game. He silenced any critics by banging a double to left. Stan Musial followed with his customary key hit, a homer over the right field screen. Robinson scored ahead of Williams and the game was now 4–2.

In the second inning, Parnell pitched to only three batters, but enough to hurt. Willard Marshall drew a free pass to first before Eddie Kazak singled to left to move Marshall to second. In a wild streak, Parnell then struck Andy Seminick with a pitch. He was pulled by manager Lou Boudreau, who called on Virgil Trucks. Trucks was a right-hander for the New York Yankees who finished the season with a sparkling 21–10 record. His first batter was Don Newcombe, who had replaced Spahn on the mound. Newcombe, one of six Brooklyn Dodgers selected to the team, was a pretty good hitting pitcher in his day.

Not this inning he wasn't. Newcombe ended the inning with a long drive that appeared to have chances of clearing the center field wall for a homer, or at least an extra base hit. But Ted Williams, the gifted outfielder that he was, made a spectacular leaping catch to rob the Nationals of any additional scoring.

With the one run scored, the Nationals were close to the Americans, 4–3.

The Nationals then took the lead for the first time that day in the third inning when Jackie Robinson's speedy base-running and singles by Stan Musial and Johnny Mize amounted to two more runs.

The Americans pecked away with two more in the fourth to take the lead, 6-5. The runs scored on a grounder by Philadelphia's Eddie Joost, whose hopper to first baseman Gil Hodges took a tricky bounce for an error on the play.

All was quiet until the sixth when the Americans added two more runs on Joe DiMaggio's double off Vern Bickford. The ball crashed against the left centerfield wall and scored Dom DiMaggio, Joe's brother, and St. Louis Browns third-sacker Bob Dillinger. The Americans now led, 8-5.

The Nationals didn't give up. In their bottom of the sixth, Ralph Kiner played long ball with A.L. pitcher Lou Brissie by taking Brissie over the 351-foot mark for a two-run homer. Jackie Robinson scored to put the N.L. within one, 8-7.

It was no use, however, as N.L. manager Billy Southworth paraded seven pitchers to the hill. That and a leaky infield, who committed five errors leading to four unearned runs on the afternoon, lost the game. Manager Lou Boudreau called these miscues "the turning point."

The real turning point for the A.L. squad proved to be Joe DiMaggio. A three-run splurge in the seventh by the Americans put the game away for good at the expense of Howie Pollet, the N.L.'s new relief pitcher. Joe Gordon doubled, scoring on Dom DiMaggio's single, and two more runs came in off Pat Dillinger's one bagger and Dale Mitchell's scoring double to left. Dom DiMaggio and Dillinger trucked across the plate to end the day's scoring and the game.

Virgil Trucks was credited with the victory, while Don Newcombe suffered the loss.

But the real boost to the Americans was having good ole Joltin' Joe.

July 11, 1950

Comiskey Park

Red Schoendienst was not named by the fans to the N.L. All-Star squad for the 1950 All-Star contest. Instead, manager Burt Shotten added Schoendienst to the roster and raised some eyebrows when the young Cardinals second-sacker was inserted as Jackie Robinson's replacement in the late innings.

Schoendienst, leading the league with a .341 batting mark, had told several teammates before he entered the game, "I'm going to homer if I ever get into this game."

It isn't known whether Schoendienst received a spiritual visit from above, but his prediction came true when he powered a Ted Gray home run ball into the left field seats to help his National League team jump past the American League 4–3 in 14 innings. The blast ended the Americans' series domination over the Nationals, and it was the first time the Nationals had beaten the Americans in an A.L. ball park. It was also the first extra-inning All-Star game. The series record now stood at 12–5 in favor of the Americans.

Schoendienst, who had only three homers on the season, was mobbed by his teammates as he crossed home plate. The bench began clearing from the moment Schoendienst connected. There was never any doubt that his hit would land in the front row seats of the upper left field stands some 375 feet away.

Many of the 46,127 paid remained till the very end, only to tell their friends afterwards about the dog-eat-dog battle they saw between the two clubs. Schoendienst's homer, the second homer on the day, also ended what had become a marathon affair which lasted three hours and 19 minutes.

Neither starting pitcher was around to taste the fruits of victory or the agony of defeat, depending on what side of the field they were on. Vic Raschi was Casey Stengel's pick to open the game on the mound for the not-so-mighty Americans. Robin Roberts, the Philadelphia Phillies $25,000 bonus baby, took the hill for the Nationals. Both pitched extraordinarily well.

Raschi gave up two runs on two hits; Roberts one run on three hits in three-inning stretches. The Nationals were the first to score, with Jackie Robinson roaring home on Enos Slaughter's triple in the first inning.

The 1950 All-Star Game

National League	AB	R	H	PO	A	E
Jones (Phillies) 3b	7	0	1	2	3	0
Kiner (Pirates) lf	6	1	2	1	0	0
Musial (Cardinals) 1b	5	0	0	11	1	0
Robinson (Dodgers) 2b	4	1	1	3	2	0
Wyrostek (Reds) rf	2	0	0	0	0	0
Slaughter (Cardinals) cf–rf	4	1	2	3	0	0
Schoendienst (Cardinals) 2b	1	1	1	1	1	0
Sauer (Cubs) rf	2	0	0	1	0	0
Pafko (Cubs) cf	4	0	2	4	0	0
Campanella (Dodgers) c	6	0	0	13	2	0
Marion (Cardinals) ss	2	0	0	0	2	0
Konstanty (Phillies) p	0	0	0	0	0	0
Jansen (Giants) p	2	0	0	1	0	0
Snider (Dodgers) ph	1	0	0	0	0	0
Blackwell (Reds) p	1	0	0	0	1	0
Roberts (Phillies) p	1	0	0	0	0	0
Newcombe (Dodgers) p	0	0	0	0	1	0
Sisler (Phillies) ph	1	0	1	0	0	0
Reese (Dodgers) ss	3	0	0	2	4	0
Totals	52	4	10	42	17	0

American League	AB	R	H	PO	A	E
Rizzuto (Yankees) ss	6	0	2	2	2	0
Doby (Indians) cf	6	1	2	9	0	0
Kell (Tigers) 3b	6	0	0	2	4	0
Williams (Red Sox) lf	4	0	1	2	0	0
D. DiMaggio (Red Sox) lf	2	0	0	1	0	0
Dropo (Red Sox) 1b	3	0	1	8	1	0
Fain (Athletics) 1b	3	0	1	2	1	0
Evers (Tigers) rf	2	0	0	1	0	0
J. DiMaggio (Yankees) rf	3	0	0	3	0	0
Berra (Yankees) c	2	0	0	2	0	0
Hegan (Indians) c	3	0	0	7	1	0
Doerr (Red Sox) 2b	3	0	0	1	4	0
Coleman (Yankees) 2b	2	0	0	0	0	1
Raschi (Yankees) p	0	0	0	0	0	0
Michaels (Senators) ph	1	1	1	0	0	0
Lemon (Indians) p	0	1	0	1	0	0
Houtteman (Tigers) p	1	0	0	1	0	0
Reynolds (Yankees) p	1	0	0	0	0	0
Henrich (Yankees) ph	1	0	0	0	0	0
Gray (Tigers) p	0	0	0	0	0	0
Feller (Indians) p	0	0	0	0	0	0
Totals	49	3	8	42	13	1

```
National League ........... 0 2 0 0 0 0 0 0 1 0 0 0 0 1 - 4
American League........... 0 0 1 0 2 0 0 0 0 0 0 0 0 0 - 3
```

DP—Nationals 1, Americans 1. LOB—Nationals 9, Americans 6. 2B—Michaels, Doby, Kiner. 3B—Slaughter, Dropo. HR—Kiner, Schoendienst. RBIs—Slaughter, Sauer, Kell (2), Williams, Kiner, Schoendienst. WP—Roberts. PB—Hegan.

National League	IP	H	R	ER	BB	SO
Roberts	3	3	1	1	1	1
Newcombe	2	3	2	2	1	1
Konstanty	1	0	0	0	0	2
Jansen	5	1	0	0	0	6
Blackwell (W)	3	1	0	0	0	2
American League	IP	H	R	ER	BB	SO
Raschi	3	2	2	2	0	1
Lemon	3	1	0	0	0	2
Houtteman	3	3	1	1	1	0
Reynolds	3	1	0	0	1	2
Gray (L)	1⅓	3	1	1	0	1
Feller	⅔	0	0	0	1	1

Umpires—McGowan, Rommel, and Stevens (A.L.), Pinelli, Conian, and Robb (N.L.). Time—3:19. Attendance—46,127.

But the Americans tied the game in the second when George Kell knocked in Cass Michaels from third with a scoring fly ball to Enos Slaughter.

Bob Lemon, Cleveland Indians ace, took over pitching chores in the top of the fourth and held the N.L. scoreless for the same. Don Newcombe, subbing for Roberts, did the same with A.L. hitters when he entered the game.

The game finally broke open in the fifth when the Americans suddenly became serious about winning by pounding across two runs off Newcombe. Bob Lemon walked and Larry Doby doubled, placing runners at second and third, with one out. Lemon scored on George Kell's deep fly to center fielder Andy Pafko, who just entered the game. Then, Ted Williams cracked his only single of the day to right to send Doby home with the second run of the inning. The score was 3–2, Americans.

But the Nationals were hungry for a victory. Regrouping, Ralph Kiner led off against Art Houtteman, now pitching for the Americans, with a solo home run into the left field stands to even the score at three apiece.

Kiner's smash sent the game into extra innings until Schoendienst blew out the lights with his dramatic home run in the 14th inning.

Ewell Blackwell, who pitched the last three innings, picked up the victory, allowing only one hit. Ted Gray took the loss.

Besides Schoendienst, Larry Jansen was another hero for the Nationals. He hurled five shutout innings, the longest stint in relief, striking out six to tie a record set by Carl Hubbell in 1934 and matched by Johnny Vander Meer in 1943.

The game was a bitter defeat for the Americans since it was learned afterwards that Ted Williams, who made a leaping catch of Ralph Kiner's deep drive in the first inning, had played the entire game with a fractured wrist. In great pain, Williams remained in the game and had one RBI-scoring single in four at-bats. Unfortunately, the injury lost Williams to the Red Sox for the rest of the season.

The National League should also be credited with having enough adversity to win. Prior to the contest, a swirl of controversy clouded the game. Evidently, manager Burt Shotten got himself in a heap of trouble when he said he was going to ignore the fan's selections for the starting center fielder. Instead, he was planning to start his own team's center fielder, Dodger Duke Snider.

A flurry of calls and letters flooded the office of Commissioner A.B. "Happy" Chandler, who reacted by ordering Shotten to abide by the fans' favorites.

Shotten got the message, and alternated Enos Slaughter and Andy Pafko in center. However, Shotten supposedly snubbed another outfielder on the roster, Hank Sauer, for personal differences.

Fortunately, Schoendienst was on Shotten's good side or the game might have had a different ending.

July 10, 1951

Briggs Stadium

A four–home run barrage highlighted the most explosive attack by the National League to date. Fence-clearing blows by Stan Musial, Gil Hodges, Bob Elliott, and Ralph Kiner paced the Nationals to a 8–3 drubbing of the Americans before 52,075 amazed fans. The game was at Briggs Stadium in connection with Detroit's 250th birthday as a city.

But the Nationals ruined the festivities by boosting their win streak to two games, trailing the Americans, 12–6, in the series edge. The four home runs accounted for six of the Nationals' eight runs. The Americans, who were 7–5 favorites to win the contest, did everything they could to lose.

Robin Roberts showed the way with his second starting assignment in as many years for the National League. N.L. manager Eddie Sawyer really had no other choice in the matter, since his other eight pitchers had all worked regular season matchups two days before the All-Star affair. Preacher Rowe and Don Newcombe were other possibilities, but they worked relief in respective games before the interleague contest, too. Roberts, who led the 1950 Phils to a World Championship, allowed one run on four hits in two innings of work and struck out none.

A.L. skipper Casey Stengel reached into his magic bag and pulled out Ned Garver, sensational St. Louis Browns ace, to face Roberts in the battle of arms. Stengel could have used Yankee lefty Eddie Lopat, Cleveland's Bob Lemon, or Detroit's Freddie Hutchinson. Garver was a much sought after commodity by division leading clubs, however. With the last place Browns, he had won 11, or half of his team's *total* wins on the year.

Stengel was wise in his decision to go with Garver, who matched Roberts pitch for pitch, since the hurler lasted the full three innings and gave up only one run on one hit.

The one run he allowed came in the first when Richie Ashburn doubled, advanced to third, and scored on Alvin Dark's short fly to center.

The Americans got even in the home half of the second when Ferris Fain's triple sent Yogi Berra home, who had singled in his first at bat.

With the score deadlocked 1–1, the Nationals put the game away in the fourth when Casey Stengel replaced Garver with Eddie Lopat. Lopat was

The 1951 All-Star Game

National League	AB	R	H	PO	A	E
Ashburn (Phillies) cf	4	2	2	4	1	0
Snider (Dodgers) cf	0	0	0	0	0	0
Dark (Giants) ss	5	0	1	0	3	0
Reese (Dodgers) ss	0	0	0	0	1	0
Musial (Cardinals) lf–rf	4	1	2	0	0	0
Westlake (Cardinals) lf	0	0	0	0	0	0
J. Robinson (Dodgers) 2b	4	1	2	3	1	1
Schoendienst (Cardinals) 2b	0	0	0	0	0	0
Hodges (Dodgers) 1b	5	2	2	6	0	0
Elliott (Braves) 3b	2	1	1	1	1	0
Jones (Phillies) 3b	2	0	0	3	0	0
Ennis (Phillies) rf	2	0	0	0	0	0
Kiner (Pirates) lf	2	1	1	1	0	0
Wyrostek (Reds) lf	1	0	0	0	0	0
Campanella (Dodgers) c	4	0	0	9	1	0
Roberts (Phillies) p	0	0	0	0	0	0
Slaughter (Cardinals) ph	1	0	0	0	0	0
Maglie (Giants) p	1	0	0	0	0	0
Newcombe (Dodgers) p	2	0	1	0	1	0
Blackwell (Reds) p	0	0	0	0	0	0
Totals	39	8	12	27	9	1

American League	AB	R	H	PO	A	E
D. DiMaggio (Red Sox) cf	5	0	1	1	0	0
Fox (White Sox) 2b	3	0	1	3	1	1
Doerr (Red Sox) ph–2b	1	0	1	1	0	0
Kell (Tigers) 3b	3	1	1	4	2	0
Williams (Red Sox) lf	3	0	1	3	0	0
Busby (White Sox) lf	0	0	0	0	0	0
Berra (Yankees) c	4	1	1	4	2	1
Wertz (Tigers) rf	3	1	1	2	0	0
Rizzuto (Yankees) ss	1	0	0	1	2	0
Fain (Athletics) 1b	3	0	1	5	0	0
E. Robinson (White Sox) 1b	1	0	0	0	1	0
Carrasquel (White Sox) ss	2	0	1	0	3	0
Minoso (White Sox) ph–rf	2	0	0	2	0	0
Garver (Browns) p	1	0	0	0	0	0
Lopat (Yankees) p	0	0	0	0	0	0
Doby (Indians) ph	1	0	0	0	0	0
Hutchinson (Tigers) p	0	0	0	0	0	0
Stephens (Red Sox) p	1	0	0	0	0	0
Parnell (Red Sox) p	0	0	0	0	0	0
Lemon (Indians) p	0	0	0	1	0	0
Hegan (Indians) ph	1	0	1	0	0	0
Totals	35	3	10	27	11	2

National League .... 1 0 0 3 0 2 1 1 0 – 8
American League........................ 0 1 0 1 1 0 0 0 0 – 3

DP—Americans, 1. LOB—Nationals 8, Americans 9. 2B—Ashburn, Hegan. 3B—Fain, Williams. HR—Musial, Elliott, Wertz, Kell, Hodges, Kiner. RBIs—Fain, Musial, Elliott (2), Wertz, Kell, Hodges (2). SAC HIT—Kell. PB—Campanella.

National League	IP	H	R	ER	BB	SO
Roberts	2	4	1	1	1	1
Maglie (W)	3	3	2	2	1	1
Newcombe	3	2	0	0	0	3
Blackwell	1	1	0	0	1	2
American League	IP	H	R	ER	BB	SO
Garver	3	1	1	0	1	1
Lopat (L)	1	3	3	3	0	0
Hutchinson	3	3	3	3	2	0
Parnell	1	3	1	1	1	1
Lemon	1	2	0	0	1	1

Umpires — Passarella, Hurley, and Honochick (A.L.), Robb, Jorda, and Dascoli (N.L.). Time — 2:41. Attendance — 52,075.

---

bombed for three runs, begun with Stan Musial's homer into the second deck of the right field stands. Then Gil Hodges bounced a single to center and scored on Bob Elliott's crushing blow, a two-run shot and the second homer of the inning. The score jumped to 4–1, Nationals.

After Roberts exited, New York Giants hurler Sal Maglie came in to pitch relief for the winning Nationals. But he surrendered a fourth-inning home run to Vic Wertz to pull the Americans within striking distance, 4–2.

Maglie was replaced by Freddie Hutchinson in the fifth. The Americans drew one step closer in the bottom of that inning when George Kell powered his homer to account for the Americans' final run of the game.

Now 4–3, the Nationals concluded their show of power in the eighth when Ralph Kiner walloped his blast to end the scoring and the game, 8–3.

Even though Sal Maglie was credited with the victory, Don Newcombe also sparkled in three innings of relief, from the sixth through the eighth, by striking out three. Ewell Blackwell finished up in the ninth. Eddie Lopat received the loss.

One sad note: Joe DiMaggio, who was named an honorary member of the A.L. squad, announced his retirement at the end of the season with the New York Yankees. His spirit from the game was sorely missed. DiMaggio never played in the 1951 game, because of a nagging leg injury.

Richie Ashburn was the National League's hitting standout: a single, double, two runs scored, and a stolen base. He also played well in the field; he cut off another American scoring threat in the sixth by hauling down Vic Wertz's long drive to right center field.

Even though the ballgame was strictly a home run contest, manager Eddie Sawyer was pleased by the power his players packed into their performances. He told reporters, "Don't lose sight of the pitching. Newcombe and Maglie were great. Roberts obviously didn't have it, so I pulled him out."

Clearly the National League had plenty to win.

July 14, 1952

Shibe Park

Sweet revenge that didn't go Sauer was the story at Shibe Park on a rain-filled evening which saw a 45-minute downpour cut the game short after five innings, and the National League beat the American League 3–2. A rain-soaked 32,785 showed up to watch the two teams battle.

Slugger Hank Sauer, who was overlooked by manager Burt Shotten in the 1950 contest, paved the way with his 430-foot fourth-inning blast to account for the National League's final tally. Sauer entered the game with 23 round-trippers and 69 RBIs to lead the Nationals' offense.

In a postgame interview, one reporter asked Sauer, "I wonder how Shotten feels?"

Sauer replied, "I've never felt badly toward anybody, but I wanted no part of that guy."

The Americans must have felt the same way about Sauer.

A.L. skipper Casey Stengel, managing his fourth All-Star duel, went with Vic Raschi (8–2) as his opening starter. Leo Durocher, piloting the N.L. club, named Curt Simmons of the Phils to stop the mighty Americans.

The Nationals struck against Raschi first, with Jackie Robinson's first-inning home run to forge his team in front, 1–0. Raschi was pulled out of the game after only two innings; he gave up the one run on Robinson's clout and struck out three.

Curt Simmons meanwhile blanked the Americans with one-hit ball over his three-inning drive. He gave way to Cub ace, Bob Rush, in the fourth. Rush found himself on the end of the Americans' final scoring drive in the top of that inning. The Americans netted three scratch singles, pushing across two runs to take the lead, 2–1. Minnie Minoso slashed Rush's first pitch into the right field corner for a double. Then Eddie Robinson bounced a tricky single past Jackie Robinson to drive Minoso home with the tying run. Bobby Avila of Cleveland put the Americans in front with another scratch single past Robinson. Rush was the eventual winner.

Bob Lemon, who took over for Raschi in the third, couldn't hold the lead in his half of the fourth. He struck Stan Musial with an inside pitch, then watched Hank Sauer smack his game-winning two-run homer to dead center.

The 1952 All-Star Game

American League	AB	R	H	PO	A	E
D. DiMaggio (Red Sox) cf	2	0	1	1	0	0
Doby (Indians) cf	0	0	0	0	0	0
Bauer (Yankees) rf	3	0	1	2	0	0
Jensen (Senators) rf	0	0	0	0	0	0
Mitchell (Indians) lf	1	0	0	1	0	0
Minoso (White Sox) lf	1	1	1	0	0	0
Rosen (Indians) 3b	1	1	0	3	1	0
Berra (Yankees) c	2	0	0	6	0	0
E. Robinson (White Sox) 1b	2	0	1	1	0	0
Avila (Indians) 2b	2	0	1	0	0	0
Rizzuto (Yankees) ss	2	0	0	1	0	0
Raschi (Yankees) p	0	0	0	0	0	0
McDougald (Yankees) ph	1	0	0	0	0	0
Lemon (Indians) p	1	0	0	0	0	0
Shantz (Athletics) p	0	0	0	0	0	0
Totals	18	2	5	15	1	0

National League	AB	R	H	PO	A	E
Lockman (Giants) 1b	3	0	0	5	0	0
J. Robinson (Dodgers) 2b	3	1	1	2	2	0
Musial (Cardinals) cf	2	1	0	1	0	0
Sauer (Cubs) lf	2	1	1	0	0	0
Campanella (Dodgers) c	1	0	0	5	1	0
Slaughter (Cardinals) rf	2	0	1	0	0	0
Thomson (Giants) 3b	2	0	0	1	1	0
Hamner (Phillies) ss	1	0	0	1	3	0
Simmons (Phillies) p	0	0	0	0	0	0
Reese (Dodgers) ph	1	0	0	0	0	0
Rush (Cubs) p	1	0	0	0	0	0
Totals	18	3	3	15	7	0

American League.................................... 0 0 0 2 0 - 2
National League .... 1 0 0 2 0 - 3
Game shortened by rain.

DP—Nationals 1. LOB—Americans 3, Nationals 3. 2B—DiMaggio, Minoso, Slaughter. HR—J. Robinson, Sauer. HBP—By Lemon (Musial).

American League	IP	H	E	ER	BB	SO
Raschi	2	1	1	1	0	3
Lemon (L)	2	2	2	2	2	0
Shantz	1	0	0	0	0	3

National League	IP	H	E	R	BB	SO
Simmons	3	1	0	0	1	3
Rush (W)	2	4	2	2	1	1

Umpires — Barlick, Boggess, and Warneke (N.L.), Berry, Summers, and Soar (A.L.).
Time — 1:29. Attendance — 32,785.

Lemon was credited with the loss.

Afterwards, Casey Stengel didn't want to blame anyone on his team for the defeat, but he did say, "How did I know it was going to rain? Sure I had good men I could have used for pinch hitters sitting on the bench, but I might have needed them later. And besides, Lemon is a pretty good pitcher."

Not enough to stop Sauer.

July 14, 1953

Crosley Field

The 1953 All-Star contest could have appropriately been renamed "The Enos Slaughter Show." With a capacity crowd of 30,846 at Crosley Field, in 80-degree weather, and millions more watching on television, Enos Slaughter was a one-man army as he paraded the National League past the American League 5–1 in a game that was as one-sided as the score indicates.

The Americans were shut out until the ninth when they produced their first and only run on three hits. But, by and large, the Americans were never in the ball game after the fifth, when a two-run burst by the Nationals broke a scoreless tie. The Nationals assaulted four A.L. pitchers for 10 hits, handing Casey Stengel's American Leaguers their fourth straight loss.

Slaughter, 37, was appearing in his 10th All-Star game. He came through with two base hits, a base on balls, two runs scored, and a spectacular somersault catch in the sixth of Harvey Kuenn's bid for extra bases. Slaughter did it all ... with a little help.

The game was primarily a pitching duel through the fifth, with the Phils' Robin Roberts facing the White Sox' Bill Pierce. Roberts was 14–6 on the season; Pierce was 10–5. Both starters breezed through the first three innings without allowing a run. N.L. manager Chuck Dressen then called on veteran ace Warren Spahn to keep the game close. Spahn, 11–3 with Milwaukee, hurled a solid two innings of relief. He gave way to Curt Simmons, another Phillies' pitcher, in the sixth. N.L. manager Chuck Dressen asked Simmons to keep the string of zeroes going, and he did just that. Simmons yielded one hit in two innings. But Simmons' counterpart, New York's Allie Reynolds, wasn't so fortunate in his relief outing.

In the fourth, Eddie Mathews of Milwaukee started it when he was hit on the foot by a pitch. With two gone, Reynolds walked Slaughter. Up stepped Richie Ashburn, batting for Spahn, who bounced a single to center to score Mathews. Reese then punched a one-bagger to right to bring Slaughter home with the second tally of the inning.

It seemed the Nationals had their best luck against right-handers. Reynolds gave up two runs, Cleveland's Mike Garcia one, and St. Louis' Satchel Paige two, all of whom threw from the right side.

The 1953 All-Star Game

American League	AB	R	H	PO	A	E
Goodman (Red Sox) 2b	2	0	0	1	1	0
Fox (White Sox) 2b	1	0	0	1	0	0
Vernon (Senators) 1b	3	0	0	6	0	0
Fain (White Sox) 1b	1	1	1	1	1	0
Bauer (Yankees) rf	2	0	0	3	0	0
Mize (Yankees) ph	1	0	1	0	0	0
Mantle (Yankees) cf	2	0	0	0	0	0
Hunter (Browns) ph	0	0	0	0	0	0
Doby (Indians) cf	1	0	0	1	1	0
Rosen (Indians) 3b	4	0	0	2	4	0
Zernial (Athletics) lf	2	0	1	1	0	0
Minoso (White Sox) lf	2	0	2	0	0	0
Berra (Yankees) c	4	0	0	4	0	0
Carrasquel (White Sox) ss	2	0	0	2	1	0
Kell (Red Sox) ph	1	0	0	0	0	0
Rizzuto (Yankees) ss	0	0	0	1	0	0
Pierce (White Sox) p	1	0	0	0	0	0
Reynolds (Yankees) p	0	0	0	0	0	0
Kuenn (Tigers) ph	1	0	0	0	0	0
Garcia (Indians) p	0	0	0	1	0	0
E. Robinson (Athletics) ph	1	0	0	0	0	0
Paige (Browns) p	0	0	0	0	0	0
Totals	31	1	5	24	8	0

National League	AB	R	H	PO	A	E
Reese (Dodgers) ss	4	0	2	1	1	0
Hamner (Phillies) ss	0	0	0	0	0	0
Schoendienst (Cardinals) 2b	3	0	0	0	3	0
Williams (Giants) 2b	0	0	0	2	0	0
Musial (Cardinals) lf	4	0	2	3	0	0
Kluszewski (Reds) 1b	3	0	1	5	0	0
Hodges (Dodgers) ph–1b	1	0	0	1	0	0
Campanella (Dodgers) c	4	1	1	6	2	0
Mathews (Braves) 3b	3	1	0	0	0	0
Bell (Reds) cf	3	0	0	4	0	0
Snider (Dodgers) ph–cf	0	1	0	1	0	0
Slaughter (Cardinals) rf	3	2	2	4	0	0
Roberts (Phillies) p	0	0	0	0	1	0
Kiner (Cubs) ph	1	0	0	0	0	0
Spahn (Braves) p	0	0	0	0	0	0
Ashburn (Phillies) ph	1	0	1	0	0	0
Simmons (Phillies) p	0	0	0	0	0	0
J. Robinson (Dodgers) ph	1	0	0	0	0	0
Dickson (Pirates) p	1	0	1	0	0	0
Totals	32	5	10	27	7	0

```
American League.........................  0 0 0 0 0 0 0  1 – 1
National League .........................  0 0 0 0 2 0 1 2  x – 5
```

DP—Americans 1. LOB—Nationals 7, Americans 6. 2B—Reese. RBIs—Ashburn, Reese (2), Slaughter, Dickson, Minoso. SB—Slaughter. HPB—By Reynolds (Mathews).

American League	IP	H	R	ER	BB	SO
Pierce	3	1	0	0	0	1
Reynolds (L)	2	2	2	2	1	0
Garcia	2	4	1	1	1	2
Paige	1	3	2	2	1	0
National League	IP	H	R	ER	BB	SO
Roberts	3	1	0	0	1	2
Spahn (W)	2	0	0	0	1	2
Simmons	2	1	0	0	1	1
Dickson	2	3	1	1	0	0

Umpires—Conlan, Donatelli, Engeln (N.L.), Stevens, McKinley, and Napp (A.L.). Time—2:19. Attendance—30,846.

The one run off Garcia came in the seventh. Slaughter set the groundwork with a single, followed by a headfirst slide into second for a stolen base. Pee Wee Reese, 0-for-13 in eight previous All-Star games, broke his slump with a double to score Slaughter with the third run of the game.

The Nationals feasted for two more runs off Satchel Paige in the eighth. Paige, 47, was the oldest player ever to appear in All-Star competition. He entertained the audience with his variety of pitches. He threw slow stuff, and then almost bounced the ball to the plate. Roy Campanella wasn't fooled, however. He bounced a single past Paige to center. It was Campy's first All-Star hit in 17 trips to the plate. Slaughter got another clutch hit, bouncing a single up the middle, to score Campanella. Murry Dickson then laced a double to left to bring Duke Snider, who had walked, home with the Nationals' fifth run of the contest.

Pittsburgh's Murray Dickson, who knocked in the N.L.'s last run, also relieved for his team in the ninth. Along with his run-scoring hit, Dickson will be remembered for giving up the Americans' only run of the game. It came when singles by Ferris Fain, Johnny Mize, and Minnie Minoso produced a run.

Besides Slaughter's hitting and fielding exhibition, two Cincinnati Reds crashed the starting lineup: powerful Ted Kluszewski and Gus Bell, father of third baseman Buddy Bell.

But on the American side of the field, the day was filled with frustration. Not even the Yankee coterie could bring the Americans to their feet. Mickey Mantle, playing with a pulled leg muscle, went hitless. So did Yogi Berra, and Hank Bauer. Allie Reynolds' poor outing on the mound further disgraced the men in pinstripes.

Ted Williams, a Marine Corps captain on leave, was on hand to throw out the first ball. Someone believed that his presence would provide some much needed inspiration for his A.L. contemporaries. What they needed most, instead, was his bat.

Or another Enos Slaughter.

July 13, 1954

Municipal Stadium

There wasn't a power shortage this year at Cleveland's Municipal Stadium. Manager Walt Alston, scratching his head after a dramatic 11–9 defeat to the American League, said, "In spite of all the homers out there today, Fox's blow beat us. We put everything we had [into it]. It could have gone either way."

Alston may have been right as the game produced six home runs (four by the American League), a game record 20 runs, 31 hits (the most by two teams), and the most hits by a winning team, with 17. But Nellie Fox's little blooping single in the ninth inning proved the crushing blow, driving in two runs and breaking Casey Stengel's four-game losing streak.

Yet the real hero was Al Rosen, who, known as "The Hebrew Hammer," clobbered two home runs for a five-RBI day, tying the All-Star record. In fact, several Cleveland players starred in the show, and why not? The Indians were streaking to a divisional crown, edging the second-place Yankees by eight games with an amazing 111–43 mark. Bobby Avila, who was one reason for the Indians' season-long success, smacked three singles and knocked in two in All-Star play. And Larry Doby cracked a pinch homer in the eighth to send the game into extra innings at 9–9. Together these three players drove in eight out of the Americans' 11 runs. Even Indian pitching ace Bob Lemon cooled down the Nationals with a fine two-thirds of an inning of relief.

Rosen, along with Fox, was mobbed in the clubhouse after the game. Up until the All-Star break, Rosen had been slumping because of a stiff right index finger, which he could hardly wrap around the bat. Rosen, who received the most votes of any plate position, admitted he was afraid of becoming "this year's goat." He said, "I didn't sleep a wink last night worrying whether I'd be an All-Star game goat. I even asked before the game to be taken out after my first time at bat."

Stengel, ignoring Rosen's request, strutted around the dressing room beaming, "That Rosen really was something. They did it all. I told you fellows we hit home runs, too."

That he did, although it appeared early to be just another pitcher's contest.

The 1954 All-Star Game

National League	AB	R	H	PO	A	E
Hamner (Phillies) 2b	3	0	0	0	0	0
Schoendienst (Cardinals) 2b	2	0	0	1	0	0
Dark (Giants) ss	5	0	1	1	2	0
Snider (Dodgers) cf–rf	4	2	3	2	0	0
Musial (Cardinals) rf–lf	5	1	2	2	1	0
Kluszewski (Reds) 1b	4	2	2	5	0	0
Hodges (Dodgers) 1b	1	0	0	1	0	0
Jablonski (Cardinals) 3b	3	1	1	1	0	0
Jackson (Cubs) 3b	2	0	0	0	1	0
Robinson (Dodgers) lf	2	1	1	0	0	0
Mays (Giants) cf	2	1	1	1	1	0
Campanella (Dodgers) c	3	0	1	9	0	0
Burgess (Phillies) c	0	0	0	1	0	0
Roberts (Phillies) p	1	0	0	0	0	0
Mueller (Giants) ph	1	0	1	0	0	0
Antonelli (Giants) p	0	0	0	0	0	0
Thomas (Pirates) ph	1	0	0	0	0	0
Spahn (Braves) p	0	0	0	0	0	0
Grissom (Giants) p	0	0	0	0	0	0
Bell (Reds) ph	1	1	1	0	0	0
Conley (Braves) p	0	0	0	0	0	0
Erskine (Dodgers) p	0	0	0	0	0	0
Totals	40	9	14	24	5	0
American League	**AB**	**R**	**H**	**PO**	**A**	**E**
Minoso (White Sox) lf–rf	4	1	2	1	0	1
Piersall (Red Sox) rf	0	0	0	0	0	0
Avila (Indians) 2b	3	1	3	1	1	0
Keegan (White Sox) p	0	0	0	0	0	0
Stone (Senators) p	0	0	0	0	0	0
Doby (Indians) ph–cf	1	1	1	0	0	0
Mantle (Yankees) cf	5	1	2	2	0	0
Trucks (White Sox) p	0	0	0	0	0	0
Berra (Yankees) c	4	2	2	5	0	0
Rosen (Indians) 1b–3b	4	2	3	7	0	0
Boone (Tigers) 3b	4	1	1	1	3	0
Vernon (Senators) ph–1b	1	0	0	1	0	0
Bauer (Yankees) rf	2	0	1	1	0	0
Porterfield (Senators) p	1	0	0	0	0	0
Fox (White Sox) 2b	2	0	1	1	0	0
Carrasquel (White Sox) ss	5	1	1	5	4	0
Ford (Yankees) p	1	0	0	0	0	0
Consuegra (White Sox) p	0	0	0	0	0	0
Lemon (Indians) p	0	0	0	0	0	0
Williams (Red Sox) ph–lf	2	1	0	2	0	0
Noren (Yankees) lf	0	0	0	0	0	0
Totals	39	11	17	27	8	1

National League .... 0 0 0 5 2 0 0 0 2 – 9
American League........................ 0 0 4 1 2 1 0 3 x – 11

DP—Americans 1. LOB—Nationals 6, Americans 9. 2B—Robinson, Mueller, Snider. HR—Rosen (2), Boone, Kluszewski, Bell, Doby. RBIs—Rosen (5), Boone, Kluszewski (3), Jablonski, Robinson (2), Mueller, Avila (2), Bell (2), Doby, Fox (2). SAC FLY—Avila.

National League	IP	H	R	ER	BB	SO
Roberts	3	5	4	4	2	5
Antonelli	2	4	3	3	0	2
Spahn	⅔	4	1	1	1	0
Grissom	1⅓	0	0	0	2	0
Conley (L)	⅓	3	3	3	1	0
Erskine	⅔	1	0	0	0	1

American League	IP	H	R	ER	BB	SO
Ford	3	1	0	0	1	0
Consuegra	⅓	5	5	5	0	0
Lemon	⅔	1	0	0	0	0
Porterfield	3	4	2	2	0	1
Keegan	⅔	3	2	2	0	1
Stone (W)	⅓	0	0	0	0	0
Trucks	1	0	0	0	0	0

Umpires—Rommel (A.L.), plate; Ballanfant (N.L.), first base; Honochick (A.L.), second base; Stewart (A.L.), third base; Gorman (N.L.), left field; Paparella (A.L.), right field (first 4½ innings). Stewart (N.L.), plate; Honochick (A.L.), first base; Ballanfant (N.L.), second base; Rommel (A.L.), third base; Gorman (N.L.), left field; Paparella (A.L.), right field (last four innings). Time—3:10. Attendance—68,751.

Whitey Ford, a 25-year-old New York Yankees left-hander, was manager Casey Stengel's choice to pitch against the Phils' Robin Roberts. Ford's selection had game brokers panicking since the young staffer had been erratic in compiling a spotty 7-8 record. Also, with the A.L. seeking to break a four-game All-Star losing streak, Ford would have to stop a power-packed N.L. lineup stacked with such left-handed sluggers as Ted Kluszewski, Duke Snider, and Stan Musial. Willie Mays, the young Giants rookie standout with 31 home runs, could also provide some punch. Mays was making his first All-Star game appearance. Going into the game, the Nationals clearly had the edge in the power department, as the Americans' greatest home run threat was Mickey Mantle.

There was no scoring until the third when the Americans finally got to Roberts for three runs. With Minnie Minoso and teammate Bobby Avila on base, Rosen strode to the plate and slammed a Roberts pitch for a 380-foot homer over the portable fence in left center for a 3-0 lead. Ray Boone followed with another home run to make it 4-0; his blast sent the mostly Indian-minded faithful of 68,751, the second largest All-Star crowd, into a frenzy.

In the end, Roberts surrendered four runs, all earned, five hits, walked two and struck out five in his three-inning stretch. Ford, who was suspect by his mediocre record, surprised everyone with three shutout innings. He struck out one and gave up only one hit.

When Ford left the game in the fourth, the Nationals took turns scoring as they pounded across five runs, with Ted Kluszewski powering his first home run in All-Star play. The Nationals entered the fifth with the lead for the first time, 5-4, only to relinquish it.

Al Rosen clubbed his second homer of the day, a two-run blast off reliever Johnny Antonelli, into the lower left field seats some 400 feet away to tie the score at 7-all. Yogi Berra, who singled, scored ahead of Rosen.

The Nationals battled back in the eighth on Gus Bell's pinch-hit homer to take another short-lived lead, 9-7. But the Americans bounced back in their half of the inning on Larry Doby's pinch-homer to tie the game and send it into extra innings.

Then, in the fateful ninth, Gene Conley, a 6'8" Milwaukee Braves rookie, set up the winning runs for the Americans by watching Mickey Mantle and Yogi Berra single, before walking Rosen. Walt Alston had enough and called on Carl Erskine to face the sly Nellie Fox. Both Alston and Erskine were stunned when Fox dropped a single to center to score Mantle and Berra and win the game in a fancy comeback fashion, 11-9.

The winning pitcher was Dean Stone of the Washington Senators. Conley suffered the loss.

And to Rosen — the honor of not becoming another American League goat.

July 12, 1955

Milwaukee County Stadium

At age 34, Stan Musial was playing his fourth All-Star game, but, for the first time, not as a starter. He didn't enter the game until the fourth inning when he replaced left fielder Del Ennis. At first, Musial didn't make good with the bat; he struck out in the fourth, grounded into a double play in the seventh, and tapped out to second base in the ninth.

Musial, suffering his worst All-Star performance, came up to the plate in the twelfth inning with the score deadlocked 5–5, and whispered to catcher Yogi Berra, "I'm tired." Immediately afterward, Musial ripped hurler Frank Sullivan's first pitch over the boards in right to win the game, 6–5. It was the National League's fifth victory in the last six games and cut the A.L.'s edge to 13 victories against nine defeats. Musial's blast sent the crowd of 45,643 home cheering after playing hosts to Milwaukee's first All-Star contest. The game was the second extra-inning affair in the history of the event.

Musial told reporters that none of his teammates ever gave up. Trailing 5–0 as late as the seventh inning, the Nationals clawed back to win after they had been down for the count. Mickey Mantle's 425-foot four-bagger led the Americans to a four-run outburst in the first inning off N.L. starter Robin Roberts (13–7), who was starting his fifth All-Star game. Mantle's homer came with two men on base, Nellie Fox, safe on a lead off single, and Ted Williams, who walked. The first run of the inning was produced when Harvey Kuenn scored on a wild pitch by Roberts.

The Americans scored their fifth run in the sixth on a combination single by Yogi Berra and an infield out by Mickey Vernon. The run was earned off the St. Louis Cardinal left-handed curveball specialist, Harvey Haddix. Haddix zipped through the fourth and fifth frames unblemished, except for the one run.

Chicago's Billy Pierce blanked the Nationals for three perfect innings. Pierce (5–6) was a surprise selection by A.L. manager Al Lopez. Lopez could also count on the services of Early Wynn (11–4) and Whitey Ford (10–4) if anything went wrong. Pierce, who started the 1953 All-Star game, came close to his old form by striking out three and pitching one-hit ball.

Early Wynn hurled the middle three innings and kept goose eggs next

The 1955 All-Star Game

American League	AB	R	H	PO	A	E
Kuenn (Tigers) ss	3	1	1	1	0	0
Carrasquel (White Sox) ss	3	0	2	1	3	1
Fox (White Sox) 2b	3	1	1	2	0	0
Avila (Indians) 2b	1	0	0	1	2	0
Williams (Red Sox) lf	3	1	1	1	0	0
Smith (Indians) lf	1	0	0	0	0	0
Mantle (Yankees) cf	6	1	2	3	0	0
Berra (Yankees) c	6	1	1	8	2	0
Kaline (Tigers) rf	4	0	1	6	0	0
Vernon (Senators) 1b	5	0	1	8	0	0
Finigan (Athletics) 3b	3	0	0	2	0	0
Rosen (Indians) 3b	2	0	0	0	0	1
Pierce (White Sox) p	0	0	0	0	0	0
Jensen (Red Sox) ph	1	0	0	0	0	0
Wynn (Indians) p	0	0	0	0	1	0
Power (Athletics) ph	1	0	0	0	0	0
Ford (Yankees) p	1	0	0	0	1	0
Sullivan (Red Sox) p	1	0	0	0	0	0
Totals	44	5	10	33	9	2

National League	AB	R	H	PO	A	E
Schoendienst (Cardinals) 2b	6	0	2	3	2	0
Ennis (Phillies) lf	1	0	0	1	0	0
Musial (Cardinals) ph–lf	4	1	1	0	0	0
Snider (Dodgers) cf	2	0	0	3	0	0
Mays (Giants) cf	3	2	2	3	0	0
Kluszewski (Reds) 1b	5	1	2	9	1	0
Mathews (Braves) 3b	2	0	0	0	3	1
Jackson (Cubs) 3b	3	1	1	0	0	0
Mueller (Giants) rf	2	0	1	0	0	0
Aaron (Braves) ph–rf	2	1	2	0	0	0
Banks (Cubs) ss	2	0	0	2	1	0
Logan (Braves) ss	3	0	1	1	1	0
Crandall (Braves) c	1	0	0	1	0	0
Burgess (Phillies) ph–c	1	0	0	2	0	0
Lopata (Phillies) ph–c	3	0	0	10	0	0
Roberts (Phillies) p	0	0	0	1	1	0
Thomas (Pirates) ph	1	0	0	0	0	0
Haddix (Cardinals) p	0	0	0	0	2	0
Hodges (Dodgers) ph	1	0	1	0	0	0
Newcombe (Dodgers) p	0	0	0	0	0	0
Baker (Cubs) ph	1	0	0	0	0	0
Jones (Cubs) p	0	0	0	0	0	0
Nuxhall (Reds) p	2	0	0	0	1	0
Conley (Braves) p	0	0	0	0	0	0
Totals	45	6	13	36	12	1

American League	4	0	0	0	0	1	0	0	0	0	0 – 5
National League	0	0	0	0	0	0	2	3	0	0	1 – 6

DP—Nationals 1, Americans 1. LOB—Americans 12, Nationals 8. 2B—Kluszewski, Kaline. HR—Mantle, Musial. RBIs—Mantle (3), Vernon, Logan, Jackson, Aaron, Musial. SAC HITS—Pierce, Avila. HPB—By Jones (Kaline). WP—Roberts. PB—Crandall.

American League	IP	H	R	ER	BB	SO
Pierce	3	1	0	0	0	3
Wynn	3	3	0	0	0	1
Ford	1⅔	5	5	3	1	0
Sullivan (L)	3⅓	4	1	1	1	4
National League	IP	H	R	ER	BB	SO
Roberts	3	4	4	4	1	0
Haddix	3	3	1	1	0	2
Newcombe	1	1	0	0	0	1
Jones	⅔	0	0	0	2	1
Nuxhall	3⅓	2	0	0	3	5
Conley (W)	1	0	0	0	0	3

Umpires—Barlick, Boggess, and Secory (N.L.), Soar, Summners, and Runge (A.L.). Time—3:17. Attendance—45,643.

---

to the National League's score. He struck out one and scattered three hits.

For a while, the Americans were riding on their way to a comfortable shutout win, until the Nationals pecked away at Whitey Ford in the seventh. In an inning and two-thirds, the N.L.'s slugging brigade scored five runs, three earned, on five hits. Ford, last year's hero, was this year's goat. Willie Mays singled, and Hank Aaron walked. Johnny Logan, another Milwaukee Brave, blew the Americans shutout bid by punching a single to left to drive in Mays. Then pinch-hitter Stan Lopata of the Phils bounced a grounder to White Sox shortstop Chico Carrasquel, who fumbled the ball, leaving Lopata safe. With Logan forced at second, Aaron scored from third with the second run of the frame. The Nationals were closing in on the Americans, 5-2.

The National Leaguers pounded on Ford once more in the eighth, driving across three runs to even the game at five. With Red Schoendienst and Stan Musial out on grounders, Willie Mays, Ted Kluszewski and Ransom Jackson each singled. Manager Al Lopez pulled out Ford after Mays scored, and his relief ace Frank Sullivan was called on to close out the inning. It took some effort on Sullivan's part, but the Nationals scored two more runs on a single by Hank Aaron and on an errant throw by Al Kaline, to allow the final run to come home.

Cincinnati southpaw Joe Nuxhall threw three scoreless innings of relief through the 11th, with Milwaukee's Gene Conley, an 11-game winner, fanning the side in the 12th before Musial's game-winning homer.

Conley was credited with his first victory in All-Star play. Sullivan, pitching in his first interleague contest, went down to his first defeat.

After Musial put the game away for good with his clutch hit, N.L. skipper Leo Durocher was all smiles in the dressing room. He told a legion of scribes, "When they were five runs behind, they kept saying, 'We've got to get six.' They were like a bunch of college kids."

With Musial as the head cheerleader.

July 10, 1956

Griffith Stadium

Washington, D.C., has never been without its share of controversies, political or otherwise, including the 1956 All-Star game, which became famous for the Cincinnati fan ballot box stuffing episode.

The Reds were roaring along in first place at the time, and five players were named to N.L. starting berths, which didn't seem unusual for a front-running team. What was unusual, however, was the fact that three other Reds were voted runners-up to three of the five named Red starters! As a result, a few suspecting eyes reviewed the matter and uncovered a scandal involving several Cincinnati radio stations and newspapers, all guilty of promoting a "ballot stuffing campaign." Fans from all over the country cried "foul," even though the number of Reds players didn't affect the game's outcome.

This time a Redbird starred—not from Cincinnati either—but from St. Louis. His name was third baseman Ken Boyer. Boyer placed the ballot box controversy out of his mind and went three-for-five at the plate to lead his N.L. squad to a 7–3 win over the Americans, before 28,843 fans. Boyer was not only impressive offensively, but he made several key defensive plays to harass the opposition throughout the game.

Until Boyer's exploits, the game was a pretty tame affair through the first three innings, in which Pittsburgh's Bob Friend, 11–7,—and the first Pirate to start an All-Star game—dueled Billy Pierce, top winner in the majors with a 13–3 record, of the White Sox.

The Nationals broke open the game in the third on Roy McMillan's walk, a sacrifice by Friend, who won the game, and Johnny Temple's RBI single.

In the meantime, Warren Spahn replaced Friend in the fourth and blanked the opposition until sixth. Before that, the Nationals erupted for two more runs in the fourth off A.L. reliever Whitey Ford of the Yankees. Ford surrendered a single to Ken Boyer, and then a pinch-homer to Willie Mays, scoring Boyer, and extending the Nationals lead to 3–0.

Ford was gone after only an inning and was replaced by Jim Wilson, who was milked for another run in the fifth when Boyer's single to center scored

The 1956 All-Star Game

National League	AB	R	H	PO	A	E
Temple (Reds) 2b	4	1	2	2	3	0
Robinson (Reds) lf	2	0	0	1	0	0
Snider (Dodgers) ph–cf	3	0	0	1	0	0
Musial (Cardinals) rf–lf	4	1	1	2	0	0
Aaron (Braves) lf	1	0	0	0	0	0
Boyer (Cardinals) 3b	5	1	3	3	1	0
Bell (Reds) cf	1	0	0	2	0	0
Mays (Giants) cf–rf	3	2	1	2	0	0
Long (Pirates) 1b	2	0	0	6	0	0
Kluszewski (Reds) ph–1b	2	1	2	2	0	0
Bailey (Reds) c	3	0	0	3	1	0
Campanella (Dodgers) c	0	0	0	1	0	0
McMillan (Reds) ss	3	1	2	1	5	0
Friend (Pirates) p	0	0	0	0	0	0
Repulski (Cardinals) ph	1	0	0	0	0	0
Spahn (Braves) p	1	0	0	0	0	0
Antonelli (Giants) p	1	0	0	1	0	0
Totals	36	7	11	27	10	0
American League	AB	R	H	PO	A	E
Kuenn (Tigers) ss	5	0	1	2	3	0
Fox (White Sox) 2b	4	1	2	1	0	0
Williams (Red Sox) lf	4	1	1	2	0	0
Mantle (Yankees) cf	4	1	1	0	0	0
Berra (Yankees) c	2	0	2	10	1	0
Lollar (White Sox) c	2	0	1	4	0	0
Kaline (Tigers) rf	3	0	1	0	0	0
Piersall (Red Sox) rf	1	0	0	1	0	0
Vernon (Red Sox) 1b	2	0	0	4	0	0
Power (Athletics) ph–1b	2	0	1	3	0	0
Kell (Orioles) 3b	4	0	1	0	1	0
Pierce (White Sox) p	0	0	0	0	1	0
Simpson (Athletics) ph	1	0	0	0	0	0
Ford (Yankees) p	0	0	0	0	0	0
Wilson (White Sox) p	0	0	0	0	1	0
Martin (Yankees) ph	1	0	0	0	0	0
Brewer (Red Sox) p	0	0	0	0	0	0
Boone (Tigers) ph	1	0	0	0	0	0
Score (Indians) p	0	0	0	0	0	0
Wynn (Indians) p	0	0	0	0	0	0
Sievers (Senators) ph	1	0	0	0	0	0
Totals	37	3	11	27	7	0

National League .... 0 0 1 2 1 1 2 0 0 – 7
American League......................... 0 0 0 0 0 3 0 0 0 – 3

DP—Nationals 1. LOB—Nationals 7, Americans 7. 2B—Kluszewski (2). HR—Mays, Williams, Mantle, Musial. RBIs—Temple, Mays (2), Boyer, Williams (2), Mantle, Kluszewski. SB—Temple. SAC HIT—Friend. WP—Brewer, 2.

National League	IP	H	R	ER	BB	SO
Friend (W)	3	3	0	0	0	3
Spahn	2	4	3	3	0	1
Antonelli	4	4	0	0	0	1
American League	IP	H	R	ER	BB	SO
Pierce (L)	3	2	1	1	1	5
Ford	1	3	2	2	1	2
Wilson	1	2	1	1	0	1
Brewer	2	4	3	3	1	2
Score	1	0	0	0	1	1
Wynn	1	0	0	0	0	0

Umpires — Berry, Hurley, and Flaherty (A.L.), Pinelli, Gore, and Jackowski (N.L.).
Time — 2:45. Attendance — 28,843.

Temple from second. Then, in the bottom of that inning, Boyer made his first defensive gem of the evening by spearing a hot smash that would have gone down the line for extra bases.

The Nationals led 5-0 in the sixth when Ted Kluszewski scored from third on Tom Brewer's wild pitch. Brewer came in to relieve Wilson at the top of that inning.

Warren Spahn, meanwhile, held the Americans scoreless until the sixth when a pair of homers, a two-run shot by Ted Williams, scoring Nellie Fox, and a solo blast by Mickey Mantle made it a 5-3 game. Spahn, who pitched brilliantly the first two innings, was taken out in favor of Johnny Antonelli, who promptly retired the Americans in order.

But the Americans never challenged the Nationals' lead again, as Mantle's homer became the A.L.'s last major offensive threat. Two more runs were added by the Nationals in the seventh, however, when Stan Musial homered with Willie Mays, who walked, on board to cap the scoring and the game at 7-3.

Afterwards, Ken Boyer was voted the game's MVP, while N.L. manager Walt Alston was criticized for pitching Antonelli four innings, one over the maximum. Alston's move went uncontested, however, since a pitcher is allowed to go three innings *after* the one into which he has come in as a reliever.

But that rule didn't include ballot stuffing.

July 9, 1957

Sportsman Park

Minnie Minoso wasn't sure if Casey Stengel would play him in the 1957 All-Star game. The American League squad was pretty well-represented by the likes of Ted Williams, Joe DiMaggio, Bobby Doerr, Lou Boudreau, and Tommy Henrich, so it was doubtful his bat or glove would be needed.

As it turned out, Minoso was a ninth-inning replacement for the aging Ted Williams, and did more in that one single inning than others did in nine to help his teammates squeak past the National Leaguers, 6–5.

Minoso drove in some insurance runs with a run-scoring double in the ninth, padding the Americans lead to 6–2, until the Nationals came back with three of their own. But Minoso saved possibly three more runs from crossing the plate with two great defensive plays.

Gus Bell tried to advance from first to third on Ernie Banks' one-out single, but Minoso's throw to third baseman Frank Malzone gunned him down. Had Bell not elected to leg out the extra base, the National Leaguers might have still been playing. So with two outs and Banks on second with the tying run, N.L. manager Walt Alston chose Gil Hodges to pinch-hit in this clutch situation. Hodges drove relief pitcher Don Mossi's second pitch on a low line to left that sounded like trouble from the moment Hodges connected. But Minoso, playing Hodges right, sprinted hard to spear the drive for the third out and saved the Americans' second All-Star win since 1949. The victory boosted the Americans' overall margin in the series to 14–10.

For the most part, the game was all American League from the start. The Nationals didn't put up their first marker on the board until the seventh inning. Up until then, two American League pitchers had blanked the senior circuit on just three hits, beginning with 25-year-old Jim Bunning of the Detroit Tigers. Bunning was named as Casey Stengel's starting pitcher when Early Wynn, Stengel's original candidate, pitched a regular season game the day before and could only come on in relief.

Bunning, 8–4 on the season, no-hit the Nationals by striking out one during his three-inning stretch. Bunning was a noted speedball artist on the mound, and his game-ending statistics certainly showed that.

Walt Alston went with Phillies left-hander, Curt Simmons. Simmons

The 1957 All-Star Game

American League	AB	R	H	PO	A	E
Kuenn (Tigers) ss	2	0	0	0	1	0
McDougald (Yankees) ss	2	1	0	1	0	0
Fox (White Sox) 2b	4	0	0	2	4	0
Kaline (Tigers) rf	5	1	2	1	1	0
Mantle (Yankees) cf	4	1	1	4	0	0
Williams (Red Sox) lf	3	1	0	2	0	0
Minoso (White Sox) lf	1	0	1	1	1	0
Wertz (Indians) 1b	2	0	1	3	0	0
Skowron (Yankees) 1b	3	1	2	5	1	0
Berra (Yankees) c	3	0	1	6	0	0
Kell (Orioles) 3b	2	0	0	0	1	0
Malzone (Red Sox) 3b	2	0	0	1	1	0
Bunning (Tigers) p	1	0	0	0	0	0
Maxwell (Tigers) ph	1	0	1	0	0	0
Loes (Orioles) p	1	0	0	0	1	0
Wynn (Indians) p	0	0	0	0	0	0
Pierce (White Sox) p	1	1	1	1	0	0
Mossi (Indians) p	0	0	0	0	0	0
Grim (Yankees) p	0	0	0	0	0	0
Totals	37	6	10	27	11	0

National League	AB	R	H	PO	A	E
Temple (Reds) 2b	2	0	0	3	0	0
Schoendienst (Cardinals) 2b	2	0	0	0	0	1
Aaron (Braves) rf	4	0	1	2	0	0
Musial (Cardinals) 1b	3	1	1	9	0	0
Mays (Giants) cf	4	2	2	2	0	0
Bailey (Reds) c	3	1	1	2	0	0
Foiles (Pirates) ph	1	1	1	0	0	0
Robinson (Reds) lf	2	0	1	5	0	0
Bell (Reds) lf	1	0	1	0	0	0
Hoak (Reds) 3b	1	0	0	1	0	0
Mathews (Braves) ph–3b	3	0	0	1	0	0
McMillan (Reds) ss	1	0	0	2	0	0
Banks (Cubs) ph–ss	3	0	1	0	3	0
Simmons (Phillies) p	0	0	0	0	0	0
Burdette (Braves) p	1	0	0	0	0	0
Sanford (Phillies) p	0	0	0	0	0	0
Moon (Cardinals) ph	1	0	0	0	0	0
Jackson (Cardinals) p	0	0	0	0	1	0
Cimoli (Dodgers) ph	1	0	0	0	0	0
Labine (Dodgers) p	0	0	0	0	1	0
Hodges (Dodgers) ph	1	0	0	0	0	0
Totals	34	5	9	27	5	1

American League . . . . 0 2 0 0 0 1 0 0 3 – 6
National League . . . . 0 0 0 0 0 0 2 0 3 – 5

DP – Americans 1. LOB – Americans 9, Nationals 4. 2B – Musial, Skowron, Bell, Minoso. 3B – Mays. RBIs – Wertz, Kuenn, Bell (2), Berra, Kaline (2), Minoso, Mays, Banks. SAC HIT – Fox. WP – Sanford, Pierce.

American League	IP	H	R	ER	BB	SO
Bunning (W)	3	0	0	0	0	1
Loes	3	3	0	0	0	1
Wynn	⅓	3	2	2	0	0
Pierce	1⅔	2	3	3	2	3
Mossi	⅔	1	0	0	0	0
Grim	⅓	0	0	0	0	1

National League	IP	H	R	ER	BB	SO
Simmons (L)	1	2	2	2	2	0
Burdette	4	2	0	0	1	0
Sanford	1	2	1	1	0	0
Jackson	2	1	0	0	1	0
Labine	1	3	3	1	0	1

Umpires — Dascoli, Dixon, and Landes (N.L.), Napp, Stevens, and Chylak (A.L.).
Time — 2:43. Attendance — 30,693.

---

was 10–2, beating every team in the league at least once, and had started the All-Star game twice previously, in 1952 and in 1953.

Simmons may have owned N.L. hitters in his league, but A.L. batters appeared to own him during the All-Star contest. Simmons pitched one full inning and part of the second, giving up two earned runs, walked two and struck out none. Alston, baffled by his poor outing, immediately summoned Brave right-hander Lou Burdette, who pitched four solid shutout innings.

Simmons didn't last long in the top half of the second as the Americans jumped out to a 2–0 lead. Mickey Mantle singled, Ted Williams worked up a free pass, and Vic Wertz ensued with a single to center to score Mantle. Williams advanced to second, and after Yogi Berra walked, Burdette came in to put out the fire. With the bases loaded, Burdette induced George Kell to foul out and Jim Bunning to fly out. But he lost Harvey Kuenn on four balls to push across Williams with the second run of the inning. Both runs were charged to Simmons.

Jack Sanford of Philadelphia replaced Burdette in the sixth, but he was touched for another run when Bill Skowron skied a double off the right field screen. Skowron took third on Sanford's wild pitch to Yogi Berra, when Berra singled to left to drive in Skowron with the game's third run.

Then the National Leaguers broke the ice in the seventh with Early Wynn on the mound. Wynn should have stayed home, as he surrendered two earned runs in a third of an inning. Three straight hits produced the runs, starting with singles by Willie Mays and Ed Bailey and ending with pinch-hitter Gus Bell's double to left to score both Mays and Bailey. Stengel gave Wynn the hook, and saddled Billy Pierce, 12–6, of Chicago with the task of bailing his team out of the inning. Pierce did the job, until the Americans scored again in the ninth.

The Americans made their final drive with Clem Labine on the hill for the Nationals. Bill Pierce chopped an infield hit and advanced to second on Red Shoendienst's error on Gil McDougald's grounder. McDougald and Pierce were perched on first and second, with no outs, when they advanced on Nellie Fox's sacrifice fly. Al Kaline, one of three Detroit Tigers on the A.L. squad, rammed a single to left center to score McDougald and Pierce. Minnie Minoso then came in to pinch-hit for Williams, staying in the game, and struck a double to right center to score Kaline and expand the Americans' lead to 6-2.

But it almost wasn't enough. Stan Musial got the National Leaguers rolling in the home half of the ninth with a walk, and scored on Willie Mays' triple into the right field corner. Billy Pierce, still pitching for the A.L., then uncorked a wild pitch to pinch-hitter Hank Foiles, which allowed Mays to score. Foiles followed with a single to center before Gus Bell walked. This brought Casey Stengel out to the mound and Cleveland relief ace Don Mossi in as Pierce's successor. Until that inning, Pierce had allowed only one run in nine previous All-Star innings. This time he was credited with giving up three runs in an inning and a third, walking two and striking out three.

At first Mossi appeared to have the game back under control, as he struck out Eddie Mathews with a low curve ball across the plate. Mathews was so fooled that he stood looking at the called third strike. Ernie Banks wasn't fooled, however, as he singled off Frank Malzone's glove to score Foiles. It was then that Gus Bell tried taking third but was tagged out on Minoso's accurate throw. Not taking any chances, Stengel took out Mossi and asked Bob Grim to close out the game by facing pinch-hitter Gil Hodges, who lined out on a close play to Minoso to end the game.

Bunning received the victory, and Simmons the loss.

Even though Minoso made the play of the game on Bell, manager Walt Alston backed up Bell's decision to take the extra base. Alston said, "I was glad to see him try for it. It would have put us in good shape with one out and men on first and third."

Instead, Minnie Minoso sent the National League–minded 30,693 home mumbling over the National League win that could have been.

July 8, 1958

Memorial Stadium

Baltimore's Memorial Stadium was the site of the All-Star's Silver Anniversary game, with two unlikely heroes paving the way for the American League's dramatic 4-3 comeback victory over the underdog National League.

Gil McDougald and Billy O'Dell shared the spotlight as McDougald's pinch-hit single sent home the tie-breaking run in the sixth, and O'Dell, called upon to relieve in the seventh, retired the last nine batters he faced.

Vice President Richard M. Nixon was the game's guest of honor, tossing out the ceremonial first ball to the cheers of 48,829 Baltimore fans. Nixon was present on a night when both teams failed to bang out a single extra base hit; it was the second consecutive game in which no homers were clouted. Instead, the American League produced its attack on nine singles, while the National League countered with four hits, all singles.

A power show was expected from the American Leaguers with three home run leaders on the team: Jackie Jensen, tops in both leagues, with 24; Bob Cerv of Kansas City, second to Jensen with 22; and New York's pride and joy, Mickey Mantle, with 21 four-baggers. The A.L. squad also had the league's leading hitter Nellie Fox, batting .327 in the lead-off position. The N.L. also had a source of power in Giants outfielder Willie Mays, who had belted 16 homers so far on the season.

Mays contributed all right, but not with an extra base hit. Willie was the main man behind the National League's scoring drives by punching across two of his team's three runs off A.L. starter Bob Turley in the first frame.

Turley, the top winner in the majors with a 12-3 record, simply didn't have it as the American League starter. The Yankee hurler watched helplessly as Mays singled, took third on Stan Musial's base hit, and scored on Hank Aaron's sacrifice fly. Turley then hit Ernie Banks on the shoulder with an inside pitch, and walked Frank Thomas to fill the bases.

Suddenly missing his mark, Turley kept struggling as he tossed a wild pitch to Bill Mazeroski, which permitted Musial to score with the inning's second run. Turley finished the inning, but not without a visit by A.L. manager Casey Stengel. Stengel took him out after he faced two batters in the second.

The 1958 All-Star Game

National League	AB	R	H	PO	A	E
Mays (Giants) cf	4	2	1	1	0	0
Skinner (Pirates) lf	3	0	1	2	0	0
Walls (Cubs) lf	1	0	0	0	0	0
Musial (Cardinals) 1b	4	1	1	7	0	0
Aaron (Braves) rf	2	0	0	2	0	0
Banks (Cubs) ss	3	0	0	2	3	1
Thomas (Pirates) 3b	3	0	1	1	3	1
Mazeroski (Pirates) 3b	4	0	0	4	5	0
Crandall (Braves) c	4	0	0	5	0	0
Spahn (Braves) p	0	0	0	0	1	0
Blasingame (Cardinals) ph	1	0	0	0	0	0
Friend (Pirates) p	0	0	0	0	0	0
Jackson (Cardinals) p	0	0	0	0	0	0
Logan (Braves) ph	1	0	0	0	0	0
Farrell (Phillies) p	0	0	0	0	0	0
Totals	30	3	4	24	12	2

American League	AB	R	H	PO	A	E
Fox (White Sox) 2b	4	1	2	5	3	1
Mantle (Yankees) cf	2	0	1	3	0	0
Jensen (Red Sox) rf	4	0	0	1	0	0
Cerv (Athletics) lf	2	0	1	4	0	0
O'Dell (Orioles) p	0	0	0	0	0	0
Skowron (Yankees) 1b	4	0	0	8	0	0
Malzone (Red Sox) 3b	4	1	1	0	2	0
Triandos (Athletics) c	2	0	1	1	0	1
Berra (Yankees) c	2	0	0	3	0	0
Aparicio (White Sox) ss	2	1	0	1	1	0
Williams (Red Sox) ph–lf	2	0	0	1	0	0
Kaline (Tigers) lf	0	0	0	0	0	0
Turley (Yankees) p	0	0	0	0	0	0
Narleski (Indians) p	1	0	1	0	0	0
Vernon (Indians) ph	1	1	1	0	0	0
Wynn (White Sox) p	0	0	0	0	0	0
McDougald (Yankees) ph–ss	1	0	1	0	3	0
Totals	31	4	10	26	9	2

National League .... 2 1 0 0 0 0 0 0 0 - 3
American League......................... 1 1 0 0 1 1 0 0 0 - 4

DP—National 3, Americans 1. LOB—Nationals 5, Americans 7. RBIs—Skinner, Aaron, Fox, Jensen, McDougald. SAC HIT—O'Dell. SAC FLY—Aaron. SB— Mays. HBP—By Turley (Banks). WP—Turley.

National League	IP	H	R	ER	BB	SO
Spahn	3	5	2	1	0	0
Friend (L)	2⅓	4	2	1	2	0
Jackson	⅔	0	0	0	0	0
Farrell	2	0	0	0	1	4

American League	IP	H	R	ER	BB	SO
Turley	1⅔	3	3	3	2	0
Narleski	3⅓	1	0	0	1	0
Wynn (W)	1	0	0	0	0	0
O'Dell	3	0	0	0	0	2

Umpires — Rommel, McKinley, and Umont (A.L.), Gorman, Conlan, and Secory (N.L.). Time — 2:13. Attendance — 48,829.

Then it was the American League's turn against N.L. hurler Warren Spahn, manager Fred Haney's surprise selection. The 37-year-old Milwaukee southpaw had appeared in five All-Star games, starting in 1949 at Brooklyn and winning in relief in 1953 at Cincinnati. Spahn was 10–5 going into the contest, and his age clearly wasn't a handicap.

Spahn blew past the Americans in their half of the first, giving up only one run when Nellie Fox scored. Fox had reached first on Ernie Banks' errant throw to Stan Musial, which pulled the big St. Louis Cardinal off the bag, allowing Fox to take third and score on Mickey Mantle's single to center field.

Leading 2–1, the Nationals stormed back with another run off Bob Turley in the second. Willie Mays, safe on a force play, stole second and scored on Bob Skinner's single to left. Turley was yanked, and Ray Narleski replaced him. Narleski finished out the inning, holding the N.L. scoreless.

The A.L. rallied for another run in their half of the inning, and tied the game in the fifth at three a piece with Pittsburgh's Bob Friend on the mound for the Nationals. The A.L.'s winning run was driven across in the sixth when Frank Malzone singled, Yogi Berra, pinch-hitting, popped out, but Ted Williams bounced a grounder which Frank Thomas bobbled, leaving Williams safe and runners at first and second. Gil McDougald's pinch-hit single sent Malzone scurrying home with the decisive run of the ball game.

Bob Friend, the N.L.'s second pitcher, took the loss. Friend entered the contest in relief in the last of the sixth, and surrendered the Americans' final two runs. Early Wynn, last year's victim, earned the victory with an inning of solid relief.

O'Dell, on being the pitching hero of the moment, said, "I was kind of surprised when Casey picked me to the team. Then when he called on me to pitch in the seventh, he told me, 'Go hard all the way. Give it all you got.' I tried to do like he said."

So did McDougald, with flying colors.

July 7, 1959

Forbes Field
(Game One)

Whitey Ford, the A.L.'s losing pitcher, was icing his arm in the clubhouse when someone asked him why Willie Mays always hit well against him in All-Star competition. Immersing his arm in a tub of ice, Ford answered painfully, "I never have gotten him out. He hits me like he owns me."

Not even Mays himself could have said it better. The power-hitting Giants center fielder teamed up with pitcher Don Drysdale to emerge as winners over the American League 5-4. It was the N.L.'s 11th win against 15 defeats. Mays smacked a triple in the eighth off Ford to drive in the tying and winning runs. It was the third time Mays had succeeded against Ford. He hit the Yankee southpaw for two singles in the 1955 game and hammered him for a home run in the 1956 affair.

Drysdale, 9-5 with the Dodgers, was the major league's strikeout king going into the game. During the contest, he showed why by fanning Nellie Fox, Al Kaline, Rocky Colavito, and Early Wynn. The 23-year-old Van Nuys native hurled three perfect innings as manager Fred Haney's starter and was voted by the writers as the game's MVP, edging out Willie Mays by three votes, 20-17.

Drysdale came into the game having won three straight over the Braves, Reds, and Phillies. On the season, he twice fanned 11 Giants and twice performed the same against the Cubs. All nine of his victories were complete games in which he allowed a total of 12 runs.

His pitching competitor was 39-year-old Early Wynn, who was now a member of the Chicago White Sox. Wynn posted a 22-10 record that season and helped the Sox win the pennant. His repertoire of pitches earned him the description of "junkyard dog."

Junk was what he threw against the Nationals, who hit him soundly in the very first inning. In all, the N.L. outpowered their rivals with nine hits against eight. Eddie Mathews slugged a home run as the second batter in the inning to stake his club to an early 1-0 lead. Mathews and teammate Hank Aaron were vying in the N.L. home run derby with 25 and 22 respectively.

The 1959 All-Star Game (Game One)

American League	AB	R	H	PO	A	E
Minoso (Indians) lf	5	0	0	0	1	0
Fox (White Sox) 2b	5	1	2	3	0	0
Kaline (Tigers) cf	3	1	1	1	0	0
Kuenn (Tigers) cf	1	1	0	0	0	0
Skowron (Yankees) 1b	3	0	2	3	0	0
Power (Indians) 1b	1	1	1	2	0	0
Colavito (Indians) rf	3	0	1	1	0	0
Williams (Red Sox) ph	0	0	0	0	0	0
McDougald (Yankees) ss	0	0	0	0	0	0
Triandos (Orioles) c	4	0	1	8	0	0
Mantle (Yankees) rf	0	0	0	0	0	0
Killebrew (Senators) 3b	3	0	0	0	1	0
Bunning (Tigers) p	0	0	0	0	0	0
Runnels (Red Sox) ph	0	0	0	0	0	0
Sievers (Senators) ph	0	0	0	0	0	0
Ford (Yankees) p	0	0	0	0	1	0
Daley (Athletics) p	0	0	0	0	0	0
Aparicio (White Sox) ss	3	0	0	4	2	0
Lollar (White Sox) p	1	0	0	1	0	0
Wynn (White Sox) p	1	0	0	1	0	0
Duren (Yankees) p	1	0	0	0	0	0
Malzone (Red Sox) 3b	2	0	0	0	0	0
Totals	34	4	8	24	5	0
National League	AB	R	H	PO	A	E
Temple (Reds) 2b	2	0	0	1	3	0
Musial (Cardinals) ph	1	0	0	0	0	0
Face (Pirates) p	0	0	0	0	0	0
Antonelli (Giants) p	0	0	0	0	0	0
Boyer (Cardinals) ph-3b	1	1	1	1	0	0
Mathews (Braves) 3b	3	1	1	2	1	1
Groat (Pirates) ph	0	0	0	0	0	0
Elston (Cubs) p	0	0	0	0	0	0
Aaron (Braves) rf	4	1	2	2	0	0
Mays (Giants) cf	4	0	1	2	0	0
Banks (Cubs) ss	3	1	2	1	2	0
Cepeda (Giants) 1b	4	0	0	6	0	0
Moon (Dodgers) lf	2	0	0	1	0	0
Crandall (Braves) c	3	1	1	10	0	0
Drysdale (Dodgers) p	1	0	0	0	0	0
Burdette (Braves) p	1	0	0	0	0	0
Mazeroski (Pirates) 2b	1	0	1	1	1	0
Totals	30	5	9	27	7	1

```
American League.........................  0  0  0  1  0  0  0  3  0 – 4
National League ........................  1  0  0  0  0  0  2  2  x – 5
```

DP—Americans 1. LOB—Americans 8, Nationals 4. 2B—Banks (2), Triandos.
3B—Mays. HR—Mathews, Kaline. RBIs—Kaline, Power, Triandos (2), Mathews,
Aaron, Mays, Crandall, Mazeroski. SAC HIT—Groat. WP—Elston.

American League	IP	H	R	ER	BB	SO
Wynn	3	2	1	1	1	3
Duren	3	1	0	0	1	4
Bunning	1	3	2	2	0	1
Ford (L)	⅓	3	2	2	0	0
Daley	⅔	0	0	0	0	1

National League	IP	H	R	ER	BB	SO
Drysdale	3	0	0	0	0	4
Burdette	3	4	1	1	0	2
Face	1⅔	3	3	3	2	2
Antonelli (W)	⅓	0	0	0	1	0
Elston	1	1	0	0	0	1

Umpires—Barlick, Donatelli, and Crawford (N.L.), Runge, Paparella, and Rice (A.L.). Time—2:33. Attendance—35,277.

The Americans got that run back in the fourth at the expense of Lou Burdette, Drysdale's successor, who threw up a home run ball to Detroit Tiger slugger Al Kaline with the bases empty. The score was tied 1-1. It proved to be the only extra-base hit for the Stengel-managed A.L. squad.

Detroit ace Jim Bunning tried holding the game close in the seventh, but he was sacked for two runs on a double by Ernie Banks, and singles by Del Crandall and Bill Mazeroski.

From then on it appeared as if the National League had the game in the bag, with Roy Face, the forkballing Pittsburgh relief ace, coming in to retire the side in order in the seventh. Face was 12–0 with the parent club and had fashioned a microscopic 0.83 earned run average in 32 relief appearances. But, in the eighth, Face fell on hard times as he pitched like a rookie. After taking care of the first two batters, he gave up a line single to Nellie Fox. Fox was playing in the game along with shortstop Luis Aparicio, another White Sox, who were touted before the game as "the greatest double-play combination." Harvey Kuenn walked; then Vic Power, who was not on speaking terms with Stengel, bolted a shot to center to score Fox. Ted Williams, pinch-hitting for Colavito, walked to load the bases. Williams, 40, was the oldest player on either team's roster. Oriole catcher Gil Triandos followed with a base hit over the third-base bag to drive in two runs and give the Americans a slim 4–3 lead.

Face was taken out of the game, the first time he failed to finish a job since Memorial Day, 1958, and was replaced by Johnny Antonelli. Antonelli retired Chicago's Sherm Lollar to end the inning.

Then, before a boisterous pro–National League crowd, the N.L. made their dramatic comeback with Ken Boyer launching a single to left. Boyer later moved to second on Pirate Dick Groat's bunt along first. Hank Aaron powered Boyer home with the tying run on a single past shortstop Gil McDougald. Aaron came all the way around to score when Willie Mays unloaded a 440-foot triple off Whitey Ford, who came in to pitch for the A.L. in the eighth.

The National League walked off with a 5–4 decision, and Antonelli posted the victory while Ford earned the loss.

Ryne Duren, the nearsighted Yankee, threw blanks from the fourth through the sixth, striking out four and facing only eight men in three innings until Aaron singled.

Stengel used every pitcher except Hoyt Wilhelm and Billy Pierce, and the game was the 15th contest for the ageless Ted Williams. Williams, batting .317, was chosen to the game along with Stan Musial, who was appearing in his 16th All-Star contest with a .315 batting mark. First-timers to this interleague matchup included Drysdale, Orlando Cepeda (the youngest player at 21), Dick Groat, Vada Pinson, Roy Face, Don Elston, Bill White and Joe Cunningham for the Nationals; and Harmon Killebrew, Pete Runnels, Bud Daley, and Rocky Colavito for the Americans.

On his key triple, Willie Mays said, "I was just looking to get a base hit when I came up. So what happens? I wind up with a triple."

And a share of the hero's cup with Don Drysdale.

August 3, 1959

Los Angeles Coliseum (Game Two)

Don Drysdale, the Dodger "wonder kid," was called on to face 20-year-old Baltimore rookie, Jerry Walker, in the season's second All-Star matchup and first "doubleheader" in the event's history.

Drysdale had performed his spell of magic over the opposition in the first 1959 contest, and now he was asked to repeat the same, this time before a capacity crowd of 55,105 fans at the Los Angeles Coliseum (then home of the Los Angeles Dodgers). The Coliseum was not built for baseball, but the Dodgers made do. A portable fence was lifted in left and it was that screen which created many years of controversy until the Dodgers moved to their permanent residence at Dodger Stadium.

The game, besides marking Drysdale's second appearance, also marked the first time that either manager was allowed to pick their own starting lineups. A.L. skipper Casey Stengel took advantage of this rare opportunity by stocking his lineup with powerful left-handed swingers to face the right-hander Drysdale. Stengel's strategy paid off as the Americans bombed Drysdale for four hits and three runs in a nightmarish second and third innings. But Drysdale couldn't hold on as the Nationals went down to defeat, 5–3.

The scoring started in the first, when Hank Aaron's sacrifice fly scored Johnny Temple, who had doubled. Then, in the second, Frank Malzone crushed a homer over the left field fence for the A.L.'s first run.

The damage to Drysdale was far from over. In the third, Yogi Berra belted a two-run homer over the right field fence, with Nellie Fox on base to account for the A.L.'s second scoring drive off Drysdale and extend the Americans' lead to 3–1.

Frank Robinson narrowed the margin in the fifth to 3–2, when he slammed an Early Wynn pitch deep into the left center field bleachers. Wynn had come in to replace Walker in the top of the fourth.

The Americans went hitless after their first two run-scoring innings, but

The 1959 All-Star Game (Game Two)

American League	AB	R	H	PO	A	E
Runnels (Red Sox) 1b	3	0	0	9	0	0
Power (Indians) 1b	1	0	0	4	0	0
Fox (White Sox) 2b	4	1	2	3	1	0
Williams (Red Sox) lf	3	0	0	0	0	0
Kaline (Tigers) lf–cf	2	0	0	0	0	0
Berra (Yankees) c	3	1	1	2	0	0
Lollar (White Sox) c	0	0	0	2	0	0
Mantle (Yankees) cf	3	0	1	3	0	0
O'Dell (Orioles) p	0	0	0	0	0	0
McLish (Indians) p	0	0	0	0	0	0
Maris (Athletics) rf	2	0	0	1	0	0
Colavito (Indians) rf	2	1	1	0	0	0
Malzone (Red Sox) 3b	4	1	1	1	6	0
Aparicio (White Sox) ss	3	0	0	1	2	0
Walker (Orioles) p	1	0	0	0	0	0
Woodling (Orioles) ph	1	0	0	0	0	0
Wynn (White Sox) p	0	0	0	1	0	0
Wilhelm (Orioles) p	0	0	0	0	0	0
Kubek (Yankees) ph–lf	1	1	0	0	0	0
Totals	33	5	6	27	9	0

National League	AB	R	H	PO	A	E
Temple (Reds) 2b	2	1	1	1	1	0
Gilliam (Dodgers) ph–3b	2	1	1	0	0	0
Boyer (Cardinals) 3b	2	0	0	0	1	0
Neal (Dodgers) 2b	1	0	0	0	2	0
Aaron (Braves) rf	3	0	0	2	0	0
Mays (Giants) cf	4	0	0	3	0	0
Banks (Cubs) ss	4	0	0	2	0	1
Musial (Cardinals) 1b	0	0	0	3	1	0
Robinson (Reds) 1b	3	1	3	3	0	1
Moon (Dodgers) lf	2	0	0	1	0	0
Crandall (Braves) c	2	0	1	7	1	0
Smith (Cardinals) c	2	0	0	5	0	0
Drysdale (Dodgers) p	0	0	0	0	0	0
Mathews (Braves) ph	1	0	0	0	0	0
Conley (Phillies) p	0	0	0	0	1	0
Cunningham (Cardinals) ph	1	0	0	0	0	0
Pinson (Reds) ph	0	0	0	0	0	0
Jones (Giants) p	0	0	0	0	0	1
Groat (Pirates) ph	1	0	0	0	0	0
Face (Pirates) p	0	0	0	0	0	0
Burgess (Pirates) ph	1	0	0	0	0	0
Totals	31	3	6	27	7	3

```
American League.......................... 0 1 2 0 0 0 1 1 0 – 5
National League  ........................ 1 0 0 0 1 0 1 0 0 – 3
```

DP—Americans 1. LOB—Americans 7, Nationals 7. 2B—Temple. HR—Malzone, Berra, Robinson, Gilliam, Colavito, RBIs—Fox, Berra (2), Colavito, Malzone, Gilliam, Aaron, Robinson. SAC FLY—Aaron. SB—Aparicio.

American League	IP	H	R	ER	BB	SO
Walker (W)	3	2	1	1	1	1
Wynn	2	1	1	1	3	1
Wilhelm	1	1	0	0	0	0
O'Dell	1	1	1	1	0	0
McLish	2	1	0	0	1	2
National League	IP	H	R	ER	BB	SO
Drysdale (L)	3	4	3	3	3	5
Conley	2	0	0	0	1	2
Jones	2	1	1	0	2	3
Face	2	1	1	1	0	2

Umpires — Jackowski, Venzon, and Burkhart (N.L.), Berry, Summers, and Soar (A.L.). Time — 2:42. Attendance — 55,105.

---

came back to life in the seventh with a run off "Toothpick Sam" Jones. A walk, two infield errors, and Nellie Fox's single up the middle produced the run.

The Nationals battled back in explosive style in the seventh when Jim Gilliam belted a Billy O'Dell fastball over the left center field screen to draw his team within one, 4–3.

The score remained the same until the eighth when leadoff man Rocky Colavito poled a Roy Face pitch over the 430-foot marker to clinch a 5–3 victory for the Americans.

N.L. manager Fred Haney was dumbfounded by the defeat, while six of the game's eight runs came via the home run ball. Jerry Walker received the victory, and Drysdale was charged with the loss.

Yogi Berra won the MVP award by a landslide, even though he struck out twice. On his game-winning home run, Berra said, "I don't know about how I'd feel if I had to bat against Drysdale all the time. He throws hard enough — I know. I'd have to get used to him."

Drysdale would have obviously enjoyed a second opportunity.

July 11, 1960

Kansas City's Municipal Stadium (Game One)

With temperatures blistering above 100 degrees, Willie Mays, the San Francisco sparkplug, was as hot as the weather by pacing his National League squad to a 5–3 victory over the American League, as 30,619 spectators tried cooling off.

Mays blasted a triple, double and single on the day, and just missed hitting for the cycle with a home run shot his last time up. His drive fell short as outfielder Harvey Kuenn hauled it down. Willie's performance clearly rubbed off on his teammates, as Ernie Banks and Del Crandall joined the hit parade with solo home runs and extra base hits of their own.

In all, the N.L. outslugged the A.L. 12 hits to six. The game promised to explode with power, as each lineup contained quite an array of power hitters. The Americans could match the muscle of Chicago's Ernie Banks, Milwaukee's Hank Aaron and Eddie Mathews, and San Francisco's Willie Mays with New York's Roger Maris, Mickey Mantle, Bill Skowron, and Yogi Berra.

But all comparisons aside, the National League showed its true strength more than the Americans. The N.L. squad's victory narrowed the A.L. series edge to 16–12. Pittsburgh's Bob Friend and San Francisco's Mike McCormick pitched five shutout innings, before the Americans finally broke through with a run in the sixth.

Up until then, it was all National League. A.L. manager Al Lopez went with Boston's Bill Monbouquette as his opening hurler, but Monbouquette ran into trouble immediately. Mays welcomed the beantown right-hander with a triple to right field, scoring on Bob Skinner's opposite field single. Ernie Banks, the N.L. home run and RBI leader, kept things alive with a home run blast off Monbouquette to drive in Skinner and post the Nationals to a comfortable 3–0 lead. But it seemed as if the Nationals never got enough off Monbouquette. The senior circuit charged right back after Monbouquette in the second when Del Crandall cranked the right-hander's first pitch over the boards in left.

The 1960 All-Star Game (Game One)

National League	AB	R	H	PO	A	E
Mays (Giants) cf	4	1	3	4	0	0
Pinson (Reds) cf	1	0	0	1	0	0
Skinner (Pirates) lf	4	1	1	1	0	0
Cepeda (Giants) lf	1	0	0	0	0	0
Mathews (Braves) 3b	4	0	0	1	0	2
Boyer (Cardinals) 3b	0	0	0	0	2	0
Aaron (Braves) lf	4	0	0	0	1	0
Clemente (Pirates) rf	1	0	0	2	0	0
Banks (Cubs) ss	4	2	2	2	2	0
Groat (Pirates) ss	0	0	0	0	0	0
Adcock (Braves) 1b	3	0	2	3	0	0
White (Cardinals) 1b	1	0	0	4	0	0
Mazeroski (Pirates) 2b	2	0	1	2	2	0
Musial (Cardinals) ph	1	0	1	0	0	0
Taylor (Phillies) ph	0	0	0	0	0	0
Neal (Dodgers) 2b	0	0	0	0	0	1
Crandall (Braves) c	3	1	2	4	0	0
Burgess (Pirates) c	1	0	0	3	0	0
Friend (Pirates) p	0	0	0	0	0	0
McCormick (Giants) p	1	0	0	0	0	0
Face (Pirates) p	0	0	0	0	0	0
Larker (Dodgers) ph	1	0	0	0	0	0
Buhl (Braves) p	0	0	0	0	0	0
Law (Pirates) p	0	0	0	0	0	0
Totals	36	5	12	27	7	4

American League	AB	R	H	PO	A	E
Minoso (White Sox) lf	3	0	0	0	0	0
Lemon (Senators) lf	1	0	0	1	0	0
Malzone (Red Sox) 3b	3	0	0	1	1	0
Robinson (Orioles) 3b	2	0	0	0	0	0
Maris (Yankees) rf	2	0	0	1	0	0
Kuenn (Indians) rf	3	1	1	1	0	0
Mantle (Yankees) cf	0	0	0	2	0	0
Kaline (Tigers) cf	2	2	1	1	0	0
Skowron (Yankees) 1b	3	0	1	9	0	0
Lary (Tigers) p	0	0	0	0	0	0
Lollar (White Sox) ph	1	0	0	0	0	0
B. Daley (Athletics) p	0	0	0	0	0	1
Berra (Yankees) c	2	0	0	5	0	0
Howard (Yankees) c	1	0	0	4	0	0
Runnels (Red Sox) 2b	1	0	0	0	1	0
Fox (White Sox) 2b	2	0	1	1	3	0
Hansen (Orioles) ss	2	0	1	0	0	0
Aparicio (White Sox) ss	2	0	0	1	1	0
Monbouquette (Red Sox) p	0	0	0	0	0	0
Williams (Red Sox) ph	1	0	0	0	0	0
Estrada (Orioles) p	0	0	0	0	0	0
Coates (Yankees) p	0	0	0	0	0	0
Smith (White Sox) ph	1	0	0	0	0	0

American League	AB	R	H	PO	A	E
Bell (Indians) p	0	0	0	0	1	0
Gentile (Orioles) 1b	2	0	1	0	0	0
Totals	34	3	6	27	7	1

National League .... 3 1 1 0 0 0 0 0 0 – 5
American League........................ 0 0 0 0 0 1 0 2 0 – 3

DP – Americans 1, Nationals 1. LOB – Nationals 8, Americans 9. 2B – Banks, Mays, Adcock. 3B – Mays. HR – Banks, Crandall, Kaline. RBIs – Skinner, Banks (2), Mazeroski, Crandall, Kaline (2), Fox. SB – Skinner. HPB – By Coates (Mazeroski). WP – Friend. Balk – Friend.

National League	IP	H	R	ER	BB	SO
Friend (W)	3	1	0	0	1	2
McCormick	2⅓	3	1	0	3	2
Face	1⅔	0	0	0	0	2
Buhl	1⅓	2	2	1	1	1
Law	⅔	0	0	0	0	0

American League	IP	H	R	ER	BB	SO
Monbouquette (L)	2	5	4	4	0	2
Estrada	1	4	1	1	0	1
Coates	2	2	0	0	0	0
Bell	2	0	0	0	0	1
Lary	1	1	0	0	0	1
B. Daley	1	0	0	0	1	2

Umpires – Honochick, Chylak, and Stevens (A.L.), Gorman, Boggess, and Smith (N.L.). Time – 2:30. Attendance – 30,619.

Losing 4–0, Lopez went to Baltimore rookie Chuck Estrada, but not even Estrada (9–5) had a prayer against the power-packed National League. With two out, Ernie Banks doubled off the screen atop the left field wall, and scored on Bill Mazeroski's single.

Meanwhile, the day belonged to Mays. His performance placed him in the All-Star record book. His run in the first inning was his 10th in eight games, tying Musial and Williams.

Not even a late-inning uprising by the Americans could diminish Mays' contribution. The junior circuit added two more runs in the eighth on Al Kaline's prodigious two-run blast off reliever Bob Buhl. Vern Law, another Pirate, bailed out Buhl in the ninth to preserve the victory.

One footnote: Ted Williams and Stan Musial both drew tremendous ovations when they came to the plate. These two living legends overcame early batting slumps to be selected to the All-Star game. Musial broke three of his own records by recording his 18th All-Star hit, his 35th total base and his 56th at-bat. Williams, who pinch-hit in the second, was appearing in his 17th All-Star contest, but the best he could do was ground out.

Bill Monbouquette absorbed the loss, while Bob Friend chalked up the victory for his three innings of steady relief.

After the game, N.L. manager Walt Alston celebrated in the clubhouse by taking a towel and playfully rubbing the perspiring brow of Willie Mays.

If Alston's gesture was for good luck, Mays didn't need it.

July 13, 1960

Yankee Stadium
(Game Two)

Willie Mays moved his show east to Yankee Stadium for the second game of 1960. He led his team to a 6–0 shutout over the humbled Americans by ambushing A.L. southpaw Whitey Ford.

Mays hammered a home run, two singles, and stole a base in a winning cause. For the two All-Star games combined, Willie compiled six hits in eight at-bats—a home run, triple, double and three singles—which computed to a hefty .438 batting mark. His greatest benefactor: Whitey Ford.

Mays seemed to own Ford every time he faced him. The multitalented Giants center fielder had six successive hits off Ford in All-Star competition. Ford shook his head silently after the game in disbelief over Mays' domination of him. There weren't any complaints from the National League bench, which saw Pittsburgh's Vern Law, pitching on two days' rest, complete a two-game "sweep" over the junior circuit with two innings of work.

Besides Law, manager Walt Alston countered with five other National League hurlers: Johnny Podres, who successfully pitched two innings; Stan Williams, another Dodger, who struggled through his two innings of work; and St. Louis' Larry Jackson, Cincinatti's Bill Henry, and St. Louis' Lindy McDaniel, who finished up with one inning each.

A.L. skipper Al Lopez, searching for his first All-Star win ever, was hoping for a different outcome. Instead, Ford was racked for three runs on five hits in a game which saw four home runs and 10 hits by the N.L. The other three homers came off the bats of Stan Musial, Eddie Mathews, and Ken Boyer. The shutout, a combination eight-hit job by an assortment of six N.L. pitchers, was only the third in 29 All-Star games. The 38,362 New Yorkers, who attended this first All-Star contest at Yankee Stadium since 1939, went home disappointed. The home team just got beat ... and badly.

Eddie Mathews started the Nationals' first scoring drive in the second inning with a homer into the lower right field seats, sending teammate Joe Adcock, who singled previously, home with a 2–0 lead. Mays followed in the

The 1960 All-Star Game (Game Two)

National League	AB	R	H	PO	A	E
Mays (Giants) cf	4	1	3	5	0	0
Pinson (Reds) cf	0	0	0	0	0	0
Skinner (Pirates) lf	3	0	1	2	0	0
Cepeda (Giants) lf	2	0	0	0	0	0
Aaron (Braves) rf	3	0	0	1	0	0
Clemente (Pirates) ph–rf	0	0	0	0	0	0
Banks (Cubs) ss	3	0	1	2	3	0
Groat (Pirates) ss	1	0	0	0	1	0
Adcock (Braves) 1b	2	1	1	3	0	0
White (Cardinals) 1b	1	0	0	2	0	0
Larker (Dodgers) ph–1b	0	1	0	3	0	0
Mathews (Braves) 3b	3	1	1	0	1	0
Boyer (Cardinals) 3b	1	1	1	1	0	0
Mazeroski (Pirates) 2b	2	0	0	0	0	0
Neal (Dodgers) 2b	1	0	0	1	2	0
Taylor (Phillies) 2b	1	0	1	2	1	0
Crandall (Braves) c	2	0	0	3	0	0
S. Williams (Dodgers) p	0	0	0	0	0	0
Musial (Cardinals) ph	1	1	1	0	0	0
Jackson (Cardinals) p	0	0	0	0	0	0
Bailey (Reds) c	1	0	0	0	0	0
Law (Pirates) p	1	0	0	0	0	0
Podres (Dodgers) p	0	0	0	0	1	0
Burgess (Pirates) ph–c	2	0	0	2	0	0
Henry (Reds) p	0	0	0	0	0	0
McDaniel (Cardinals) p	0	0	0	0	0	0
Totals	34	6	10	27	9	0

American League	AB	R	H	PO	A	E
Minoso (White Sox) lf	2	0	0	1	0	0
T. Williams (Red Sox) ph	1	0	1	0	0	0
Robinson (Orioles) ph–3b	1	0	0	0	0	0
Runnels (Red Sox) 2b	2	0	0	0	1	0
Staley (White Sox) p	0	0	0	1	1	0
Kaline (Tigers) lf	1	0	1	3	0	0
Maris (Yankees) rf	4	0	0	0	0	0
Mantle (Yankees) cf	4	0	1	3	0	0
Skowron (Yankees) 1b	1	0	1	6	0	0
Power (Indians) 1b	2	0	0	5	1	0
Berra (Yankees) c	2	0	0	4	1	0
Lollar (White Sox) c	2	0	1	0	0	0
Malzone (Red Sox) 3b	2	0	0	2	2	0
Lary (Tigers) p	0	0	0	0	0	0
Smith (White Sox) ph	1	0	0	0	0	0
Bell (Indians) p	0	0	0	0	1	0
Hansen (Orioles) ss	4	0	2	2	4	0
Ford (Yankees) p	0	0	0	0	0	0
Kuenn (Indians) ph	1	0	0	0	0	0

American League	AB	R	H	PO	A	E
Wynn (White Sox) p	0	0	0	0	0	0
Fox (White Sox) ph–2b	3	0	1	0	1	0
Totals	33	0	8	27	12	0

National League . . . . 0 2 1 0 0 0 1 0 2 – 6
American League. . . . . 0 0 0 0 0 0 0 0 0 – 0

DP – Nationals 2, Americans 1. LOB – Nationals 5, Americans 12. 2B – Lollar.
HR – Mathews, Mays, Musial, Boyer. RBIs – Mays, Mathews (2), Boyer (2), Musial.
SB – Mays.

National League	IP	H	R	ER	BB	SO
Law (W)	2	1	0	0	0	1
Podres	2	1	0	0	3	1
S. Williams	2	2	0	0	1	2
Jackson	1	1	0	0	0	0
Henry	1	1	0	0	0	0
McDaniel	1	1	0	0	0	0

American League	IP	H	R	ER	BB	SO
Ford (L)	3	5	3	3	0	1
Wynn	2	0	0	0	0	2
Staley	2	2	1	1	1	0
Lary	1	1	0	0	1	0
Bell	1	2	2	2	2	0

Umpires – Chylak, Honochick, and Stevens (A.L.), Boggess, Gorman, and Smith
(N.L.). Time – 2:42. Attendance – 38,362.

---

third by clouting a homer of his own deep into the left field stands. The score
was now 3–0.

Lopez tried weathering the storm with an assortment of relief artists, but
it was all to no avail. Stan Musial, the 39-year-old St. Louis Cardinal
favorite, appearing in his 19th All-Star game, slammed a pinch homer into
the upper deck in right to score the Nationals' fourth run of the game in the
seventh. It was Musial's sixth All-Star homer, breaking his own record and
smashing or tying a handful of other All-Star marks.

Musial drew the biggest ovation of the day, next to Ted Williams, who
kept his consecutive streak of All-Star appearances alive by making his 18th.
He pinch-hit for Minnie Minoso in the seventh and came through with a
sharp single to right.

But not even Williams' historic single took the sting out of this defeat,
as Ken Boyer, another St. Louis Cardinal, stepped up in the ninth and ended
all scoring with a two-run homer to left. Dodger Norm Laker, who walked
to open the inning, scored ahead of Boyer.

In two games, the National Leaguers pounded out 22 hits, including six homers, three doubles, and a triple, and scored a total of 11 runs. Meanwhile, the Americans were handcuffed to a total of three runs on 14 hits.

The triumph was manager Walt Alston's third in five games, and the third straight defeat for skipper Al Lopez.

Whitey Ford was ticketed with the loss, and Vern Law with the victory.

And Mays — another chance for Alston to rub his forehead for good luck.

July 11, 1961

Candlestick Park (Game One)

It was one of the weirdest finishes in All-Star game history. The site: Candlestick Park, San Francisco, where anything can happen—and did. Noted for its gales of wind, Candlestick Park was far from a baseball player's haven for the 30th annual midsummer classic.

The windblown conditions created a comedy of errors—seven in all, five by the Nationals. This matchup will also go down in baseball annals for the windstorm that knocked N.L. reliever Stu Miller off the mound for the first balk of his career, advancing two runners and almost costing his team the game. It was likewise a game from which third sacker Ken Boyer didn't save clippings for his scrapbooks. He made two miscues on the day, which he attributed to the abnormal conditions.

But once the dust and, more importantly, the wind cleared, the final results were unlike any previous interleague contest: the Nationals saw their lead suddenly vanish in the final innings, but, miraculously, recaptured it to win in ten innings on Roberto Clemente's run-scoring single, 5–4. The victim: Baltimore knuckleballer Hoyt Wilhelm, whose knuckler didn't knuckle. The win cut the Americans' All-Star lead to 16–14, and it was the 10th N.L. victory in the last 14 contests.

The pitching matchup was also slightly lopsided. The Milwaukee Braves' 40-year-old ace Warren Spahn took the mound against Yankee lefty Whitey Ford. It seemed to be quite a mismatch even on paper. Ford entered the game, his sixth such appearance, with the niftiest record in the majors, 16 wins against only two losses. His All-Star record was something else altogether. In five previous appearances he worked a total of nine innings, lost two games and built up an astronomical 10.00 earned run average. Meanwhile, Ford was facing a pitching legend in Spahn. With 296 victories under his belt, Spahn was making his seventh appearance, and third straight, in All-Star play. The balding Brave had a 1–0 record in interleague play and had been selected to the N.L. All-Star roster a dozen times in all.

Both managers, Danny Murtaugh of the National League and Paul

The 1961 All-Star Game (Game One)

American League	AB	R	H	PO	A	E
Temple (Indians) 2b	3	0	0	1	2	0
Gentile (Orioles) ph-1b	2	0	0	2	0	1
Cash (Tigers) 1b	4	0	1	6	1	0
Fox (White Sox) 2b	0	2	0	1	0	0
Mantle (Yankees) cf	3	0	0	3	0	0
Kaline (Tigers) cf	2	1	1	1	0	0
Maris (Yankees) rf	4	0	1	3	0	0
Colavito (Tigers) lf	4	0	0	1	0	0
Kubek (Yankees) ss	4	0	0	1	2	1
Romano (Indians) c	3	0	0	7	0	0
Berra (Yankees) ph-c	1	0	0	0	0	0
Howard (Yankees) c	0	0	0	0	0	0
B. Robinson (Orioles) 3b	2	0	0	0	2	0
Bunning (Tigers) p	0	0	0	1	0	0
Brandt (Orioles) ph	1	0	0	0	0	0
Fornieles (Red Sox) p	0	0	0	0	0	0
Wilhelm (Orioles) p	1	0	0	0	0	0
Ford (Yankees) p	1	0	0	0	0	0
Lary (Tigers) p	0	0	0	0	0	0
Donovan (Senators) p	0	0	0	0	0	0
Killebrew (Twins) 3b	2	1	1	0	0	0
Howser (Athletics) 3b	1	0	0	0	1	0
Totals	38	4	4	27	8	2

National League	AB	R	H	PO	A	E
Wills (Dodgers) ss	5	0	1	0	2	0
Mathews (Braves) 3b	2	0	0	0	0	0
Purkey (Reds) p	0	0	0	1	0	0
Musial (Cardinals) ph	1	0	0	0	0	0
McCormick (Giants) p	0	0	0	0	0	0
Altman (Cubs) ph	1	1	1	0	0	0
Face (Pirates) p	0	0	0	0	0	0
Koufax (Dodgers) p	0	0	0	0	0	0
Miller (Giants) p	0	0	0	0	0	0
Aaron (Braves) ph	1	1	1	0	0	0
Mays (Giants) cf	5	2	2	3	0	0
Cepeda (Giants) lf	3	0	0	1	0	1
F. Robinson (Reds) lf	1	0	1	2	0	0
Clemente (Pirates) rf	4	1	2	2	0	0
White (Cardinals) 1b	3	0	1	7	1	0
Bolling (Braves) 2b	3	0	0	1	3	0
Zimmer (Cubs) 2b	1	0	0	0	0	1
Burgess (Pirates) c	4	0	1	13	0	1
Spahn (Braves) p	0	0	0	0	1	0
Stuart (Pirates) ph	1	0	1	0	0	0
Boyer (Cardinals) 3b	2	0	0	0	1	2
Totals	37	5	11	30	8	5

American League . . . . 0 0 0 0 0 1 0 0 2 1 – 4
National League . . . . 0 1 0 1 0 0 0 1 0 2 – 5

DP—none. LOB—Americans 6, Nationals 9. 2B—Stuart, Cash, Mays. 3B—
Clemente. HR—Killebrew, Altman. RBIs—Kaline, Colavito, Killebrew, Altman,
Mays, Clemente (2), White. SAC FLIES—Clemente, White. SB—F. Robinson.
HBP—By Wilhelm (F. Robinson). Balk—Miller. PB—Howard.

American League	IP	H	R	ER	BB	SO
Ford	3	2	1	1	0	2
Lary	0	0	1	0	0	0
Donovan	2	4	0	0	0	1
Bunning	2	0	0	0	0	2
Fornieles	⅓	2	1	1	0	0
Wilhelm (L)	1 ⅔	3	2	2	1	1
National League	IP	H	R	ER	BB	SO
Spahn	3	0	0	0	0	3
Purkey	2	0	0	0	0	1
McCormick	3	1	1	1	1	3
Face	⅓	2	2	2	0	1
Koufax	0	1	0	0	0	0
Miller (W)	1 ⅔	0	1	0	1	4

Umpires—Landes, Crawford, and Vargo (N.L.), Umont, Runge, and Drummond
(A.L.). Time—2:53. Attendance—44,115.

Richards of the American League, had the strongest faith in their selections.
And, surprisingly, neither of them were vastly disappointed.

With the help of five other pitchers, Spahn kept the Americans in check
for the first eight innings, allowing only one hit. Twelve strikeouts were
recorded by these hurlers, tying a game record. Murtaugh played the game
under the theory that keeping fresh players in and out of the lineup would
prevail, while Richards went with a set lineup with no substitutions, except
pitchers, for a full nine innings. That may have been the Americans' undoing.

The Nationals scored immediately off Ford, and his replacement, Frank
Lary of the Detroit Tigers, with tallies in the second and the fourth. Clemente
tripled and scored on Bill White's sacrifice fly. Tony Kubek misplayed Mays'
grounder for a two-base error, with Mays later rounding to score Clemente's
sacrifice fly. Richards quickly brought in Lary to douse the fire in the fourth,
but the Tiger hurler had to leave the game after throwing to Willie Mays when
his right shoulder stiffened. Senator ace Dick Donovan came in to get his
team out of the jam.

The N.L. took a comfy 3-1 lead on George Altman's pinch-blast in the
eighth off Red Sox's Mike Fornieles.

It was in the sixth that the Americans put their first tally on the scoreboard. Harmon Killebrew, the Minnesota swatter, blasted Mike McCormick's first pitch in the right field stands. Then, in the bottom of the eighth,
the A.L. scored two more runs to tie the game, 3-3.

That set the stage for Clemente's timely hit in the 10th, driving a hand-clapping Mays home with the winning run. As Clemente said to reporters afterwards, "I was going for the distance on the first pitch—and when that didn't work, I just tried to advance the runner."

Paul Richards, meanwhile, blamed part of the loss on the conditions at Candlestick: "The conditions were as near impossible as anything I've ever seen." Kansas City Athletics rookie Dick Howser agreed: "I've never seen a ball park like this. It's terrible."

So was the loss to the Americans' morale.

July 31, 1961

Fenway Park
(Game Two)

Pitching dominated a game set in a ball park that was notorious for its hitting. Instead, Fenway Park was entered into the record books for holding the first game to end in a 1–1 tie, and the first in All-Star history.

Rain prevented the game from continuing after the bottom of the ninth with a 28-minute delay, and cut short any further embarrassment for sluggers from both sides of the field. A.L. and N.L. hitters combined for only nine safeties, striking out 15 times between them.

Two celebrated hurlers took the mound: Detroit Tigers right-hander Jim Bunning (11–8) versus Cincinnati's Bob Purkey. A.L. manager Paul Richards believed Bunning was the answer to snapping the Americans' All-Star losing streak. Instead, he had to settle for a moral victory by tying.

Rocky Colavito started things out on the right foot in the first when he drilled a homer off Purkey. The drive lodged in the screen atop the 31-foot wall in left field, known to the Boston faithful as "the Green Monster." The Nationals didn't even the score until the sixth, when Don Schwall of the Red Sox, appearing in relief, gave up the equalizer. With one out, Milwaukee's Eddie Mathews drew a free pass to first. Willie Mays flied out, and Orlando Cepeda was plunked by a pitch, setting runners at first and second. Eddie Kasko advanced Mathews to third on a high hopping single to center, leaving the rest up to Bill White of the Cardinals. White whistled Schwall's first pitch up the middle for a base hit to score Mathews. The score was now 1–1, which it remained until the end.

Even though the game had little real action, there were some interesting sidelights to report: Roger Maris and Tony Kubek of the Yankees were side-lined with leg injuries, forcing them out of the lineup. Four members of the Los Angeles Dodgers crashed the N.L. roster: Maury Wills, Johnny Rose-boro, Sandy Koufax, and Don Drysdale.

Yet, the biggest newsmaker, next to the rain, was 33-year-old Stu Miller. A "junk" pitcher by trade, Miller struck out the side in the eighth. His victims: Mickey Mantle, Elston Howard, and Roy Sievers. Miller's performance was

The 1961 All-Star Game (Game Two)

National League	AB	R	H	PO	A	E
Wills (Dodgers) ss	2	0	1	1	1	0
Aaron (Braves) rf	2	0	0	1	0	0
Miller (Giants) p	0	0	0	0	0	0
Mathews (Braves) 3b	3	1	0	0	2	0
Mays (Giants) cf	3	0	1	1	0	0
Cepeda (Giants) lf	3	0	0	0	0	0
Clemente (Pirates) rf	2	0	0	0	0	0
Kasko (Reds) ss	1	0	1	2	4	0
Banks (Cubs) ss	1	0	0	0	0	0
White (Cardinals) 1b	4	0	2	11	1	0
Bolling (Braves) 2b	4	0	0	3	2	0
Burgess (Pirates) c	1	0	0	2	0	0
Roseboro (Dodgers) c	3	0	0	6	0	0
Purkey (Reds) p	0	0	0	0	1	0
Stuart (Pirates) ph	1	0	0	0	0	0
Mahaffey (Phillies) p	0	0	0	0	0	0
Musial (Cardinals) ph	1	0	0	0	0	0
Koufax (Dodgers) p	0	0	0	0	0	0
Altman (Cubs) rf	1	0	0	0	0	0
Totals	32	1	5	27	11	0

American League	AB	R	H	PO	A	E
Cash (Tigers) 1b	4	0	0	11	0	0
Colavito (Tigers) lf	4	1	1	3	0	0
Kaline (Tigers) rf	4	0	2	1	0	0
Mantle (Yankees) cf	3	0	0	2	0	0
Romano (Indians) c	1	0	0	1	0	0
Maris (Yankees) ph	1	0	0	0	0	0
Howard (Yankees) c	2	0	0	6	0	0
Aparicio (White Sox) ss	2	0	0	1	3	0
Sievers (White Sox) ph	1	0	0	0	0	0
Temple (Indians) 2b	2	0	0	2	3	0
B. Robinson (Orioles) 3b	3	0	1	0	3	0
Bunning (Tigers) p	1	0	0	0	0	0
Schall (Red Sox) p	1	0	0	0	0	0
Pascual (Twins) p	1	0	0	0	0	0
Totals	30	1	4	27	9	0

National League	0	0	0	0	0	1	0	0	0 – 1
American League	1	0	0	0	0	0	0	0	0 – 1

Game called because of rain.

DP – Nationals 2. LOB – Nationals 7, Americans 5. 2B – White. HR – Colavito. RBIs – White, Colavito. SB – Kaline. HBP – By Schwall (Cepeda). PB – Burgess.

National League	IP	H	R	ER	BB	SO
Purkey	2	1	1	1	2	2
Mahaffey	2	0	0	0	1	0
Koufax	2	2	0	0	0	1
Miller	3	1	0	0	0	5

American League	IP	H	R	ER	BB	SO
Bunning	3	0	0	0	0	1
Schwall	3	5	1	1	1	2
Pascual	3	0	0	0	1	4

Umpires — Napp, Flaherty, and Smith (A.L.), Secory, Sudol, and Pelekoudas (N.L.). Time — 2:27. Attendance — 31,851.

---

reminiscent of Carl Hubbell's 1934 All-Star game strike out string, even though Miller fell short of the record.

Unfortunately, each team also fell short in the win department.

July 10, 1962

D.C. Stadium
(Game One)

Maury Wills was the cover story on most sport magazines in America in 1962. He stole the Dodgers to a divisional tie with San Francisco with a then-record breaking 102 steals on the season. He was to the Dodgers what Reggie Jackson was to the Yankees, "The straw that stirs the drink."

The speed merchant he was, Wills literally stole the show — and the game — for the National League with a 3-1 victory at Washington's D.C. Stadium before 45,480 fans, including President John F. Kennedy.

A Washington native, Wills attended schools in the area while prepping for his baseball career. It was only fitting that he should star in a game before the hometown crowd. Everywhere "local boy makes good" angles sprouted up in newspapers. Even Casey Stengel, the N.L.'s first base coach, added that Wills was "the man who did it" (helped them win).

No argument there. Wills used his bat and his powerful legs to capture the Nationals' 11th victory in the last 15 games, pulling close to the Americans, 16-15-1, in the series.

Wills scored his team's first and third runs with an exhibition of base-running that convinced everyone at the time he was the best in the business. The fleet-footed Maury scooted home with the first run on Dick Groat's single off losing pitcher Camilo Pascual. Wills set himself in scoring position by stealing second off catcher Earl Battey. Battey didn't even bother throwing.

The Nationals took a 2-0 lead when Roberto Clemente's third hit of the game advanced Groat to second. Groat eventually moved to third and scored on Orlando Cepeda's ground out to second.

Then, in the eighth, Wills continued his swiftness on the base paths. After blooping a single in front of Rocky Colavito, Wills took second on Colavito's throwing error. Packing one of the strongest arms in the game, Colavito tried throwing behind Wills to catch him off guard, but his throw trickled back to the backstop. Wills later scored on Felipe Alou's foul fly down the right field line.

All in all, four Los Angeles baseball players had their hands in the

The 1962 All-Star Game (Game One)

National League	AB	R	H	PO	A	E
Groat (Pirates) ss	3	1	1	3	3	0
Davenport (Giants) 3b	1	0	1	0	1	0
Clemente (Pirates) rf	3	0	3	2	0	0
F. Alou (Giants) rf	0	0	0	0	0	0
Mays (Giants) cf	3	0	0	3	0	0
Cepeda (Giants) 1b	3	0	0	2	2	0
Purkey (Reds) p	0	0	0	0	0	0
Callison (Phillies) ph	1	0	1	0	0	0
Shaw (Braves) p	0	0	0	1	0	0
T. Davis (Dodgers) lf	4	0	0	2	0	0
Boyer (Cardinals) 3b	2	0	0	1	0	0
Banks (Cubs) 1b	2	0	0	4	1	0
Crandall (Braves) c	4	0	0	5	0	0
Mazeroski (Pirates) 2b	2	0	0	1	0	0
Bolling (Braves) 2b	2	0	0	1	3	0
Drysdale (Dodgers) p	1	0	0	1	0	0
Marichal (Giants) p	0	0	0	0	0	0
Musial (Cardinals) ph	1	0	1	0	0	0
Wills (Dodgers) ph–ss	1	2	1	1	1	0
Totals	33	3	8	27	11	0

American League	AB	R	H	PO	A	E
Rollins (Twins) 2b	2	1	1	1	3	0
Robinson (Orioles) 3b	0	0	0	1	0	0
Moran (Angels) 2b	3	0	1	0	0	0
Richardson (Yankees) 2b	1	0	0	1	0	0
Maris (Yankees) cf	2	0	0	2	0	0
Landis (White Sox) cf	1	0	0	2	0	0
Mantle (Yankees) rf	1	0	0	0	0	0
Colavito (Tigers) ph–lf	1	0	0	1	0	0
Gentile (Orioles) 1b	3	0	0	8	0	0
Wagner (Angels) rf–lf	4	0	0	4	0	0
Battey (Twins) c	2	0	0	4	1	0
Romano (Indians) c	2	0	1	1	0	0
Aparicio (White Sox) ss	4	0	1	3	2	0
Bunning (Tigers) p	0	0	0	0	0	0
L. Thomas (Angels) ph	1	0	0	0	0	0
Pascual (Twins) p	1	0	0	0	1	0
Donovan (Indians) p	0	0	0	0	0	0
Siebern (Athletics) ph	1	0	0	0	0	0
Pappas (Orioles) p	0	0	0	0	0	0
Totals	29	1	4	28	7	0

```
National League  ........................ 0 0 0 0 0 2 0 1 0 – 3
American League........................ 0 0 0 0 0 1 0 0 0 – 1
```

DP — Nationals 1, Americans 1. LOB — Nationals 5, Americans 7. 2B — Clemente. 3B — Aparicio. RBIs — Groat, Cepeda, Maris, F. Alou. SAC FLIES — Maris, F. Alou. SB — Mays, Wills. HBP — By Drysdale (Rollins), by Shaw (Robinson).

National League	IP	H	R	ER	BB	SO
Drysdale	3	1	0	0	1	3
Marichal (W)	2	0	0	0	1	0
Purkey	2	2	1	1	0	1
Shaw	2	1	0	0	1	1
American League	IP	H	R	ER	BB	SO
Bunning	3	1	0	0	0	2
Pascual (L)	3	4	2	2	1	1
Donovan	2	3	1	1	0	0
Pappas	1	0	0	0	0	0

Umpires — Hurley, Stewart, and Schwartz (A.L.), Donatelli, Venzon, and Steiner (N.L.). Time — 2:33. Attendance — 45,480

---

game. Don Drysdale engaged in a mound duel with Jim Bunning for the first three frames. Two members of the Los Angeles Angels, Leon Wagner and Billy Moran, made contributions to the A.L. squad as starters. Wagner had four put-outs in the field, even though he was a disappointment at bat, while Moran went one-for-three. His hit set up the Americans' only scoring drive of the day in the sixth, after Minnesota's Rich Rollins blooped a leadoff single and sped to third on Moran's one-sacker off the Reds' Bob Purkey. Rollins trotted home on Roger Maris' sacrifice fly to center.

Five All-Star records were set during this two hour and 23 minute contest. Mays stole his third base to share the record with Detroit's Charley Gehringer, and the people's choice, Stan Musial, rewrote four of his marks. Musial earned his 20th All-Star hit, giving him 40 total bases and 60 at-bats, and it was his 22nd All-Star appearance.

For Wills, stealing a win was what he knew best.

July 30, 1962

Wrigley Field
(Game Two)

Los Angeles Angels' outfielder Leon ("Daddy Wags") Wagner was suffering a horrendous slump at the plate prior to the All-Star game, his second such appearance. Up until then, he had compiled an impressive sheet of statistics: 28 homers and 69 RBIs. But, lately, he had lost his stroke and was hoping it would return.

Fortunately for the downtrodden American League, Wagner found his power in time to snap the A.L.'s four-game losing streak in a big way with a 9–4 win over the Nationals, before 38,359 in the Windy City.

Wagner, going three-for-four at the plate, told reporters in the clubhouse: "Maybe I'm back in the groove now. I haven't been hitting good lately. I felt strong at the beginning of the season, but I'm a little weak now." Leon credited his manager Bill Rigney, the A.L.'s first base coach, as the added inspiration for his resurgence. "He takes special interest in me," said Wagner, his pleasant round-face all smiles while teammates congratulated him. "I go all out for him. I never had a manager take an interest in me before."

Luckily, someone finally did. Wagner almost single-handedly destroyed National League pitching. He clubbed a tide-turning two-run homer and also banged out two singles, besides making the outstanding defensive play of the game.

It was the American League all the way, after Wagner unloaded his big blast to break a 1–1 tie in the fourth inning. Instead of the National League finally tying in the standings, the Americans extended their superiority to 17–15–1.

Don Drysdale hurled for the Nationals, substituting for Johnny Podres, the game's original starter. Big D, as he was nicknamed, pitched two scoreless innings and scored the N.L.'s first run in the bottom of the second after spanking a solid double off Washington's Dave Stenhouse. Pete Runnel's pinch-hit homer off losing pitcher Art Mahaffey tied the score in the third, until Wagner's big clout in the fourth.

Wagner also went into action in the sixth, but this time defensively. He

The 1962 All-Star Game (Game Two)

American League	AB	R	H	PO	A	E
Rollins (Twins) 3b	3	0	1	0	1	0
B. Robinson (Orioles) 3b	1	1	0	0	1	0
Moran (Angels) 2b	4	0	1	1	4	0
Berra (Yankees) ph	1	0	0	0	0	0
Richardson (Yankees) ph–2b	0	1	0	2	0	0
Maris (Yankees) cf	4	2	1	4	0	0
Colavito (Tigers) rf	4	1	1	2	0	0
Gentile (Orioles) 1b	4	0	1	10	0	0
Battey (Twins) c	2	1	0	2	0	0
Kaline (Tigers) ph	0	1	0	0	0	0
Howard (Yankees) c	2	0	0	2	0	0
Wagner (Angels) lf	4	1	3	1	0	0
L. Thomas (Angels) lf	0	0	0	1	0	0
Aparicio (White Sox) ss	2	0	0	2	3	0
Tresh (Yankees) ss	2	0	1	0	4	0
Stenhouse (Senators) p	0	0	0	0	0	0
Runnels (Red Sox) ph	1	1	1	0	0	0
Herbert (White Sox) p	1	0	0	0	0	0
Aguirre (Tigers) p	2	0	0	0	0	0
Pappas (Orioles) p	0	0	0	0	0	0
Totals	37	9	10	27	13	0

National League	AB	R	H	PO	A	E
Groat (Pirates) ss	3	0	2	3	3	1
Wills (Dodgers) ss	1	0	0	0	1	0
Clemente (Pirates) rf	2	0	0	2	0	0
F. Robinson (Reds) rf	3	0	0	1	0	0
Mays (Giants) cf	2	0	2	2	0	0
Aaron (Braves) cf	2	0	0	1	0	0
Cepeda (Giants) 1b	1	0	0	2	0	0
Banks (Cubs) 1b	2	1	1	1	1	0
T. Davis (Dodgers) lf	1	0	0	0	1	1
Musial (Cardinals) ph–lf	2	0	0	0	1	0
Williams (Cubs) lf	1	0	0	2	0	0
Boyer (Cardinals) 3b	3	0	1	1	2	0
Mathews (Braves) 3b	1	0	0	0	0	2
Crandall (Braves) c	1	0	0	3	0	0
Roseboro (Dodgers) c	3	1	1	6	0	0
Mazeroski (Pirates) 2b	1	0	0	0	0	0
Altman (Cubs) ph	1	0	0	0	0	0
Gibson (Cardinals) p	0	0	0	0	0	0
Farrell (Colts) p	0	0	0	0	0	0
Ashburn (Mets) ph	1	1	1	0	0	0
Marichal (Giants) p	0	0	0	0	0	0
Callison (Phillies) ph	0	0	0	0	0	0
Podres (Dodgers) p	1	1	1	0	0	0
Mahaffey (Phillies) p	0	0	0	0	0	0
Bolling (Braves) 2b	3	0	1	3	1	0
Totals	35	4	10	27	10	4

```
American League....................... 0  0  1  2  0  1  3  0  2 – 9
National League ...................... 0  1  0  0  0  0  1  1  1 – 4
```

DP – Americans 2. LOB – Americans 6, Nationals 7. 2B – Podres, Tresh, Bolling, Maris. 3B – Banks. HR – Runnels, Wagner, Colavito, Roseboro. RBIs – Groat (2), Runnels, Wagner (2), Tresh, Colavito (4), Williams, Maris, Roseboro. HBP – By Stenhouse (Groat). WP – Marichal 2, Stenhouse.

American League	IP	H	R	ER	BB	SO
Stenhouse	2	3	1	1	1	1
Herbert (W)	3	3	0	0	0	0
Aguirre	3	3	2	2	0	2
Pappas	1	1	1	1	1	0
National League	IP	H	R	ER	BB	SO
Drysdale	2	2	0	0	0	2
Mahaffey (L)	2	2	3	3	1	1
Gibson	2	1	1	1	2	1
Farrell	1	3	3	3	1	2
Marichal	2	2	2	1	0	2

Umpires – Conlan, Burkhart, and Forman (N.L.), McKinley, Rice, and Kinnamon (A.L.). Time – 2:28. Attendance – 38,359.

---

made the catch of the afternoon, skidding along on his wishbone for several yards after stabbing a pinch-hit drive off George Altman's bat. It brought Leon a much-deserved rousing ovation.

Another Angel, second baseman Billy Moran, also starred by teaming up with shortstop Luis Aparicio for two double plays in two very crucial innings.

The Americans finally put the game away in the seventh on Rocky Colavito's three-run homer, even though the Nationals came back with three runs of their own on Johnny Roseboro's homer and Ernie Banks' run-scoring triple.

Chicago's Ray Herbert, a last minute sub for Angel Ken McBride, was credited with the victory.

And Wagner regained the hope that his home run swat had finally returned.

July 9, 1963

Municipal Stadium

Willie Mays never ceased to amaze his baseball contemporaries. In this, his 14th All-Star game, Mays maintained his interleague domination by driving in a pair of runs, scoring twice, stealing two bases, and making an acrobatic catch to lead the favored Nationals to an easy 5–3 victory over the Americans.

The Americans seemed defenseless—even though they outhit the National Leaguers 11 to 6—with someone like Mays on the other side. It spelled the 12th win out of the last 18 games for the Nationals after being mauled in the early years of the All-Star skirmishing.

Willie entered the contest with a .417 batting average to his name in 13 All-Star appearances, and he added to that in the second inning by putting his team ahead 1–0. A.L. starter Ken McBride of the Angels, who didn't figure in the decision, walked Mays to open the inning. McBride, 9–6 on the season with a 2.71 earned run average, wasn't particularly sharp in his first All-Star assignment. Mays stole second and rounded for home on Dick Groat's single. Somehow, McBride escaped any further trouble.

The Americans scored the equalizer against Cincinnati's Jim O'Toole, the N.L.'s opening hurler, in that same inning. O'Toole, 16–6 at the All-Star break with a sparkling 2.01 earned run average, yielded the tying run on singles by Angels' outfielder Leon Wagner and Ken McBride. O'Toole's early going shakiness was blamed on a bad case of "butterflies."

Once the junior circuit tied up the score, Mays played a major role in the Nationals forging ahead with two more markers in the third inning. A single by Tommy Davis, a run-scoring safety by Mays, followed by his second theft, and Ed Bailey's single put the N.L. on top, 3–1.

Larry Jackson, replacing O'Toole in the fourth, tried protecting this slim-margined lead, but was unsuccessful in his bid. The Americans clawed back to tie the score for the second time on Albie Pearson's double (the only extra base hit of the day). Pearson scored on Frank Malzone's single, with Malzone scoring on Earl Battey's single to center.

But Mays proved unstoppable. He broke the stalemate in the fifth after Tommy Davis walked to open the inning. A fielding error by Bobby Richard-

The 1963 All-Star Game

National League	AB	R	H	PO	A	E
T. Davis (Dodgers) lf	3	1	1	2	1	0
Snider (Mets) ph–lf	1	0	0	0	0	0
Aaron (Braves) rf	4	1	0	3	0	0
White (Cardinals) 1b	4	1	1	5	3	0
Mays (Giants) cf	3	2	1	1	0	0
Clemente (Pirates) cf	0	0	0	0	0	0
Bailey (Giants) c	1	0	1	4	1	0
Musial (Cardinals) ph	1	0	0	0	0	0
Culp (Pirates) p	0	0	0	0	1	0
Santo (Cubs) 3b	1	0	1	0	0	0
Boyer (Cardinals) 3b	3	0	0	0	0	0
McCovey (Giants) ph	1	0	0	0	0	0
Drysdale (Dodgers) p	0	0	0	0	0	0
Groat (Cardinals) ss	4	0	1	2	2	0
Javier (Cardinals) 2b	4	0	0	4	1	0
O'Toole (Reds) p	1	0	0	0	0	0
Jackson (Cubs) p	1	0	0	1	0	0
Edwards (Reds) c	2	0	0	5	0	0
Totals	34	5	6	27	9	0

American League	AB	R	H	PO	A	E
Fox (White Sox) 2b	3	0	1	3	1	0
Richardson (Yankees) 2b	2	0	0	0	1	1
Pearson (Angels) cf	4	1	2	4	0	0
Tresh (Yankees) cf	0	0	0	0	0	0
Kaline (Tigers) rf	3	0	0	2	0	0
Allison (Twins) rf	1	0	0	0	0	0
Malzone (Red Sox) 3b	3	1	1	1	3	0
Bouton (Yankees) p	0	0	0	0	0	0
Pizarro (White Sox) p	0	0	0	0	0	0
Killebrew (Twins) ph	1	0	0	0	0	0
Radatz (Red Sox) p	0	0	0	0	0	0
Wagner (Athletics) lf	3	1	2	1	0	0
Howard (Yankees) c	1	0	0	5	0	0
Battey (Twins) c	2	0	1	1	0	0
Yastrzemski (Red Sox) lf	2	0	0	1	0	0
Pepitone (Yankees) 1b	4	0	0	8	0	0
Versalles (Twins) ss	1	0	1	0	2	0
Aparicio (Orioles) ss	1	0	0	0	0	0
McBride (Angels) p	1	0	1	0	0	0
Bunning (Tigers) p	0	0	0	0	0	0
Robinson (Orioles) 3b	2	0	2	1	1	0
Totals	34	3	11	27	8	1

National League	0	1	2	0	1	0	0	1	0	–	5
American League	0	1	2	0	0	0	0	0	0	–	3

DP – Nationals 3. LOB – Nationals 5, Americans 7. 2B – Pearson. RBIs – Mays (2), Bailey, Santo, Groat, Malzone, Battey, McBride. SAC HIT – Bunning. SB – Mays (2), White. HBP – By O'Toole (Versalles).

National League	IP	H	R	ER	BB	SO
O'Toole	2	4	1	1	0	1
Jackson (W)	2	4	2	2	0	3
Culp	1	1	0	0	0	0
Woodeshick	2	1	0	0	1	3
Drysdale	2	1	0	0	0	2
American League	IP	H	R	ER	BB	SO
McBride	3	4	3	3	2	1
Bunning (L)	2	0	1	0	1	0
Bouton	1	0	0	0	0	0
Pizarro	1	0	0	0	0	0
Radatz	2	2	1	1	0	5

Umpires — Soar, Smith, and Haller (A.L.), Jackowski, Pryor, and Harvey (N.L.).
Time — 2:20. Attendance — 44,160.

---

son, and Mays' infield out drove Davis home with the go-ahead run. Then, in the eighth, relief ace Dick Radatz yielded the fifth and final run of the game when Bill White singled, stole second, and breezed home on Ron Santo's single.

Mays undoubtedly gave the 44,160 fans their money's worth in the eighth when he robbed Joe Pepitone of an extra-base hit, maybe even a home run, against the 410-foot marker in deep center field. Mays crashed against the boards, wrenching his ankle, but hung on to the ball for the out.

Larry Jackson, who hurled three solid innings of relief, went home with the victory for the Nationals, while Jim Bunning, the A.L.'s victim, took the defeat.

Al Dark, the N.L. manager, employed 19 National Leaguers opposed to Ralph Houk's 21. The game also marked Stan Musial's 24th All-Star appearance, and his last.

But, for Mays, he showed why he was really an all-star.

July 7, 1964

Shea Stadium

A last minute addition to the National League roster proved to be the deciding factor in the 35th annual All-Star game at New York's new Shea Stadium.

A 25-year-old Philadelphia Phillies power-slugging outfielder named Johnny Callison smashed a three-run homer off Boston's Dick Radatz in the last of the ninth to send his National League team home with a 7–4 triumph over the underdog Americans. Overwhelmingly voted the game's most valuable player, Callison was added as an extra man to the roster by N.L. manager Walt Alston the day before the matchup. Callison's home run feat was reminiscent of Ted Williams' three-run homer in the final minutes of the 1946 All-Star game. It was the N.L.'s sixth win in seven decisions.

Radatz walked off the mound completely disgusted, shaking his head as if he had just been through a nightmare. One moment his team was on its way to snapping its losing streak against the Nationals, then the tide suddenly turned in the opposite direction. Up until Radatz's collapse, the young Boston hurler had kept the Nationals in check during the seventh and eighth innings. He would have been named the A.L.'s star of the day if Willie Mays hadn't ignited his team in the final inning.

Nicknamed "The Monster," Radatz faced but six batters in the seventh and eighth. His team was leading 4–3 in the bottom of the ninth until the Nationals produced four surprise runs. Willie Mays walked and scored on Orlando Cepeda's single to open the inning, and then there was Callison's three-run drive.

For most of the game, however, the Americans seemed to have the best shot at holding the lead. At the end of five innings, the N.L. was ahead 3–1, but in the sixth the A.L. deadlocked the score on Brooks Robinson's two-run triple. Willie Mays, flawless in the field all day, tried making a diving catch of Robinson's liner but the ball rolled by him to the wall.

Angels shortstop Jim Fregosi, 22, the youngest player on either team, put his team in front for the first time in the seventh when he knocked in Elston Howard with a sacrifice fly to center. Fregosi, who later managed the Angels, was making his first All-Star appearance as the lead-off hitter.

The 1964 All-Star Game

American League	AB	R	H	PO	A	E
Fregosi (Angels) ss	4	1	1	4	1	0
Oliva (Twins) rf	4	0	0	0	0	0
Radatz (Red Sox) p	1	0	0	0	0	0
Mantle (Yankees) cf	4	1	1	2	0	0
Hall (Twins) cf	0	0	0	0	0	0
Killebrew (Twins) lf	4	1	3	0	0	0
Hinton (Senators) lf	0	0	0	0	0	0
Allison (Twins) 1b	3	0	0	9	0	0
Pepitone (Yankees) 1b	0	0	0	1	0	1
Robinson (Orioles) 3b	4	0	2	1	2	0
Richardson (Yankees) 2b	4	0	1	0	4	0
Howard (Yankees) c	3	1	0	9	0	0
Chance (Angels) p	1	0	0	0	1	0
Wyatt (Athletics) p	0	0	0	0	1	0
Siebern (Orioles) ph	1	0	0	0	0	0
Pascual (Twins) p	0	0	0	0	1	0
Colavito (Athletics) ph–rf	2	0	1	0	0	0
Totals	35	4	9	26	10	1

National League	AB	R	H	PO	A	E
Clemente (Pirates) rf	3	1	1	1	0	0
Short (Phillies) p	0	0	0	0	1	0
Farrell (Colts) p	0	0	0	0	0	0
White (Cardinals) ph	1	0	0	0	0	0
Marichal (Giants) p	0	0	0	0	0	0
Groat (Cardinals) ss	3	0	1	0	0	0
Cardenas (Reds) ph–ss	1	0	0	1	0	0
Williams (Cubs) lf	4	1	1	1	0	0
Mays (Giants) cf	3	1	0	7	0	0
Cepeda (Giants) 1b	4	0	1	6	0	0
Flood (Cardinals) ph	0	1	0	0	0	0
Boyer (Cardinals) 3b	4	1	2	0	2	0
Torre (Braves) c	2	0	0	5	0	0
Edwards (Reds) c	1	1	0	5	0	0
Hunt (Mets) 2b	3	0	1	1	0	0
Aaron (Braves) ph	1	0	0	0	0	0
Drysdale (Dodgers) p	0	0	0	0	3	0
Stargell (Pirates) ph	1	0	0	0	0	0
Bunning (Phillies) p	0	0	0	0	0	0
Callison (Phillies) ph–rf	3	1	1	0	0	0
Totals	34	7	8	27	6	0

American League . . . . 1 0 0 0 0 2 1 0 0 – 4
National League . . . . 0 0 0 2 1 0 0 0 4 – 7

DP – none. LOB – Americans 7, Nationals 3. 2B – Groat, Colavito. 3B – Robinson. HR – Williams, Boyer, Callison. RBIs – Killebrew, Williams, Boyer, Groat, Robinson (2), Fregosi, Callison (3). SAC FLY – Fregosi. SB – Mays. HBP – By Farrell (Howard). WP – Drysdale. PB – Torre.

American League	IP	H	R	ER	BB	SO
Chance	3	2	0	0	0	2
Wyatt	1	2	2	2	0	0
Pascual	2	2	1	1	0	1
Radatz (L)	2⅔	2	4	4	2	5
National League	IP	H	R	ER	BB	SO
Drysdale	3	2	1	0	0	3
Bunning	2	2	0	0	0	4
Short	1	3	2	2	0	1
Farrell	2	2	1	1	1	1
Marichal	1	0	0	0	0	1

Umpires—Sudol, Secory, and Harvey (N.L.), Paparella, Chylak, and Salerno (A.L.). Time—2:37. Attendance—50,844.

The pitchers during the first three innings of the contest were Don Drysdale of the Dodgers and Dean Chance of the Angels. Drysdale, 6'6" and 210 pounds, entered the game with an 11–7 record, including 11 complete games, three shutouts, and a 2.06 earned run average. In 162 innings, Big D had struck out 120 batters.

On the other hand, Chance, 23, had made 15 starts on the regular season, completing three and compiling a 5–5 record with a 2.19 earned run average. Chance was also known for his blazing fastball, striking out 85 batters in 111 innings. This was his first All-Star assignment.

Both matched each other, pitch for pitch, hurling three shutout innings. Chance only surrendered two hits, no runs, and struck out two. Drysdale gave up one unearned run, but struck out three.

Following Drysdale, Jim Bunning, Chris Short, and Dick Farrell paraded to the mound, until Juan Marichal of the Giants pitched to three batters in the ninth to pick up the victory.

Dean Chance was followed by John Wyatt and Camilo Pascual, all of whom kept the game air-tight for the Americans until Radatz lost it in the final innings.

Along with Callison's clout, Billy Williams of the Cubs and Ken Boyer of the Cardinals crushed solo homers. Attendance was 50,850, the second largest since 55,105 crammed the Los Angeles Coliseum in 1959.

Meanwhile, Callison saw his first All-Star plate appearance become one for the record books.

July 13, 1965

Metropolitan Stadium

The amazing Willie Mays was at it again. No American or National league park could stop him. That included Bloomington's Metropolitan Stadium before a sellout crowd of 46,706, where Mays paced the National League to its third straight victory, 6–5, and seventh out of the last eight decisions.

Mays started things out with a bang and finished in the same explosive fashion by scoring the first and last runs for the Nationals. Willie motored home with the victory run in the seventh inning on Ron Santo's bad-hop single. As A.L. manager Al Lopez, winless in three attempts, said, "The bad hop beat us. It was just one of those things."

Santo's bouncer had the makings of an easy double play ball, but it suddenly took a National League skip on shortstop Zoilo Versalles, who tried falling on the ball in vain. It was ruled as an infield hit, yet the most important on an explosive afternoon which saw five home runs and a dazzling pitching performance by Juan Marichal, high-kicking right-hander from the San Francisco Giants.

Marichal hooked up for battle with Baltimore's Milt Pappas during the first three frames, but Pappas didn't survive. The Nationals, as one writer put it, "ran out of scoreboard space" by racking up five runs during a lopsided first two innings.

Mays was involved in the first scoring drive. Batting leadoff, he slammed the second pitch of the game 398 feet into the left center field bleachers, and before Pappas recovered, Richie Allen followed with a single and scored ahead of Joe Torre's two-run bomb and second homer of the inning. Quickly behind 3–0, Lopez removed Pappas and called on Jim Grant to shut the door on the mighty National League. Unfortunately, a third homer, a two-run shot by Willie Stargell off Grant, ensued in the second to stake the Nationals to a comfortable 5–0 lead.

Meanwhile, Marichal threw beebees as he gunned down the first six batters he faced, and gave up only one single to Vic Davillo in the third. The Americans finally came alive when Reds ace Jim Maloney was substituted for Marichal in the fourth. Maloney was a welcome replacement, as the singles

The 1965 All-Star Game

National League	AB	R	H	PO	A	E
Mays (Giants) cf	3	2	1	4	0	0
Aaron (Braves) rf	5	0	1	0	0	0
Stargell (Pirates) lf	3	2	2	1	0	0
Clemente (Pirates) lf	2	0	0	0	0	0
Allen (Phillies) 3b	3	0	1	0	1	0
Santo (Cubs) 3b	2	0	1	2	0	0
Torre (Braves) c	4	1	1	5	1	0
Banks (Cubs) 1b	4	0	2	11	0	0
Rose (Reds) 2b	2	0	0	1	5	0
Wills (Dodgers) ss	4	0	1	2	3	0
Cardenas (Reds) ss	0	0	0	0	0	0
Marichal (Giants) p	1	1	1	0	0	0
Rojas (Phillies) ph	1	0	0	0	0	0
Maloney (Reds) p	0	0	0	0	0	0
Drysdale (Dodgers) p	0	0	0	0	0	0
F. Robinson (Reds) ph	1	0	0	0	0	0
Koufax (Dodgers) p	0	0	0	0	0	0
Farrell (Astros) p	0	0	0	0	0	0
Williams (Cubs) ph	1	0	0	0	0	0
Gibson (Cardinals) p	0	0	0	1	0	0
Totals	36	6	11	27	10	0
American League	AB	R	H	PO	A	E
McAuliffe (Tigers) ss	3	2	2	3	0	0
McDowell (Indians) p	0	0	0	0	1	0
Oliva (Twins) ph–rf	2	0	1	0	0	0
B. Robinson (Orioles) 3b	4	1	1	1	2	0
Alvis (Indians) 3b	1	0	0	0	0	0
Killebrew (Twins) 1b	3	1	1	7	1	0
Colavito (Indians) rf	4	0	1	1	0	0
Fisher (White Sox) p	0	0	0	1	1	0
Pepitone (Yankees) ph	1	0	0	0	0	0
Horton (Tigers) lf	3	0	0	2	0	0
Mantilla (Red Sox) 2b	2	0	0	1	1	0
Richardson (Yankees) 2b	2	0	0	2	1	0
Davalillo (Indians) cf	2	0	1	1	0	0
Versalles (Twins) ss	1	0	0	0	2	0
Battey (Twins) c	2	0	0	4	1	0
Freehan (Tigers) c	1	0	1	4	0	0
Pappas (Orioles) p	0	0	0	0	1	0
Grant (Twins) p	0	0	0	0	0	0
Kaline (Tigers) ph	1	0	0	0	0	0
Richert (Senators) p	0	0	0	0	0	0
Hall (Twins) ph–cf	2	1	0	0	0	0
Totals	34	5	8	27	11	0

National League .... 3 2 0 0 0 0 1 0 0 – 6
American League........................ 0 0 0 1 4 0 0 0 0 – 5

DP—Americans 2, Nationals 1. LOB—Nationals 7, Americans 8. 2B—Oliva. HR—
Mays, Torre, Stargell, McAuliffe, Killebrew. RBIs—Mays, Stargell (2), Santo, Torre
(2), McAuliffe (2), Killebrew (2), Colavito. SAC HIT—Rose. WP—Maloney.

National League	IP	H	R	ER	BB	SO
Marichal	3	1	0	0	0	0
Maloney	1⅔	5	5	5	2	1
Drysdale	⅓	0	0	0	0	0
Koufax (W)	1	0	0	0	2	1
Farrell	1	0	0	0	1	0
Gibson	2	2	0	0	1	3
American League	IP	H	R	ER	BB	SO
Pappas	1	4	3	3	1	0
Grant	2	2	2	2	1	3
Richert	2	1	0	0	0	2
McDowell (L)	2	3	1	1	1	2
Fisher	2	1	0	0	0	0

Umpires—Stevens, DiMuro, and Valentine (A.L.), Weyer, Williams, and Kibler
(N.L.). Time—2:45. Attendance—46,706.

---

by Dick McAuliffe and Rocky Colavito scored the first American League
run.

It was bombs away in the fifth when McAuliffe and Harmon Killebrew
both unloaded two-run shots over the 400-foot marker, tying the game at
5–5. Lopez was riding his hopes on Killebrew and Rocky Colavito for supply-
ing most of his team's power. He wasn't disappointed with their offense, but
the big disappointment was his pitching staff.

National League batters went through them like they were going out of
style. Lopez threw an assortment of hurlers to the lions after Pappas failed,
including Pete Richert, Sam McDowell, and Eddie Fisher.

Although Jim Maloney was charged with all of the Americans' five runs,
his successors shut out the Americans on two hits over the final six innings.
Don Drysdale, Sandy Koufax (who was credited with the win), Dick Farrell,
and Bob Gibson made the victory a team effort, much to the satisfaction of
manager Gene Mauch of the Phillies.

Mays' performance turned out lucky even though he played in the game
without his batting helmet. Apparently, the "Say Hey, Kid" forgot to pack
his batting helmet the night he left from Philadelphia. So he borrowed Cub
outfielder Billy Williams' hat for good measure.

On the win, Mauch said, "We played it to win, if we could. If they hadn't
won it the way they did, they would have thought of another way."

So would Willie Mays.

July 12, 1966

Busch Stadium

The 1966 All-Star game featured Sandy Koufax in his first starting assignment for the National League, bringing along with him a 100 mph fastball. That wasn't the only heat American Leaguers contended with, however. It was a sweltering 106 degrees at game time, and on the grass surface of Busch Stadium it was about ten degrees hotter for the players.

Thus, combining Koufax's heater and mother nature's, the National Leaguers sweated out a 2–1 triumph over the American Leaguers in ten innings. It was the fourth extra-inning All-Star contest, all won by the Nationals.

Koufax's opponent was Denny McLain, who had posted 13 victories on the season, along with two one-hitters and two two-hitters. A.L. skipper Sam Mele of Minnesota realized the matchup would be a close one — and close it was.

Maury Wills drove in the winning run, before 49,936 soggy citizens, with one out in the 10th to finish the game in grand style. Catcher Tim McCarver opened the extra round with a single, advancing to second on a bunt by Ron Hunt. Wills then singled to right field off his former teammate Pete Richert of the Senators, to score McCarver with the margin of victory.

Wills was 5-for-14 in six previous All-Star contests for a .357 batting average. Despite his last-inning heroics, MVP honors were awarded to Brooks Robinson who raised his All-Star average to .391 with three hits, including a triple off Koufax to set up the Americans' only run of the game. As Robinson said after learning he had won the award, "This is nice getting the MVP, but it's nicer to win."

Nobody will argue with that. After Denny McLain held N.L. batters hitless for three innings, Jim Kaat of the Twins did just the opposite. He got himself in a jam immediately. Mays extended his All-Star hit record with his 22nd safety, a single, and stopped at second on Roberto Clemente's base hit. Willie McCovey, another Giant, next forced Clemente, moving Mays to third. Mays later scored when the sure-fielding Brooks Robinson fumbled Ron Santo's tricky bouncer. It was Mays' 19th run, another record, and the Nationals' first of the game.

The 1966 All-Star Game

American League	AB	R	H	PO	A	E
McAuliffe (Tigers) ss	3	0	0	1	1	0
Stottlemyre (Yankees) p	0	0	0	0	0	0
Colavito (Indians) ph	1	0	0	0	0	0
Siebert (Indians) p	0	0	0	0	0	0
Richert (Senators) p	0	0	0	0	1	0
Kaline (Tigers) cf	4	0	1	3	0	0
Agee (White Sox) cf	0	0	0	1	0	0
F. Robinson (Orioles) lf	4	0	0	2	0	0
Oliva (Twins) rf	4	0	0	0	0	0
B. Robinson (Orioles) 3b	4	1	3	4	4	0
Scott (Red Sox) 1b	2	0	0	4	1	0
Cash (Tigers) ph–1b	2	0	0	4	0	0
Freehan (Tigers) c	2	0	1	4	0	0
Battey (Twins) c	1	0	0	1	0	0
Knoop (Angels) 2b	2	0	0	3	1	0
Richardson (Yankees) 2b	2	0	0	1	1	0
McClain (Tigers) p	1	0	0	0	1	0
Kaat (Twins) p	0	0	0	0	0	0
Killebrew (Twins) ph	1	0	1	0	0	0
Fregosi (Angels) ss	2	0	0	0	1	0
Totals	35	1	6	28	11	0

National League	AB	R	H	PO	A	E
Mays (Giants) cf	4	1	1	3	0	0
Clemente (Pirates) rf	4	0	2	2	0	0
Aaron (Braves) lf	4	0	0	2	0	0
McCovey (Giants) 1b	3	0	0	10	1	0
Santo (Cubs) 3b	4	0	1	2	2	0
Torre (Braves) c	3	0	0	5	0	0
McCarver (Cardinals) c	1	1	1	1	0	0
Lefebvre (Dodgers) 2b	2	0	0	2	0	0
Hunt (Mets) 2b	1	0	0	0	1	0
Cardenas (Reds) ss	2	0	0	2	2	0
Stargell (Pirates) ph	1	0	0	0	0	0
Wills (Dodgers) ss	1	0	1	1	1	0
Koufax (Dodgers) p	0	0	0	0	0	0
Flood (Cardinals) ph	1	0	0	0	0	0
Bunning (Phillies) p	0	0	0	0	0	0
Allen (Phillies) ph	1	0	0	0	0	0
Marichal (Giants) p	0	0	0	0	0	0
Hart (Giants) ph	1	0	0	0	0	0
Perry (Giants) p	0	0	0	0	0	0
Totals	33	2	6	30	7	0

American League . . . . 0 1 0 0 0 0 0 0 0 0 – 1
National League . . . . 0 0 0 1 0 0 0 0 0 1 – 2

One out when winning run scored.

DP – Nationals 1. LOB – Americans 5, Nationals 5. 2B – Clemente. 3B – B. Robinson. RBIs – Santo, Wills. SAC HIT – Hunt. WP – Koufax.

American League	IP	H	R	ER	BB	SO
McClain	3	0	0	0	0	3
Kaat	2	3	1	1	0	1
Stottlemyre	2	1	0	0	1	0
Siebert	2	0	0	0	0	1
Richert (L)	⅓	2	1	1	1	0
National League	IP	H	R	ER	BB	SO
Koufax	3	1	1	1	0	1
Bunning	2	1	0	0	0	2
Marichal	3	3	0	0	0	2
Perry (W)	2	1	0	0	1	1

Umpires — Barlick, Vargo, and Engel (N.L.), Umont, Honochick, and Neudecker (A.L.). Time — 2:19. Attendance — 49,936.

It stayed that way until Wills' clutch hit in the tenth.

Another member of the San Francisco Giants also pitched: spitballing right-hander Gaylord Perry, who worked the 10th to pick up the victory.

Before Perry's entrance, Jim Bunning and Juan Marichal contained the A.L., and Mel Stottlemyre and Sonny Siebert handcuffed the Nationals on one hit until Richert blew the game in the 10th.

Honorary coaches for the contest were Ted Williams and Casey Stengel. Vice President Hubert H. Humphrey threw out the first ball, but ducked out of the proceedings early because of the heat.

This was also Walt Alston's fifth managerial success in seven All-Star starts, and the able Dodger pilot's fourth win in a row.

But finally escaping the heat was another reason to celebrate.

July 11, 1967

Anaheim Stadium

Lately, marathon games seemed to be the order of the day whenever the National and American leagues got together for their annual "dream game." It was as if nobody really wanted to win.

Such was the case at Anaheim Stadium, home of the California Angels, where a sunbaked mob of 46,309 witnessed a record 30 strikeouts and 15 innings before Cincinnati's Tony Perez put an end to such misery with a solo home run blast over the left field wall. Perez's four-bagger posted a 2–1 victory for the N.L., and their fifth in a row over the Americans.

What was billed as "a power show" proved to be a power *shortage,* even though all three runs were produced by homers. Richie Allen exploded one off Dean Chance in the second, Brooks Robinson connected off Ferguson Jenkins in the sixth, and Perez finished the long ball hitting against Catfish Hunter with his jackpot blow in the 15th.

Offensively, both sides appeared even. The N.L.'s celebrated band of fence busters combined for a team batting average of .306, compared to A.L.'s .273 team mark. Yet, the none-too-comforting statistic that frightened the Americans was the fact that the National League had captured 15 out of the last 20 games. This was surely no time to rest on one's laurels. That especially held true since the Americans were minus the services of Frank Robinson and Al Kaline, both out with nagging injuries. The A.L.'s sole source of power rested on the shoulders of slugger Harmon Killebrew, the A.L.'s number one run producer with 22 homers and 62 RBIs.

But hitting never dominated the game, as both teams were limited to a total of 17 hits. Instead, pitching surprisingly ruled the game. Of the thirty strikeouts, the list of victims included Roberto Clemente, the N.L.'s MVP and number two hitter, who fanned four times, celebrated pinch hitters Mickey Mantle and Willie Mays, and Richie Allen, the pride of Philadelphia, who homered and then was fanned three straight times. Other three-time strikeout victims included Gene Alley, and Tony Oliva, the two-time A.L. batting champion. Overall, the Americans won the "K" race, whiffing a total of 17 times to the Nationals' thirteen. Of the 30 strikeouts, 11 were on called strikes. Some players complained that the game's starting time (4:15 p.m.)

The 1967 All-Star Game

National League	AB	R	H	PO	A	E
Brock (Cardinals) lf	2	0	0	1	0	0
Mays (Giants) ph–cf	4	0	0	3	0	0
Clemente (Pirates) rf	6	0	1	6	0	0
Aaron (Braves) cf–lf	6	0	1	2	0	0
Cepeda (Cardinals) 1b	6	0	0	6	2	0
Allen (Phillies) 3b	4	1	1	0	2	0
Perez (Reds) 3b	2	1	1	0	3	0
Torre (Braves) c	2	0	0	4	1	0
Haller (Giants) c	1	0	0	7	0	0
Banks (Cubs) ph	1	0	1	0	0	0
McCarver (Cardinals) c	2	0	2	7	0	0
Mazeroski (Pirates) 2b	4	0	0	7	1	0
Drysdale (Dodgers) p	0	0	0	0	0	0
Helms (Reds) ph	1	0	0	0	0	0
Seaver (Mets) p	0	0	0	0	0	0
Alley (Pirates) ss	5	0	0	1	3	0
Marichal (Giants) p	1	0	0	0	0	0
Jenkins (Cubs) p	1	0	0	0	0	0
Wynn (Astros) ph	1	0	1	0	0	0
Short (Phillies) p	0	0	0	0	1	0
Staub (Astros) ph	1	0	1	0	0	0
Cuellar (Astros) p	0	0	0	0	0	0
Rose (Reds) ph–2b	1	0	0	1	0	0
Totals	51	2	9	45	13	0

American League	AB	R	H	PO	A	E
B. Robinson (Orioles) 3b	6	1	1	0	6	0
Carew (Twins) 2b	3	0	0	2	3	0
McAuliffe (Tigers) 2b	3	0	0	3	2	0
Oliva (Twins) cf	6	0	2	4	0	0
Killebrew (Twins) 1b	6	0	0	15	1	0
Conigliaro (Red Sox) rf	6	0	0	4	0	0
Yastrzemski (Red Sox) lf	4	0	3	2	0	0
Freehan (Tigers) c	5	0	0	13	0	0
Petrocelli (Red Sox) ss	1	0	0	0	0	0
McGlothin (Angels) p	0	0	0	0	0	0
Mantle (Yankees) ph	1	0	0	0	0	0
Peters (White Sox) p	0	0	0	0	1	0
Mincher (Angels) ph	1	0	1	0	0	0
Agee (White Sox) pr	0	0	0	0	0	0
Downing (Yankees) p	0	0	0	0	0	0
Alvis (Indians) ph	1	0	0	0	0	0
Hunter (Athletics) p	1	0	0	0	0	0
Berry (White Sox) ph	1	0	0	0	0	0
Chance (Twins) p	0	0	0	0	0	0
Fregosi (Angels) ph–ss	4	0	1	2	3	0
Totals	49	1	8	45	16	0

```
National League ........ 0 1 0 0 0 0 0 0 0 0 0 0 0 0 1 – 2
American League........ 0 0 0 0 0 1 0 0 0 0 0 0 0 0 0 – 1
```

DP—Americans 2. LOB—Nationals 5, Americans 7. 2B—Yastrzemski, McCarver.
HR—Allen, B. Robinson, Perez. RBIs—Allen, Perez, B. Robinson. SAC HITS—
Fregosi, Freehan, Mazeroski. SB—Aaron.

National League	IP	H	R	ER	BB	SO
Marichal	3	1	0	0	0	3
Jenkins	3	3	1	1	0	6
Gibson	2	2	0	0	0	2
Short	2	0	0	0	1	1
Cuellar	2	1	0	0	0	2
Drysdale (W)	2	1	0	0	0	2
Seaver	1	0	0	0	1	1
American League	IP	H	R	ER	BB	SO
Chance	3	2	1	1	0	1
McGlothin	2	1	0	0	0	2
Peters	3	0	0	0	0	4
Downing	2	2	0	0	0	2
Hunter (L)	5	4	1	1	0	4

Umpires—Runge (A.L.), plate; Secory (N.L.), first base; Dimuro (A.L.), second
base; Burkhart (N.L.), third base; Ashford (A.L.), left field line; Pelekoudas (N.L.),
right field line. Time—3:41. Attendance—46,309.

---

cast shadows over the home plate area, thus making it difficult to see.

Whatever the reasons, managers Hank Bauer of the Baltimore Orioles
and Walt Alston of the Los Angeles Dodgers were placing bets on the pitching outlasting the hitting. And they were right. Their pitching opponents
were Dean Chance, an 11-game winner for the Minnesota Twins, and San
Francisco Giants 12-game winner, Juan Marichal.

Amid the sultry, steaming 92-degree heat, Marichal and Chance dueled
each other, pitch for pitch. Marichal, the high-kicking Cuban, surrendered
only one hit and struck out three. Chance, meanwhile, gave up only one
earned run on Richie Allen's blast, struck out one, and surrendered just the
one hit in three innings.

Afterwards, pitching sparkled on both sides. Walt Alston called upon
Ferguson Jenkins, Bob Gibson, Chris Short, Mike Cuellar, Don Drysdale,
and Tom Seaver to hold the Americans at bay. Drysdale was credited with
the victory.

Jenkins, the Cubs' 11-game winner, tied an All-Star pitching mark by
striking out six in three innings. The old mark was set by Carl Hubbell in
1934.

The Americans' pitching corp also handcuffed National League hitters,
using the likes of Jim McGlothin, Gary Peters, Al Downing, and Catfish
Hunter. Hunter took the loss. Of them, Peters mowed down nine in a row

from the sixth through the eighth, including four by strikeout. McGlothin, 9–2 with the Angels, gave up an infield hit to Hank Aaron but that was quickly rubbed out by a double play. Hunter, the only A.L. pitcher to fail in relief, took the loss.

Meanwhile, Hunter's teammates set a record which no All-Star squad since has been able to match.

July 9, 1968

Astrodome

This was Don Drysdale's year. He had reached the pinnacle of his success as a member of the Los Angeles Dodgers. The ol' pro performed two fabulous feats that season: he hurled six consecutive shutouts and 58⅔ scoreless innings. To top it off, Drysdale was selected to open the All-Star game for the fifth time, the most by any pitcher in the game.

Drysdale didn't let his teammates down as he overpowered the Americans, blanking them on three hits, 1–0. N.L. skipper Red Schoendienst played the percentages perfectly. Drysdale had been scored upon only once in seven All-Star appearances, this coming in the second game in 1959. Meanwhile, the 1968 contest was not only the first 1–0 decision in the history of the event, but a game of several other firsts: the first played in the South, the first played indoors, and the first played on artificial grass.

It also added up to a frustrating night for both sides under the 'Dome. For the second year in a row, the game turned into a pitching duel. Manager Dick Williams countered with the crafty Cleveland Indian sidewinder, Luis Tiant, as his choice to beat Drysdale. But Tiant made only one mistake: he surrendered one run which was the difference of the game.

Willie Mays got to Tiant first in the top of the first inning with a single to left, his 23rd All-Star hit. Tiant, the loser, tried picking Mays off first but threw the ball away. Mays steamed into second base, and strutted into third after Tiant, still unnerved, wild-pitched Curt Flood. Willie McCovey bounced into a double play, scoring Mays with the lone run of the game.

The game from then on was dull by comparison. National League staffers held the Americans to three hits, while American hurlers limited the Nationals to just five hits. The two other American League hits were doubles, by Jim Fregosi and Tony Olivia, but both with two out.

As in the 1967 contest, strikeouts played an important role in the victory. This time, 20 whiffs were recorded in the game, combining the arms of 12 pitchers.

Manager Red Schoendienst summed up the contest best when he said, "It's just like it's been all season — the pitchers are in charge."

The 1968 All-Star Game

American League	AB	R	H	PO	A	E
Fregosi (Angels) ss	3	0	1	1	6	0
Campaneris (A's) ss	1	0	0	1	0	0
Carew (Twins) 2b	3	0	0	2	2	0
Johnson (Orioles) 2b	1	0	0	1	1	0
Yastrzemski (Red Sox) cf–lf	4	0	0	0	0	0
Howard (Senators) rf	2	0	0	0	0	0
Oliva (Twins) rf	1	0	1	2	0	0
Horton (Tigers) lf	2	0	0	1	0	0
Azcue (Indians) c	1	0	0	5	0	0
Josephson (White Sox) c	0	0	0	0	0	0
Killebrew (Twins) 1b	1	0	0	4	0	0
Powell (Orioles) 1b	2	0	0	2	0	0
Freehan (Tigers) c	2	0	0	4	0	0
McClain (Tigers) p	0	0	0	0	0	0
McDowell (Indians) p	0	0	0	0	0	0
Mantle (Yanks) ph	1	0	0	0	0	0
Stottlemyre (Yankees) p	0	0	0	0	0	0
John (White Sox) p	0	0	0	0	0	0
Robinson (Orioles) 3b	2	0	0	0	1	0
Wert (Tigers) 3b	1	0	1	1	0	0
Tiant (Indians) p	0	0	0	0	0	0
Harrelson (Red Sox) ph	1	0	0	0	0	0
Odom (A's) p	0	0	0	0	0	0
Monday (A's) cf	2	0	0	0	0	0
Totals	30	0	3	24	10	1
National League	AB	R	H	PO	A	E
Mays (Giants) cf	4	1	1	0	0	0
Flood (Cardinals) lf	1	0	0	1	0	0
M. Alou (Pirates) lf	1	0	1	1	0	0
Javier (Cardinals) 2b	0	0	0	0	0	0
McCovey (Giants) 1b	4	0	0	10	0	0
Aaron (Braves) rf	3	0	1	1	0	0
Santo (Cubs) 3b	2	0	1	1	1	0
Perez (Reds) 3b	0	0	0	0	1	0
Helms (Reds) 2b	3	0	1	1	2	0
Reed (Braves) p	0	0	0	0	0	0
Koosman (Mets) p	0	0	0	0	0	0
Grote (Mets) c	2	0	0	3	0	0
Carlton (Cardinals) p	0	0	0	0	1	0
Staub (Astros) ph	1	0	0	0	0	0
Seaver (Mets) p	0	0	0	0	0	0
F. Alou (Braves) lf	0	0	0	0	0	0
Kessinger (Cubs) ss	2	0	0	1	1	0
Williams (Cubs) ph–ss	1	0	0	0	0	0
Cardenas (Reds) ss	0	0	0	0	1	0
Drysdale (Dodgers) p	1	0	0	0	0	0
Marichal (Giants) p	0	0	0	0	0	0

National League	AB	R	H	PO	A	E
Haller (Dodgers) c	2	0	0	6	0	0
Bench (Reds) c	0	0	0	2	0	0
Totals	27	1	5	27	8	0

American League . . . . 0 0 0 0 0 0 0 0 0 - 0
National League . . . . 1 0 0 0 0 0 0 0 x - 1

DP — Americans 2. LOB — Americans 3, Nationals 8. 2B — Fregosi, Helms, Oliva, Wert. SB — Aaron. WP — Tiant.

American League	IP	H	R	ER	BB	SO
Tiant (L)	2	2	1	0	2	2
Odom	2	0	0	0	2	2
McClain	2	1	0	0	2	1
McDowell	1	1	0	0	0	3
Stottlemyre	⅓	0	0	0	0	1
John	⅔	1	0	0	0	1

National League	IP	H	R	ER	BB	SO
Drysdale (W)	3	1	0	0	0	0
Marichal	2	0	0	0	0	3
Carlton	1	0	0	0	0	1
Seaver	2	2	0	0	0	5
Reed	⅔	0	0	0	0	1
Koosman	⅓	0	0	0	0	1

Umpires — Crawford (N.L.), plate; Napp (A.L.), first base; Steiner (N.L.), second base; Kinnamon (A.L.), third base; Wendelstedt (N.L.), right field line; Odom (A.L.), left field line. Time — 2:10. Attendance — 48,321.

July 23, 1969

Robert F. Kennedy Stadium

Baseball was celebrating its 100th anniversary in 1969, and Willie McCovey, the Giants' famed "Bay Bomber," was in a festive mood. He cranked two homers, joining Arky Vaughan, Ted Williams, and Al Rosen as the only hitters to belt two in a game, to propel his National League team to a 9–3 thrashing of the Americans.

This ceremonial contest, played before a rain-spattered 45,259, was delayed a day because of flash flooding in the Washington, D.C., area. Maybe afterwards the American League wished the game had been delayed permanently, especially after the N.L. scored eight runs during the first three innings on 10 hits before the A.L. pitchers could provide any relief.

A.L. manager Mayo Smith of the Tigers was rightfully upset, however. His original starting day pitcher, Tiger 31-game winner Denny McLain, was a no-show. McLain was granted permission to fly home for a dentist's appointment the day of the scheduled game, provided he would return to Washington in time for the contest. As it turned out, McLain didn't arrive in time to open the game, but appeared after the fourth inning.

Meanwhile, Smith enlisted the Yanks' Mel Stottlemyre as his choice to duel N.L. ace Steve Carlton. But Stottlemyre didn't have a chance against the National League bombers. In two innings, he surrendered three runs, two earned, on four hits. Smith yanked him immediately and asked Oakland's John "Blue Moon" Odom to restore order in the bottom of the second. But Odom turned several shades of blue as N.L. batters raked him over the coals. A parade of sluggers knocked him out after a third of an inning, scoring five runs, four of which were earned, on five hits, including Willie McCovey's first home run blast and a two-run shot by Cincinnati Reds catcher Johnny Bench.

Down 3–0, the Americans pecked away at the lead with single runs off Carlton in the second and third, both coming from home runs by Frank Howard and Bill Freehan. Other than that, Carlton was perfect. He allowed only two runs on two hits, striking out two, in three full innings.

With a big lead, N.L. manager Red Schoendienst employed five of his nine pitchers — Bob Gibson, Bill Singer, Jerry Koosman, Larry Dierker, and Phil Nierko — to blank the Americans over the final six frames.

The 1969 All-Star Game

National League	AB	R	H	PO	A	E
Alou (Pirates) cf	4	1	2	5	0	0
Kessinger (Cubs) ss	3	0	0	0	0	0
Mays (Giants) ph	1	0	0	0	0	0
Menke (Astros) ss	1	0	0	1	0	0
Aaron (Braves) rf	4	1	1	0	0	0
Singer (Dodgers) p	0	0	0	0	0	0
Beckert (Cubs) 2b	1	0	0	0	0	0
McCovey (Giants) 1b	4	2	2	2	0	0
L. May (Reds) 1b	1	0	0	3	0	0
Santo (Cubs) 3b	3	0	0	2	1	0
Perez (Reds) 3b	1	0	0	1	1	0
Jones (Mets) lf	4	2	2	3	0	0
Rose (Reds) lf	1	0	0	2	0	0
Bench (Reds) c	3	2	2	4	0	0
Hundley (Cubs) c	1	0	0	3	0	0
Millan (Braves) 2b	4	1	1	1	1	0
Koosman (Mets) p	0	0	0	0	0	0
Dierker (Astros) p	0	0	0	0	0	0
Niekro (Braves) p	0	0	0	0	1	0
Carlton (Cardinals) p	2	0	1	0	1	0
Gibson (Cardinals) p	0	0	0	0	0	0
Banks (Cubs) ph	1	0	0	0	0	0
Clemente (Pirates) lf	1	0	0	0	0	0
Totals	40	9	11	27	5	0

American League	AB	R	H	PO	A	E
Carew (Twins) 2b	3	0	0	0	2	0
Andrews (Red Sox) 2b	1	0	0	0	0	0
Jackson (A's) cf-rf	2	0	0	2	0	0
Yastrzemski (Red Sox) lf	1	0	0	1	0	0
F. Robinson (Orioles) lf	2	0	0	0	0	0
Blair (Orioles) cf	2	0	0	2	0	0
Powell (Orioles) 1b	4	0	1	9	1	0
Howard (Senators) lf	1	1	1	0	0	1
Smith (Red Sox) pr-lf-rf	2	1	0	0	0	0
Bando (A's) 3b	3	0	1	0	1	0
Culp (Red Sox) p	0	0	0	0	0	0
White (Yankees) ph	1	0	0	0	0	0
Petrocelli (Red Sox) ss	3	0	1	1	3	0
Fregosi (Angels) ss	1	0	0	0	0	0
Freehan (Tigers) c	2	1	2	4	0	0
Roseboro (Twins) c	1	0	0	6	0	0
C. May (White Sox) ph	1	0	0	0	0	0
Stottlemyre (Yankees) p	0	0	0	1	0	0
Odom (A's) p	0	0	0	0	0	0
Knowles (Senators) p	0	0	0	0	0	0
Killebrew (Twins) ph	1	0	0	0	0	0
McClain (Tigers) p	0	0	0	0	0	0
Mincher (Pilots) ph	1	0	0	0	0	0

American League	AB	R	H	PO	A	E
McNally (Orioles) p	0	0	0	0	0	0
B. Robinson (Orioles) 3b	1	0	0	1	1	0
Totals	33	3	6	27	8	1

National League .... 1 2 5 1 0 0 0 0 0 – 9
American League.......................... 0 1 1 1 0 0 0 0 0 – 3

DP – none. LOB – Nationals 7, Americans 5. 2B – Millan, Carlton, Petrocelli. HR – Bench, Howard, McCovey (2). RBIs – Bench (2), Howard, McCovey (3), Millan (2), Carlton, Freehan (2). WP – Stottlemyre.

National League	IP	H	R	ER	BB	SO
Carlton (W)	3	2	2	2	1	2
Gibson	1	2	1	1	1	2
Singer	2	0	0	0	0	0
Koosman	1⅔	1	0	0	0	1
Dierker	⅓	1	0	0	0	0
Niekro	1	0	0	0	0	2

American League	IP	H	R	ER	BB	SO
Stottlemyre (L)	2	4	3	2	0	1
Odom	⅓	5	5	4	0	0
Knowles	⅔	0	0	0	0	0
McClain	1	1	1	1	2	2
McNally	2	1	0	0	1	1
McDowell	2	0	0	0	0	4
Culp	1	0	0	0	0	2

Umpires – Flaherty (A.L.), plate; Donatelli (N.L.), first base; Stewart (A.L.), second base; Gorman (N.L.), third base; Springstead (A.L.), left field line; Venzon (N.L.), right field line. Time – 2:38. Attendance – 45,259.

For the A.L., skipper Mayo Smith's staff kept him in the race once Odom was removed. With the exception of McLain, who surrendered McCovey's second homer in the fourth, Darrel Knowles, Dave McNally, Sam McDowell, and Ray Culp held the Nationals to just two safeties over the final six innings.

Odom entered himself into the All-Star record books by giving up five hits in an inning. He joined the ranks of such hurlers as Tex Hughson (1944), and Sandy Consuegra (1954), as the only other pitchers to surrender five hits in an inning. Denny McLain replaced Odom and he too placed himself into the All-Star history books by tossing McCovey's second homer of the day.

Johnny Bench also missed writing his name in next to McCovey's, when a sixth inning drive fell inches short of his second home run. His blast was caught just above the seven-foot fence by Carl Yastrzemski.

The only other no-show on the day, next to McLain, was President Richard M. Nixon. An avid baseball fan, Nixon was set to throw out the game's first ball, but, due to the rain delay, he was unable to attend the following day since he was scheduled to meet the returning Apollo 11 astronauts.

McCovey, meanwhile, provided his own lunar orbit show with his two tape-measure home runs.

July 14, 1970

Riverfront Stadium

Pete Rose's controversial slide into catcher Ray Fosse on Jim Hickman's 12th-inning single gave the National League a 5-4 come-from-behind win at Riverfront Stadium before a partisan crowd of 51,838, including President Richard M. Nixon.

Rose and Hickman were coheroes of the contest, one which the American League almost won. Hickman, a nonstarter, singled to center as Rose headed home with the decisive run. "Charlie Hustle" decided not to slide but crash into Fosse hoping to knock the incoming throw from center fielder Amos Otis ajar. Unfortunately, Fosse never caught the ball, and went down kicking when Rose threw a body block into him to score. Fosse hurt his right shoulder on the play and was taken to a hospital for observation. Rose also banged up his shoulder, but not nearly as seriously as Fosse.

Rose claimed that if he slid into home, with Fosse blocking the plate, he would have "broken both legs." N.L. manager Gil Hodges of the Mets agreed: "If Rose slides normally, I don't think he gets there because the catcher has the line blocked. You had to take him out of there to score."

Pro that he is, Rose sent his apologies to Fosse after the game, which the 23-year-old Cleveland Indians catcher accepted. From his hospital bed, Fosse told members of the media after appearing in his first All-Star game, "I know he didn't mean to do it. It all happened so quick... I never got hit like that before... I know he didn't mean it but who knows, maybe he should've run around me."

Manager Earl Weaver of the American League made no comment on the call, but he did say he thought his team wouldn't lose. "At no time did we think we were going to lose," Weaver said. "We weren't beat until we walked into the clubhouse."

At the time, it looked just the antithesis. Tuning up on the mound were Jim Palmer of the Baltimore Orioles and Tom Seaver of the New York Mets, two Hall of Fame–bound left-handers. Both hurlers and their successors kept the game scoreless until the sixth. The National League was limited to just three hits through the first eight innings, before coming to life in the ninth and 12th to win its eighth straight contest.

The 1970 All-Star Game

American League	AB	R	H	PO	A	E
Aparicio (White Sox) ss	6	0	0	1	4	0
Yastrzemski (Red Sox) cf-1b	6	1	4	8	0	0
F. Robinson (Orioles) lf	3	0	0	1	0	0
Horton (Tigers) lf	2	1	2	1	0	0
Powell (Orioles) 1b	3	0	0	5	0	0
Otis (Royals) cf	3	0	0	2	0	0
Killebrew (Twins) 3b	2	0	1	0	0	0
Harper (Brewers) pr	0	0	0	0	0	0
B. Robinson (Orioles) 3b	3	1	2	1	1	0
Howard (Senators) lf	2	0	0	0	0	0
Oliva (Twins) rf	2	0	1	0	0	0
D. Johnson (Orioles) 2b	5	0	1	5	1	0
Wright (Angels) p	0	0	0	0	0	0
Freehan (Tigers) c	1	0	0	4	0	0
Fosse (Indians) c	2	1	1	7	0	0
Palmer (Orioles) p	0	0	0	0	0	0
McDowell (Indians) p	1	0	0	0	3	0
A. Johnson (Angels) ph	1	0	0	0	0	0
J. Perry (Twins) p	0	0	0	0	0	0
Fregosi (Angels) ph	1	0	0	0	0	0
Hunter (A's) p	0	0	0	0	0	0
Peterson (Yankees) p	0	0	0	0	0	0
Stottlemyre (Yankees) p	0	0	0	0	0	0
Alomar (Angels) 2b	1	0	0	0	0	0
Totals	44	4	12	35	9	0

National League	AB	R	H	PO	A	E
Mays (Giants) cf	3	0	0	3	0	0
G. Perry (Giants) p	0	0	0	0	2	0
McCovey (Giants) 1b	2	0	1	1	0	0
Osteen (Dodgers) pr-p	0	0	0	1	0	0
Torre (Cardinals) ph	1	0	0	0	0	0
Allen (Cardinals) 1b	3	0	0	4	0	0
Gibson (Cardinals) p	0	0	0	0	0	0
Clemente (Pirates) ph-rf	1	0	0	2	0	0
Aaron (Braves) rf	2	0	0	1	0	0
Rose (Reds) rf-lf	3	1	1	3	0	0
Perez (Reds) 3b	3	0	0	1	1	0
Grabarkewitz (Dodgers) 3b	3	0	1	0	1	0
Carty (Braves) lf	1	0	0	0	0	0
Hickman (Cubs) lf-1b	4	0	1	6	1	0
Bench (Reds) c	3	0	0	5	1	0
Dietz (Giants) c	2	1	1	2	0	0
Kessinger (Cubs) ss	2	0	2	0	0	0
Harrelson (Mets) ss	3	2	2	0	4	0
Beckert (Cubs) 2b	2	0	0	2	1	0
Gaston (Padres) cf	2	0	0	2	0	0
Seaver (Mets) p	0	0	0	0	0	0
Staub (Expos) ph	1	0	0	0	0	0
Merritt (Reds) p	0	0	0	0	0	0

National League	AB	R	H	PO	A	E
Menke (Astros) ph-ss	0	0	0	2	1	0
Morgan (Astros) 2b	2	1	1	1	2	0
Totals	43	5	10	36	14	0

```
American League.................  0  0  0  0  0  1  1  2  0  0  0  0 - 4
National League .................  0  0  0  0  0  0  1  0  3  0  0  1 - 5
```

Two out when winning run scored.

DP—none. LOB—Americans 9, Nationals 10. 2B—Oliva, Yastrzemski. 3B—B. Robinson. HR—Dietz. RBIs—Yastrzemski, Fosse, B. Robinson (2), Dietz, Mc-Covey, Clemente, Hickman. SAC FLIES—Fosse, Clemente. HBP—By J. Perry (Menke).

American League	IP	H	R	ER	BB	SO
Palmer	3	1	0	0	1	3
McDowell	3	1	0	0	3	3
J. Perry	2	1	1	1	1	3
Hunter	⅓	3	3	3	0	0
Peterson	0	1	0	0	0	0
Stottlemyre	1⅔	0	0	0	0	2
Wright (L)	1⅔	3	1	1	0	0
National League	IP	H	R	ER	BB	SO
Seaver	3	1	0	0	0	4
Merritt	2	1	0	0	0	1
G. Perry	2	4	2	2	1	0
Gibson	2	3	2	2	1	2
Osteen (W)	3	3	0	0	1	0

Umpires—Barlick (N.L.), plate; Rice (A.L.), first base; Secory (N.L.), second base; Haller (A.L.), third base; Dezelan (N.L.), left field; Goetz (A.L.), right field. Time—3:19. Attendance—51,838.

The Americans slowly built up their lead in the sixth, seventh, and eighth innings, scoring four runs while the National league squeaked across one. Carl Yastrzemski knocked in Ray Fosse with the A.L.'s first marker in the sixth on a looping single. In the seventh, another run was chased across the plate when Fosse, who might have been named the game MVP, laced a single to center to score Brooks Robinson from third. Both runs were charged against Giants spitballer Gaylord Perry, the third N.L. pitcher.

The Nationals put their first marker on the boards in the seventh, but pitcher Jim Perry of the Minnesota Twins (Gaylord's brother) escaped with minimal damage. Bud Harrelson, who eventually advanced to third, scored on a double play. The A.L. extended its lead to 4-1 in the eighth with two more runs on three hits. Bob Gibson was on the mound for the N.L., but like his predecessor, he pitched with mixed results. Singles by Carl Yastrzemski and Willie Horton set up runners at first and second, with Yaz taking third on Amos Otis's sacrifice fly to center. Horton and Yaz both scored on Brooks Robinson's triple to center.

By now the Nationals appeared to be out of the game entirely. Up until the ninth, Jim Perry and Sam McDowell held the N.L. hitters in check, until giving way to Oakland's Catfish Hunter. N.L. batters had a field day against the tobacco-chewing Hunter, driving in three runs to tie the game in the ninth. The year of the "Big Red Machine," several members of the Cincinnati Reds chipped in to produce some much-needed offense before the hometown crowd when it was desperately needed. Dick Dietz led off the last of the ninth with a solo home run, the only one of the contest. Then, singles by Bud Harrelson, Joe Morgan and Willie McCovey chased across another run, with Roberto Clemente's sacrifice fly tying it.

Going into extra innings, southpaw Claude Osteen of the Los Angeles Dodgers came in to relieve Gibson in the ninth. He did exactly what Hodges asked him, shutting the door on the Americans for three complete innings while scattering three hits. The lights finally went out at Riverfront with Jim Hickman's clutch base hit.

A member of the Chicago Cubs, Hickman was having one of his finest seasons ever (including 19 home runs), but some criticized Hodges' decision to select him over Cub outfielder Billy Williams, the fans' favorite.

But after Hickman's single, everyone understood why.

July 13, 1971

Briggs Stadium

Detroit's Briggs Stadium became a launching pad for the 1971 All-Star game by producing six home runs — three on each side — to account for all the scoring in the American League's 6–4 triumph, and snapped the N.L.'s winning streak at eight.

Reggie Jackson hit the longest homer of the evening — and of any All-Star game — a towering 520-foot blast that would have landed clear out of the stadium if it hadn't struck a light tower projecting above the right field pavillion.

Both starting pitchers, Vida Blue of the A's and Dock Ellis of the Pirates, weathered the storm until relief was in sight. Besides a record six home runs, the game featured two baseball masterminds at the helm: Earl Weaver of the Baltimore Orioles and Sparky Anderson of the Cincinnati Reds, both considered the best in the game.

For a while it looked as if Anderson's wrecking crew was going to supply all the damage that was necessary to clinch the Nationals' ninth consecutive win. Homers by Johnny Bench and Hank Aaron off Blue staked the N.L. to an early 3–0 lead. In the second inning, with Willie Stargell on base, Bench cleared the right center field fence with a wind-powered blast that set the stage for this home run contest. Aaron used his muscle in the third when he poled a drive into the upper deck in right, his first round-tripper in All-Star play.

The Nationals were rolling along comfortably until the Americans struck Dock Ellis for four runs in their home half of the third. Ellis walked Rod Carew, then retired Bobby Murcer and Carl Yastrzemski. But Frank Robinson, a horrendous 0-for-14 in All-Star competition, broke his slump with a booming home run into the right field seats, scoring Carew and closing the gap to 4–3. Robinson's homer earned him the honor of being the first player in All-Star history to homer in each league. Frank's other four-bagger came in the 1959 contest at the Los Angeles Coliseum.

If there was a greater hero in this contest, Harmon Killebrew was the top candidate. His homer in the sixth clinched the Americans victory, 6–4. Ferguson Jenkins, the Cubs' top right-hander, was the victim of Killebrew's

The 1971 All-Star Game

National League	AB	R	H	PO	A	E
Mays (Giants) cf	2	0	0	0	0	0
Clemente (Pirates) rf	2	1	1	1	0	0
Millan (Braves) 2b	0	0	0	1	1	0
Aaron (Braves) rf	2	1	1	0	0	0
May (Reds) 1b	1	0	0	6	0	0
Torre (Cardinals) 3b	3	0	0	1	0	0
Santo (Cubs) ph–3b	1	0	0	0	1	0
Stargell (Pirates) lf	2	1	0	2	0	0
Brock (Cardinals) ph	1	0	0	0	0	0
McCovey (Giants) 1b	2	0	0	4	0	0
Marichal (Giants) p	0	0	0	0	1	0
Kessinger (Cubs) ss	2	0	0	1	1	0
Bench (Reds) c	4	1	2	5	0	0
Beckert (Cubs) 2b	3	0	0	0	5	0
Rose (Reds) rf	0	0	0	0	0	0
Harrelson (Mets) ss	2	0	0	1	2	0
Jenkins (Cubs) p	0	0	0	0	0	0
Colbert (Padres) ph	1	0	0	0	0	0
Wilson (Astros) p	0	0	0	0	0	0
Ellis (Pirates) p	1	0	0	0	0	0
Davis (Dodgers) cf	1	0	1	2	0	0
Bonds (Giants) ph–cf	1	0	0	0	0	0
Totals	31	4	5	24	11	0

American League	AB	R	H	PO	A	E
Carew (Twins) 2b	1	1	0	1	2	0
Rojas (Royals) 2b	1	0	0	1	1	0
Murcer (Yankees) cf	3	0	1	1	0	0
Cuellar (Orioles) p	0	0	0	0	0	0
Buford (Orioles) ph	1	0	0	0	0	0
Lolich (Tigers) p	0	0	0	0	3	0
Yastrzemski (Red Sox) lf	3	0	0	0	0	0
F. Robinson (Orioles) rf	2	1	1	2	0	0
Kaline (Tigers) rf	2	1	1	2	0	0
Cash (Tigers) 1b	2	0	0	7	0	0
Killebrew (Twins) 1b	2	1	1	4	0	0
B. Robinson (Orioles) 3b	3	0	1	1	3	0
Freehan (Tigers) c	3	0	0	6	1	0
Munson (Yankees) cf	0	0	0	1	0	0
Aparicio (Red Sox) ss	3	1	1	1	2	0
Blue (A's) p	0	0	0	0	0	0
Jackson (A's) ph	1	1	1	0	0	0
Palmer (Orioles) p	0	0	0	0	0	0
Howard (Senators) ph	1	0	0	0	0	0
Otis (Royals) cf	1	0	0	0	0	0
Totals	29	6	7	27	12	0

National League	0	2	1	0	0	0	0	1	0 – 4
American League..........................	0	0	4	0	0	2	0	0	x – 6

DP—Nationals 2, Americans 1. LOB—Nationals 2, Americans 2. HR—Bench, Aaron, Jackson, F. Robinson, Killebrew, Clemente. RBIs—Bench (2), Jackson (2), F. Robinson (2), Aaron, Killebrew (2), Clemente. HBP—By Blue (Stargell).

National League	IP	H	R	ER	BB	SO
Ellis (L)	3	4	4	4	1	2
Marichal	2	0	0	0	1	1
Jenkins	1	3	2	2	0	0
Wilson	2	0	0	0	1	2
American League	IP	H	R	ER	BB	SO
Blue (W)	3	2	3	3	0	3
Palmer	2	1	0	0	0	2
Cuellar	2	1	0	0	1	2
Lolich	2	1	1	1	0	1

Umpires—Umont (A.L.), plate; Pryor (N.L.), first base; O'Donnell (A.L.), second base; Harvey (N.L.), third base; Denkinger (A.L.), right field; Colosi (N.L.), left field. Time—2:05. Attendance—53,559.

---

two-run shot. Reggie Jackson's clout accounted for the sixth and final run of the game.

The N.L. scored one more run on Roberto Clemente's homer off Mickey Lolich in the eighth, but came up short after that.

Even though Killebrew's homer was the game-decider, teammate Frank Robinson won MVP honors for his two-run homer that gave the A.L. its lead.

The only thing still missing from the victory was the ball Jackson sent into orbit.

July 25, 1972

Fulton County Stadium

It was "a good Morgan" victory for the National League as Joe Morgan's 10th inning single defeated the American League, 4–3, at the house that Hank Aaron built. It marked the seventh time that a game went into extra innings, and the seventh straight time the National League won.

The first five innings belonged to the pitchers, until, of course, Hank Aaron posted his N.L. squad to a 2–1 lead on his two-run homer off Indians ace Gaylord Perry in the sixth.

From then on the lead kept switching sides until it went into a virtual tie, 3–3, in the ninth. Jim Palmer and Bob Gibson opened the contest, notching a string of zeroes on the scoreboard. Gibson was disgruntled over playing in this midsummer classic, confiding to reporters that "a regular season game is more important." His comments created quite a rift between manager Danny Murtaugh and his teammates, even though he went out on the mound anyway. Palmer was also in Earl Weaver's doghouse for his comments to the media that he'd "rather be getting a tan in Ocean City, Maryland" than pitching in the All-Star game. Weaver persuaded him otherwise.

Pittsburgh's Steve Blass followed Gibson to the hill and was responsible for the first A.L. run. It came in the third when Bill Freehan walked, moved to second on Jim Palmer's sacrifice, and scored on Rod Carew's single, his first in 12 All-Star at-bats.

Meanwhile, Detroit's Mickey Lolich replaced Palmer in the fourth and blanked the opposition on one hit through two innings. Lolich entered the game as baseball's leading winner with 17 victories.

The Dodgers' Don Sutton, who succeeded Blass, worked two complete innings, retiring six straight batters after Reggie Jackson's fourth-inning double.

Gaylord Perry, Lolich's successor, fueled the fire for the Nationals in the sixth when Aaron unloaded one of his doctored pitches – apparently Perry's renowned spitter – into the left field seats. Aaron, chasing Babe Ruth's all-time home run record, received a standing ovation from the hometown crowd for his feat. Cesar Cedeno, who singled, scored ahead of Aaron with the tying run.

The 1972 All-Star Game

American League	AB	R	H	PO	A	E
Carew (Twins) 2b	2	0	1	2	3	0
Rojas (Royals) ph–2b	1	1	1	3	1	0
Murcer (Yankees) cf	3	0	0	1	0	0
Scheinblum (Royals) rf	1	0	0	1	0	0
Jackson (A's) rf–cf	4	0	2	5	0	0
Allen (White Sox) 1b	3	0	0	4	0	0
Cash (Tigers) 1b	1	0	0	3	0	0
Yastrzemski (Red Sox) lf	3	0	0	3	0	0
Rudi (A's) lf	1	0	1	0	0	0
Grich (Orioles) ss	4	0	0	0	3	0
Robinson (Orioles) 3b	2	0	0	0	1	0
Bando (A's) 3b	2	0	0	1	1	0
Freehan (Tigers) c	1	1	0	3	0	0
Fisk (Red Sox) c	2	1	1	2	0	0
Palmer (Orioles) p	0	0	0	0	0	0
Lolich (Tigers) p	1	0	0	0	0	0
Perry (Indians) p	0	0	0	0	0	0
Smith (Red Sox) ph	1	0	0	0	0	0
Wood (White Sox) p	0	0	0	0	0	0
Pinella (Royals) ph	1	0	0	0	0	0
McNally (Royals) p	0	0	0	0	1	0
Totals	33	3	6	28	10	0

National League	AB	R	H	PO	A	E
Morgan (Reds) 2b	4	0	1	3	5	0
Mays (Mets) cf	2	0	0	2	0	0
Cedeno (Astros) cf	2	1	1	0	0	0
Aaron (Braves) rf	3	1	1	0	0	0
Oliver (Pirates) rf	1	0	0	0	0	0
Stargell (Pirates) lf	1	0	0	0	0	0
Williams (Cubs) lf	2	1	1	0	0	0
Bench (Reds) c	2	0	1	3	0	0
Sanguillen (Pirates) c	2	0	1	6	0	0
May (Astros) 1b	4	0	1	13	2	0
Torre (Cardinals) 3b	3	0	1	1	2	0
Santo (Cubs) 3b	1	0	0	0	0	0
Kessinger (Cubs) ss	2	0	0	0	0	0
Carlton (Phillies) p	0	0	0	0	0	0
Stoneman (Expos) p	1	0	0	0	0	0
McGraw (Mets) p	0	0	0	0	0	0
Colbert (Padres) ph	0	1	0	0	0	0
Gibson (Cardinals) p	0	0	0	1	0	0
Blass (Pirates) p	0	0	0	0	0	0
Beckert (Cubs) ph	1	0	0	0	0	0
Sutton (Dodgers) p	0	0	0	0	0	0
Speier (Giants) ss	2	0	0	1	5	0
Totals	33	4	8	30	14	0

American League...................... 0 0 1 0 0 0 0 2 0 0 – 3
National League .... 0 0 0 0 0 2 0 0 1 1 – 4

One out when winning run scored.

DP—Americans 1, Nationals 2. LOB—Americans 3, Nationals 5. 2B—Jackson, Rudi. HR—Aaron, Rojas. RBIs—Carew, Aaron (2), Rojas (2), May. SAC HITS—Palmer, Speier. SB—Morgan.

American League	IP	H	R	ER	BB	SO
Palmer	3	1	0	0	1	2
Lolich	2	1	0	0	0	1
Perry	2	3	2	2	0	1
Wood	2	2	1	1	1	1
McNally (L)	⅓	1	1	1	1	0
National League	IP	H	R	ER	BB	SO
Gibson	2	1	0	0	0	0
Blass	1	1	1	1	1	0
Sutton	2	1	0	0	0	2
Carlton	1	0	0	0	1	0
Stoneman	2	2	2	2	0	2
McGraw (W)	2	1	0	0	0	4

Umpires—Landes (N.L.), plate; DiMuro (A.L.), first base; Weyer (N.L.), second base; Neudecker (A.L.), third base; Dale (N.L.), left field; Kunkel (A.L.), right field. Time—2:26. Attendance—53,107.

The A.L. mounted another assault in the eighth, this time against Montreal's Bill Stoneman. Carlton Fisk singled and scored when Cookie Rojas, batting for Carew, deposited a two-run homer in the left field bleachers to regain the lead for the Americans, 3–2.

Knuckleballer Wilbur Wood, the fourth A.L. pitcher, seemed to have everything under control in the bottom of the eighth, until singles by Billy Williams and Manny Sanguillen put the tying run on third with one out. Williams crossed home with the tying run on Lee May's force out.

Then, in the miracle 10th, manager Danny Murtaugh pulled some strings by calling on Nate Colbert to pinch-hit. With Dave McNally pitching, Colbert walked and advanced to second on Chris Speier's perfect sacrifice play. Morgan iced the contest with his game-winning hit.

Named the game's MVP, Morgan said of the honor, "The longer you play, the more chance you have to do something special."

As far as the National League was concerned, Morgan couldn't have picked a better time to excel.

July 24, 1973

Royals Stadium

Bobby Bonds was a National League outcast. His name was missing on the All-Star ballots, and he failed to get enough votes to qualify for a starting berth on the N.L. team. His only vote came where it counted: from manager Sparky Anderson, who added Bonds to the roster.

As Anderson said, "Bonds is the best player in the National League and I wanted him in my lineup as soon as possible."

Bonds made fans take a second look at him as he led the National League to a 7–1 pounding of the American League with a home run and double in two trips to the plate. Bonds was inserted into the game after the selected outfielder played the required first three innings. In a short amount of time, he proved his value.

Bobby electrified the sellout crowd of 40,849 when he broke the game wide open with his team leading 3–1 in the fifth. Bonds' two-run blast padded the lead, and, two innings later, Bonds stretched a single into a double and earned himself the game's MVP award.

Six of the seven N.L. pitchers used blanked the Americans on just five hits. The only run to cross the plate was scored off starter Rick Wise. Wise's successors—Claude Osteen, Don Sutton, Ed Twitchell, Dave Giusti, Tom Seaver, and Jim Brewer—did a remarkable job at holding the A.L. sluggers scoreless. The A.L. staff wasn't so lucky. It was charged with seven runs on 10 hits, three of which were homers.

The National League took charge in the third, scoring two runs off pitcher Bert Blyleven of the Minnesota Twins. Blyleven was the third A.L. hurler in three innings. A.L. starter Catfish Hunter was yanked after an inning and a third, as was Ken Holtzman after just a third of an inning. Through two innings on the mound, Blyleven was charged with two runs on two hits, walked two, and struck out none. With Pete Rose and Joe Morgan at second and third, Cesar Cedeno singled to drive Rose home with the tying run. Morgan also scored the go-ahead run on Hank Aaron's single.

Bill Singer of the California Angels was brought in to keep the game close, but he also failed. In the fourth, Johnny Bench uncorked a solo homer to lead off the inning, his third homer in All-Star competition, and Singer ·

The 1973 All-Star Game

National League	AB	R	H	PO	A	E
Rose (Reds) lf	3	1	0	1	0	0
Twitchell (Phillies) p	0	0	0	0	0	0
Giusti (Pirates) p	0	0	0	0	0	0
Mota (Dodgers) ph-lf	1	0	0	0	0	0
Brewer (Dodgers) p	0	0	0	0	0	0
Morgan (Reds) 2b	3	2	1	2	2	0
Johnson (Braves) 2b	1	0	0	1	1	0
Cedeno (Astros) cf	3	0	1	3	0	0
Russell (Dodgers) ss	2	0	0	0	2	0
Aaron (Braves) 1b	2	0	1	3	1	0
Torre (Cardinals) 1b-3b	3	0	0	5	0	0
Williams (Cubs) rf	2	0	1	0	0	0
Bonds (Giants) rf	2	1	2	0	0	0
Bench (Reds) c	3	1	1	3	0	0
Simmons (Cardinals) ph-c	1	0	0	1	1	0
Santo (Cubs) 3b	1	1	1	0	1	0
Colbert (Padres) ph	1	0	0	0	0	0
Fairly (Expos) 1b	0	0	0	4	0	0
Speier (Giants) ss	2	0	0	1	1	0
Stargell (Pirates) ph-lf	1	0	0	1	0	0
Mays (Mets) ph	1	0	0	0	0	0
Seaver (Mets) p	0	0	0	0	1	0
Watson (Astros) lf	0	0	0	0	0	0
Wise (Cardinals) p	0	0	0	0	0	0
Evans (Braves) ph	0	0	0	0	0	0
Osteen (Dodgers) p	0	0	0	0	1	0
Sutton (Dodgers) p	0	0	0	0	0	0
Davis (Dodgers) ph-cf	2	1	2	2	1	0
Totals	34	7	10	27	12	0

American League	AB	R	H	PO	A	E
Campaneris (A's) ss	3	0	0	1	2	0
Brinkman (Tigers) ss	1	0	0	1	1	0
Carew (Twins) 2b	3	0	0	5	1	0
Rojas (Royals) 2b	0	0	0	1	1	0
Mayberry (Royals) 1b	3	0	1	8	0	0
Jackson (A's) rf	4	1	1	0	0	0
Blair (Orioles) cf	0	0	0	1	0	0
Otis (Royals) cf	2	0	2	0	0	0
May (Brewers) cf-rf	2	0	0	0	0	0
Murcer (Yankees) lf	3	0	0	0	1	0
Fisk (Red Sox) c	2	0	0	3	0	0
Munson (Yankees) c	2	0	0	5	1	0
Robinson (Orioles) 3b	2	0	0	1	3	0
Bando (A's) 3b	1	0	0	0	1	0
Nelson (Rangers) 3b	0	0	0	1	0	0
Horton (Tigers) ph	1	0	0	0	0	0
Hunter (A's) p	0	0	0	0	0	0
Holtzman (A's) p	0	0	0	0	0	0
Blyleven (Twins) p	0	0	0	0	0	0
Bell (Indians) ph	1	0	1	0	0	0

American League	AB	R	H	PO	A	E
Singer (Angels) p	0	0	0	0	1	0
Kelly (White Sox) ph	1	0	0	0	0	0
Ryan (Angels) p	0	0	0	0	0	0
Spencer (Rangers) ph	1	0	0	0	0	0
Lyle (Yankees) p	0	0	0	0	0	0
Fingers (A's) p	0	0	0	0	0	0
Totals	32	1	5	27	12	0

```
National League ........................ 0 0 2 1 2 2 0 0 0 - 7
American League........................ 0 1 0 0 0 0 0 0 0 - 1
```

DP – Americans 1. LOB – Nationals 6, Americans 7. 2B – Jackson, Morgan, Mayberry. 3B – Bell. HR – Bench, Bonds, Davis. RBIs – Otis, Cedeno, Aaron, Bench, Bonds (2), Davis (2). SAC HIT – Osteen. SB – Otis. PB – Fisk.

National League	IP	H	R	ER	BB	SO
Wise (W)	2	2	1	1	0	1
Osteen	2	2	0	0	1	1
Sutton	1	0	0	0	0	0
Twitchell	1	1	0	0	0	1
Giusti	1	0	0	0	0	0
Seaver	1	0	0	0	1	0
Brewer	1	0	0	0	1	2

American League	IP	H	R	ER	BB	SO
Hunter	1 ⅓	1	0	0	0	1
Holtzman	⅔	1	0	0	0	0
Blyleven (L)	1	2	2	2	2	0
Singer	2	3	3	3	1	2
Ryan	2	2	2	2	2	2
Lyle	1	1	0	0	0	1
Fingers	1	0	0	0	0	0

Umpires – Chylak (A.L.), plate; Burkhart (N.L.), first base; Barnett (A.L.), second base; W. Williams (N.L.), third base; Luciano (A.L.), left field line; Engel (N.L.), right field line. Time – 2:45. Attendance – 40,849.

---

was haunted by the home run ball again in the fifth on Bonds' two-run blast. The Americans were now losing, 5–1, and the score became even more embarrassing when Angel strikeout king Nolan Ryan took the mound in the sixth. Ryan promptly gave up a two-run homer to Willie Davis, the second two-run blast in as many innings. Five of the N.L.'s seven runs were charged to Ryan and Singer alone.

The game was a blue-chip affair for the Los Angeles Dodgers, landing five members on the All-Star roster: shortstop Bill Russell, outfielder Willie Davis, and pitchers Don Sutton, Claude Osteen, and Jim Brewer.

Davis went 2-for-2 in his All-Star game appearance. His only other performance was in the 1971 contest in which he went one for one.

The victory boosted the National League's edge in the series to 24-18-1 and gave A.L. skipper Dick Williams indigestion.

Williams called on an assortment of pitchers—seven in all—but only two of them, Sparky Lyle and Rollie Fingers, held the National League scoreless. Bert Blyleven was charged with the loss, while Rick Wise picked up the win.

And the National League picked up another important victory, thanks to Bonds.

July 23, 1974

Three Rivers Stadium

Steve Garvey, the Los Angeles Dodgers' "Iron Man," wasn't feeling very well two weeks before the 45th summer All-Star classic. He had been suffering from a glandular infection and his cheeks were "the size of basketballs."

But Steve fully recuperated in time for the game after he had applied ice packs to his swollen jowls. Perhaps the best tonic he received was also the news that an overwhelming 1,083,489 fans had voted him the N.L.'s starting first baseman through a write-in campaign.

Still weakened, Garvey played a full nine innings (the only starter on either side to do so) at Three Rivers Stadium, collected two hits, drove in a run, scored another, made the defensive fielding play of the evening to cut short an A.L. rally, and paced the National League to a 7–2 victory. Garvey was appropriately named the game's MVP, and, as a result, he told reporters the honor didn't belong to him but to the fans. "I can't express in words themselves my thanks to the people who got me here. It's not my trophy, it's theirs," he said.

Garvey was definitely sincere by what he meant. The 25-year-old Dodger first-sacker said he was weak but determined to start and finish the game so he wouldn't disappoint his many fans. "There was no way I could thank the people unless I went out there and did the best I could. I made up my mind I'd play if I could," admitted Garvey, his cheeks still puffy but his enthusiasm at an all-time high.

Garvey's enthusiasm for the game was also felt by the 50,706 paying customers who watched the Nationals notch their 11th victory out of the last 12 decisions. Manager Yogi Berra of the Nationals was not only blessed with Garvey, but with four other stellar members of the division-leading Dodgers (also known as "The Big Blue Wrecking Crew"): Ron Cey, Jimmy Wynn, and pitchers Andy Messersmith, who started, and relief ace Mike Marshall.

Cey and Wynn contributed to the N.L. cause with several clutch hits. Cey, affectionately nicknamed "The Penguin" because he walks like one, drove in two runs with a 390-foot double and an infield out. Wynn singled and scored a run as well.

The 1974 All-Star Game

American League	AB	R	H	PO	A	E
Carew (Twins) 2b	1	1	0	0	1	0
Grich (Orioles) 2b	3	0	1	0	2	0
Campaneris (A's) ss	4	0	0	2	3	0
Jackson (A's) rf	3	0	0	3	0	0
Allen (White Sox) 1b	2	0	1	2	0	0
Yastrzemski (Red Sox) 1b	1	0	0	5	0	0
Murcer (Yankees) cf	2	0	0	0	0	0
Hendrick (Indians) cf	2	0	1	3	0	0
Burroughs (Rangers) lf	0	0	0	1	0	0
Rudi (A's) lf	2	0	0	1	0	0
B. Robinson (Orioles) 3b	3	0	0	0	0	0
Mayberry (Orioles) ph	1	0	0	0	0	0
Fingers (A's) p	0	0	0	0	0	0
Munson (Yankees) c	3	1	1	7	0	1
Perry (Indians) p	0	0	0	0	0	0
Kaline (Tigers) ph	1	0	0	0	0	0
Tiant (Red Sox) p	0	0	0	0	0	0
F. Robinson (Angels) ph	1	0	0	0	0	0
Hunter (A's) p	0	0	0	0	0	0
Chalk (Angels) 3b	1	0	0	0	0	0
Totals	30	2	4	24	6	1

National League	AB	R	H	PO	A	E
Rose (Reds) lf	2	0	0	1	0	0
Brett (Pirates) p	0	0	0	0	0	0
Brock (Cardinals) ph	1	1	1	0	0	0
Smith (Cardinals) rf	2	1	1	2	0	0
Morgan (Reds) 2b	2	0	1	3	4	0
Cash (Phillies) ph–2b	1	0	0	1	0	0
Aaron (Braves) rf	2	0	0	0	0	0
Cedeno (Astros) cf	2	0	0	2	0	0
Bench (Reds) c	3	1	2	7	0	1
Grote (Mets) c	0	0	0	1	0	0
Wynn (Dodgers) cf–rf	3	1	1	0	0	0
Matlack (Mets) p	0	0	0	0	0	0
Grubb (Padres) lf	1	0	0	0	0	0
Garvey (Dodgers) 1b	4	1	2	6	2	0
Cey (Dodgers) 3b	2	0	1	0	0	0
Schmidt (Phillies) ph–3b	0	1	0	0	1	0
Bowa (Phillies) ss	2	0	0	2	0	0
Perez (Reds) ph	1	0	0	0	0	0
Kessinger (Cubs) ss	1	1	1	1	0	0
Messersmith (Dodgers) p	0	0	0	2	1	0
Garr (Braves) ph–lf	3	0	0	0	0	0
McGlothen (Cardinals) p	0	0	0	0	0	0
Marshall (Dodgers) p	1	0	0	0	1	0
Totals	33	7	10	28	9	1

American League......................... 0 0 2 0 0 0 0 0 0 – 2
National League .... 0 1 0 2 1 0 1 2 x – 7

DP — none. LOB — Americans 8, Nationals 6. 2B — Cey, Munson, Morgan, Garvey. 3B — Kessinger. HR — Smith. RBIs — Cey (2), Allen, Garvey, Morgan, Smith, Kessinger. SAC FLY — Morgan. SAC HIT — Perry. SB — Carew, Brock. WP — Fingers.

American League	IP	H	R	ER	BB	SO
Perry	3	3	1	1	0	4
Tiant (L)	2	4	3	2	1	0
Hunter	2	2	1	1	1	3
Fingers	1	1	2	2	1	0
National League	IP	H	R	ER	BB	SO
Messersmith	3	2	2	2	3	4
Brett (W)	2	1	0	0	1	0
Matlack	1	1	0	0	1	0
McGlothen	1	0	0	0	0	1
Marshall	2	0	0	0	1	2

Umpires — Sudol (N.L.), plate; Frantz (A.L.), first base; Vargo (N.L.), second base; Anthony (A.L.), third base; Kibler (N.L.), left field; Maloney (A.L.), right field. Time — 2:37. Attendance — 50,706.

Messersmith, 11–2 on the year, was tabbed the N.L.'s opening hurler, even though he followed through with some reluctance on his part. Messersmith roundly criticized the purpose behind this annual National–American League square-off, by adding his own name to a growing list of dissenters, when he said, "Putting a lot of emphasis on this game is wrong. I think it can be taken too seriously."

A.L. manager Dick Williams of the Angels said he was taking the game very seriously, disagreeing with Messersmith on every count. Williams was so serious, in fact, that he called upon his best pitching candidate: Cleveland's spitballing Gaylord Perry. Williams was hoping that Perry, 15–3 at the All-Star break, would lead the Americans out of the interleague doldrums with a big victory.

Unfortunately, he didn't. As it turned out, Perry became Williams' greatest disappointment next to a team that sported a sluggish offense. Five N.L. hurlers, including Messersmith, limited the A.L. to just four hits. The other four pitchers to succeed Messersmith were Pittsburgh's Ken Brett, New York's Jon Matlack, St. Louis' Lynn McGlothen, and Los Angeles' Mike Marshall. Meanwhile, the American League staff of throwers — Perry, Luis Tiant, Catfish Hunter, and Rollie Fingers — surrendered a total of 10 hits for seven runs, six of which were earned.

Garvey got the game's first safety, a second-inning single, and drove in the first run in the fourth after the Americans had gone ahead, 2–1. Garvey doubled to drive in Johnny Bench with the tying run. Dodger outfielder

Jimmy Wynn advanced to third on the hit and scored the lead run on Ron Cey's ground out.

The Americans had breezed along by scoring two runs off Messersmith in the third, all on two hits and two costly walks, only to watch their lead vanish after the Nationals scored in the fourth.

From then on the National League took batting practice against A.L. hurlers, racking up four runs in the final four innings. Two of them came on Reggie Smith's towering two-run blast in the seventh.

The game also marked Hank Aaron's 23rd All-Star appearance, and last as a member of the National League. Aaron, who was planning to retire at the conclusion of the season, joined the Milwaukee Brewers as a designated hitter the following year.

The loss saddled Dick Williams with his third All-Star defeat in as many managerial attempts.

But, more importantly, the win helped soothe Garvey's pain.

July 15, 1975

Milwaukee County Stadium

The National League relied on "Dodger Power" for their second straight victory—and 12th out of the last 13—as back-to-back homers by Steve Garvey and Jimmy Wynn bolted the Nationals past the Americans, 6–3, before 51,540 baseball-fevered fans.

Wynn's and Garvey's successive blasts—both coming off A.L. starter Vida Blue—were the first in 19 years, not since Ted Williams and Mickey Mantle accomplished that feat in the 1956 interleague contest. Wynn's blast also marked the 100th homer in All-Star play. The first: Babe Ruth's in the first game in 1933. After learning that his homer was one for the record books, Wynn kidded, "Man, I should get a wristwatch for that!"

Considering the N.L.'s domination, maybe Wynn should have multiplied that order into wristwatches for all of his N.L. teammates. The game looked more like a broken record, with basically the same heroes and same team winning. The N.L. jumped out to a commanding 3–0 lead after the two Dodger homers and Johnny Bench's run-scoring single in the third.

But Milwaukee fans had a feeling that maybe this would be the night that their A.L. favorites would finally break on top, and, for one inning, it appeared as if their wish was going to come true.

In the sixth, Carl Yastrzemski's 425-foot pinch-homer sent the Americans into a virtual tie, 3–3. Tom Seaver coughed up the gopher ball after coming in to relieve Don Sutton of the Dodgers, the N.L.'s second pitcher. Sutton pitched effectively during his two-inning stint, scattering three hits and whiffing one. Sutton succeeded N.L. starter Jerry Reuss, who blanked the Americans on three hits during his full three innings of work.

Catfish Hunter kept the game locked up in a scoreless battle as he retired the first six of the seven batters he faced and appeared unbeatable, until back-to-back misplays by Claudell Washington opened the door for the Nationals. The N.L. scored three runs in the ninth to win, 6–3.

Washington misjudged two fly balls—one by Reggie Smith to center and a slicing line drive by Al Oliver—both resulting in scoring drives. Rich Gossage replaced a baffled Hunter but surrendered the clincher, a single by Bill Madlock to drive in the winning run.

The 1975 All-Star Game

National League	AB	R	H	PO	A	E
Rose (Reds) rf–lf	4	0	2	4	0	0
Carter (Expos) lf	0	0	0	1	0	0
Brock (Cardinals) lf	3	1	1	2	0	0
Murcer (Giants) rf	2	0	0	1	0	0
Jones (Padres) p	0	0	0	0	1	0
Morgan (Reds) 2b	4	0	1	0	1	0
Cash (Phillies) 2b	1	0	0	0	0	0
Bench (Reds) c	4	0	1	10	1	0
Garvey (Dodgers) 1b	3	1	2	4	1	0
Perez (Reds) ph–1b	1	0	0	1	1	0
Wynn (Dodgers) cf	2	1	1	1	0	0
Smith (Cardinals) cf–rf	2	1	1	0	0	0
Cey (Dodgers) 3b	3	0	1	0	1	0
Seaver (Mets) p	0	0	0	0	0	0
Matlack (Mets) p	0	0	0	0	1	0
Oliver (Pirates) ph–cf	1	1	1	0	0	0
Concepcion (Reds) ss	2	0	1	1	1	1
Luzinski (Phillies) ph	1	0	0	0	0	0
Bowa (Phillies) ss	0	1	0	2	0	0
Reuss (Pirates) p	1	0	0	0	0	0
Watson (Astros) ph	1	0	0	0	0	0
Sutton (Dodgers) p	1	0	0	0	0	0
Madlock (Cubs) 3b	2	0	1	0	0	0
Totals	38	6	13	27	8	1

American League	AB	R	H	PO	A	E
Bonds (Yankees) cf	3	0	0	0	1	0
Scott (Brewers) 1b	2	0	0	5	0	0
Carew (Twins) 2b	5	0	1	3	1	0
Munson (Yankees) c	2	0	1	1	1	0
Washington (A's) cf–lf	1	0	1	1	0	0
Jackson (A's) rf	3	0	1	2	0	0
Dent (White Sox) ss	1	0	0	0	1	0
Rudi (A's) lf	3	0	1	5	0	0
Hendrick (Indians) pr–rf	1	1	1	0	0	0
Nettles (Yankees) 3b	4	0	1	2	2	0
Tenace (A's) 1b–c	3	1	0	4	0	1
Campaneris (A's) ss	2	0	2	3	2	0
Lynn (Red Sox) ph–cf	2	0	0	1	0	0
Blue (A's) p	0	0	0	0	1	0
Aaron (Brewers) ph	1	0	0	0	0	0
Busby (Royals) p	0	0	0	0	0	0
Hargrove (Rangers) ph	1	0	0	0	0	0
Kaat (White Sox) p	0	0	0	0	0	0
Yastrzemski (Red Sox) ph	1	1	1	0	0	0
Hunter (Yankees) p	0	0	0	0	0	0
Gossage (White Sox) p	0	0	0	0	0	0
McRae (Royals) ph	1	0	0	0	0	0
Totals	36	3	10	27	9	1

National League .... 0 2 1 0 0 0 0 0 3 – 6
American League........................ 0 0 0 0 0 3 0 0 0 – 3

DP – none. LOB – Nationals 6, Americans 8. 2B – Oliver. HR – Garvey, Wynn, Yastrzemski. RBIs – Garvey, Wynn, Bench, Yastrzemski (3), Madlock (2), Rose. SB – Brock, Washington, Hendrick, Nettles. SAC FLY – Rose. HBP – By Reuss (Munson), by Gossage (Bowa). Balk – Busby. PB – Bench.

National League	IP	H	R	ER	BB	SO
Reuss	3	3	0	0	0	2
Sutton	2	3	0	0	0	1
Seaver	1	2	3	3	1	2
Matlack (W)	2	2	0	0	0	4
Jones	1	0	0	0	0	1
American League	**IP**	**H**	**R**	**ER**	**BB**	**SO**
Blue	2	5	2	2	0	1
Busby	2	4	1	1	0	0
Kaat	2	0	0	0	0	0
Hunter (L)	2	3	2	2	0	2
Gossage	1	1	1	1	0	0

Umpires – Haller (A.L.), plate; Pelekoudas (N.L.), first base; Springstead (A.L.), second base; Froemming (N.L.), third base; Goetz (A.L.), left field; McSherry (N.L.), right field. Time – 2:35. Attendance – 51,480.

Madlock's game-winning hit earned him the game's MVP award along with winning pitcher Jon Matlack of the Mets, who fanned four A.L. batters in two innings of relief.

Catfish Hunter was the loser, his second such defeat in interleague play.

Hank Aaron, who retired as a member of the Braves the year before, returned to baseball as a designated hitter for the Milwaukee Brewers. The 41-year-old slugger appeared before a cheering hometown throng in the second inning as a pinch hitter. It was his 24th All-Star appearance, tying him with Stan Musial and Willie Mays for the record. Much to everyone's dismay, the home run king lined out to shortstop to strand two runners and cut short a potential American League rally.

N.L. manager Walt Alston, opposing A.L. skipper Alvin Dark, was still unbeaten in seven All-Star appearances. He was visited after the game by Secretary of State Henry Kissinger, who had thrown out the first ball.

On the other hand, the only balls the Americans wished they had back were the ones Wynn and Garvey hit for homers.

July 13, 1976

Veterans Stadium

Five members of the Cincinnati Reds collected seven of the N.L.'s 10 hits as they rang in the country's Bicentennial celebration with a 7-1 whitewashing of the American League at Philadelphia's friendly Veterans Stadium.

The game wasn't even close as all six Cincy starters contributed evenly: Pete Rose, Joe Morgan, Dave Concepcion, Johnny Bench, Ken Griffey, and the game's hero, George Foster.

Detroit's Mark (The Bird) Fidrych opened the game for the Americans against San Diego Padre sensation Randy Jones, who was even more talked about than Fidrych. Jones, a stylish pitcher, was 16-3 through the first half, tying a National League record for wins at this juncture. His record even provoked talk of a 30-win season, which never materialized.

Fidrych was the complete opposite of Jones. At 21, the young right-hander had a sinking fastball and had won nine of 11 decisions with an earned run average of 1.79. Fidrych's claim to fame was his unique mound mannerisms in which he actually talked to the baseball before delivering it to the plate. His nickname, "The Bird," stemmed from the fact that he resembled *Sesame Street*'s Big Bird with his shaggy, sandy-colored hair.

But that's about all Fidrych resembled at game time. A pitcher he wasn't.

The Nationals pounded on him for four hits and two earned runs during the first inning. Pete Rose, the leadoff hitter, opened his team's attack with a single. He soon scored on Steve Garvey's fluke RBI triple to right. The fly should have been merely a single but right fielder Rusty Staub misplayed the ball's bounce on the stadium's Astroturf. Cincy's slugger George Foster, playing in his first All-Star game, drove Garvey home with the second run of the inning on a grounder to second.

Foster put the icing on the cake when he slugged a two-run homer off Catfish Hunter in the third to win a unamimous vote as the game's Most Valuable Player.

Then Cesar Cedeno added to the N.L.'s lead with a two-run homer, capping a three-run inning, off Angel southpaw Frank Tanana.

Foster had recently graduated to the head of the class as Cincinnati's newfound power slugger. A late-bloomer, the 27-year-old outfielder had

The 1976 All-Star Game

American League	AB	R	H	PO	A	E
LeFlore (Tigers) lf	2	0	1	2	0	0
Yastrzemski (Red Sox) lf	2	0	0	0	0	0
Carew (Twins) 1b	3	0	0	9	2	0
Brett (Royals) 3b	2	0	0	0	1	0
Money (Brewers) 3b	1	0	0	0	1	0
Munson (Yankees) c	2	0	0	4	0	0
Fisk (Red Sox) c	1	0	0	1	0	0
Chambliss (Yankees) ph	1	0	0	0	0	0
Lynn (Red Sox) cf	3	1	1	0	0	0
Otis (Royals) ph	1	0	0	0	0	0
Harrah (Rangers) ss	2	0	0	0	0	0
Belanger (Orioles) ss	1	0	0	1	1	0
Patek (Royals) ss	0	0	0	0	1	0
Staub (Tigers) rf	2	0	2	1	0	0
Tiant (Red Sox) p	0	0	0	0	0	0
Wynegar (Twins) ph	0	0	0	0	0	0
Tanana (Angels) p	0	0	0	1	0	0
Grich (Orioles) 2b	2	0	0	1	1	0
Garner (A's) 2b	1	0	0	1	1	0
Fidrych (Tigers) p	0	0	0	1	0	0
McRae (Royals) ph	1	0	0	0	0	0
Hunter (Yankees) p	0	0	0	0	0	0
Rivers (Yankees) ph–rf	2	0	1	2	0	0
Totals	29	1	5	24	8	0
National League	AB	R	H	PO	A	E
Rose (Reds) 3b	3	1	2	0	1	0
Oliver (Pirates) rf–lf	1	0	0	1	0	0
Garvey (Dodgers) 1b	3	1	1	6	0	0
Cash (Phillies) 2b	1	1	1	1	1	0
Morgan (Reds) 2b	3	1	1	2	3	0
Perez (Reds) 1b	0	0	0	2	0	0
Foster (Reds) cf–rf	3	1	1	3	0	0
Montefusco (Giants) p	0	0	0	0	0	0
Russell (Dodgers) ss	1	0	0	1	2	0
Luzinski (Phillies) lf	3	0	0	0	0	0
Griffey (Reds) rf	1	1	1	1	0	0
Bench (Reds) c	2	0	1	1	0	0
Cedeno (Astros) cf	2	1	1	1	0	0
Kingman (Mets) rf	2	0	0	1	0	0
Boone (Phillies) c	2	0	0	5	0	0
Concepcion (Reds) ss	2	0	1	2	3	0
Bowa (Phillies) ss	1	0	0	2	1	0
Rhoden (Dodgers) p	0	0	0	0	0	0
Cey (Dodgers) 3b	0	0	0	0	0	0
Jones (Padres) p	1	0	0	1	1	0
Seaver (Mets) p	1	0	0	0	0	0
Schmidt (Phillies) 3b	1	0	0	0	0	0
Forsch (Astros) p	0	0	0	0	0	0
Totals	33	7	10	30	12	0

```
American League..........................  0  0  0  1  0  0  0  0  0 - 1
National League .........................  2  0  2  0  0  0  0  3  x - 7
```

DP—Nationals 3, Americans 1. LOB—Americans 4, Nationals 3. 3B—Garvey, Rose. HR—Foster, Lynn, Cedeno. RBIs—Garvey, Foster (3), Lynn, Griffey, Cedeno (2). PB—Munson.

American League	IP	H	R	ER	BB	SO
Fidrych (L)	2	4	2	2	0	1
Hunter	2	2	2	2	0	3
Tiant	2	1	0	0	0	1
Tanana	2	3	3	3	1	0
National League	IP	H	R	ER	BB	SO
Jones (W)	3	2	0	0	1	1
Seaver	2	2	1	1	0	1
Montefusco	2	0	0	0	2	2
Rhoden	1	1	0	0	0	0
Forsch	1	0	0	0	0	1

Umpires—Wendelstedt (N.L.), plate; Neudecker (A.L.), first base; Olsen (N.L.), second base; Denkinger (A.L.), third base; Davidson (N.L.), left field; Evans (A.L.), right field. Time—2:12. Attendance—63,974.

---

belted 17 homers and driven in 72, while batting .338 (top mark in the majors), and this was only after the first half of the season!

On Foster, Pete Rose once said, "Foster's having an MVP year. He doesn't smoke, drink, or cuss. That doesn't have anything to do with the way he hits but it shows you what kind of guy he is. The more he plays, the more you see him."

And the more National League fans like him.

July 19, 1977

Yankee Stadium

Yankee Stadium was no longer the House that Ruth built. It had gone through a major multi-million dollar refurbishing and was completed just in time to open the 1977 season, and play host to the midsummer All-Star classic.

But, in the final analysis, the stadium's new look didn't prove too intimidating to the opposing hitters' approach to the game. The Nationals still won, even though Sparky Anderson's pregame comments were room for concern. He told reporters at the newly revamped clubhouse, "The only reason we're here is to kick the living hell out of those guys [the Americans]."

Anderson's words held true as his National League batters unloaded in the top of first with Joe Morgan's leadoff homer off Jim Palmer of the Orioles.

Palmer never got out of trouble that inning, as Dave Parker also singled and scored on George Foster's double to left center. Foster was driven home on Greg Luzinski's homer into the left field seats, with a shell-shocked Palmer and miserable 56,683 looking on as the Nationals posted four big runs on the Yankees' new million dollar scoreboard.

Palmer sailed through the second inning unblemished, but manager Billy Martin, winless as an All-Star manager, yanked Palmer after Steve Garvey led off the third with a long homer to left. Up 5–0, the Nationals didn't need any more runs as the laughs were on Billy and his A.L. squad.

But Martin wasn't laughing, nor were his teammates. Billy's starting corps was pretty decimated for several reasons. Frank Tanana of the Angels and Mark Fidrych of the Tigers were both out with arm injuries, and Nolan Ryan, another Angel, was irked over Martin not naming him to the A.L. team and remained home despite Martin's last-ditch efforts to change Ryan's mind by adding him to the roster.

Somehow, by magic, Billy's Boys managed to come out all right after a rocky start. Don Sutton and Gary Lavelle teamed up for five innings to hold the A.L. scoreless, until giving way to Tom Seaver. Seaver took the mound, but relinquished it soon as Fred Lynn and Rod Carew banged singles to set runners at first and second, with powerful Richie Zisk coming to the plate.

The 1977 All-Star Game

National League	AB	R	H	PO	A	E
Morgan (Reds) 2b	4	1	1	1	0	0
Trillo (Cubs) 2b	1	0	0	0	1	0
Garvey (Dodgers) 1b	3	1	1	1	0	0
Montanez (Braves) 1b	2	0	0	6	1	0
Parker (Pirates) rf	3	1	1	2	0	0
Templeton (Cardinals) ss	1	1	1	1	2	1
Foster (Reds) cf	3	1	1	2	0	0
Morales (Cubs) cf	0	1	0	1	0	0
Luzinski (Phillies) lf	2	1	1	2	0	0
Winfield (Padres) lf	2	0	2	1	0	0
Cey (Dodgers) 3b	2	0	0	0	0	0
Seaver (Reds) p	0	0	0	0	1	0
Smith (Dodgers) ph	1	0	1	0	0	0
Schmidt (Phillies) pr	0	0	0	0	0	0
R. Reuschel (Cubs) p	0	0	0	0	0	0
Stearns (Mets) c	0	0	0	0	0	0
Bench (Reds) c	2	0	0	4	0	0
Lavelle (Giants) p	0	0	0	0	0	0
Rose (Reds) ph–3b	2	0	0	0	1	0
Concepcion (Reds) ss	1	0	0	1	1	0
Valentine (Expos) rf	1	0	0	0	0	0
Sutton (Dodgers) p	0	0	0	0	1	0
Simmons (Cardinals) c	3	0	0	5	0	0
Gossage (Pirates) p	0	0	0	0	0	0
Totals	33	7	9	27	8	1

American League	AB	R	H	PO	A	E
Carew (Twins) 1b	3	1	1	7	0	0
Scott (Red Sox) 1b	2	1	1	4	0	0
Randolph (Yankees) 2b	5	0	1	2	6	0
Brett (Royals) 3b	2	0	0	2	1	0
Campbell (Red Sox) p	0	0	0	0	0	0
Fairly (Blue Jays) ph	1	0	0	0	0	0
Lyle (Yankees) p	0	0	0	0	0	0
Munson (Yankees) ph	1	0	0	0	0	0
Yastrzemski (Red Sox) cf	2	0	0	0	0	0
Lynn (Red Sox) cf	1	1	0	2	0	0
Zisk (White Sox) lf	3	0	2	0	0	0
Singleton (Orioles) rf	0	0	0	0	0	0
Jackson (Yankees) rf	2	0	1	0	0	0
Rice (Red Sox) rf–lf	2	0	1	1	0	0
Fisk (Red Sox) c	2	0	0	6	1	0
Wynegar (Twins) c	2	1	1	3	0	0
Burleson (Red Sox) ss	2	0	0	0	0	0
Campaneris (Rangers) ss	1	1	0	0	1	0
Palmer (Orioles) p	0	0	0	0	0	0
Kern (Indians) p	0	0	0	0	0	0
Jones (Mariners) ph	1	0	0	0	0	0
Eckersley (Indians) p	0	0	0	0	1	0
Hisle (Twins) ph	1	0	0	0	0	0

American League	AB	R	H	PO	A	E
LaRoche (Angels) p	0	0	0	0	0	0
Nettles (Yankees) 3b	2	0	0	0	1	0
Totals	35	5	8	27	11	0

National League	4 0 1 0 0 0 0 2 0 – 7
American League	0 0 0 0 0 2 1 0 2 – 5

DP—Americans 1, Nationals 1. LOB—Nationals 4, Americans 7. 2B—Foster, Winfield, Zisk, Templeton. HR—Morgan, Luzinski, Garvey, Scott. RBIs—Morgan, Foster, Luzinski (2), Garvey, Zisk (2), Randolph, Winfield (2), Scott (2). SAC HIT—Sutton. WP—Palmer, Lyle. HBP—By Lyle (Morales), by R. Reuschel (Singleton).

National League	IP	H	R	ER	BB	SO
Sutton (W)	3	1	0	0	1	4
Lavelle	2	1	0	0	0	2
Seaver	2	4	3	2	1	2
R. Reuschel	1	1	0	0	0	0
Gossage	1	1	2	2	1	2
American League	IP	H	R	ER	BB	SO
Palmer (L)	2	5	5	5	1	3
Kern	1	0	0	0	0	2
Eckersley	2	0	0	0	0	1
LaRoche	1	1	0	0	1	0
Campbell	1	0	0	0	1	2
Lyle	2	3	2	2	0	1

Umpires—Kunkel (A.L.), plate; Harvey (N.L.), first base; Phillips (A.L.), second base; Stello (N.L.), third base; Pulli (N.L.), left field; Brinkman (A.L.), right field. Time—2:34. Attendance—56,683.

Zisk drove both men home with a long double to right center. Willie Randolph knocked in the A.L.'s third run in the seventh with a single to score Butch Wynegar, making it a 5–3 game.

But the N.L.'s offense never sputtered. In the eighth, Sparky Lyle, the A.L.'s new relief pitcher, surrendered two more runs, only to have teammate George Scott gain them back in the bottom of the ninth with a two-run homer off Rich Gossage. Bert Campaneris scored ahead of Scott, but Scott's runs weren't enough. The N.L. won, 7–5, and Billy suffered his first All-Star defeat.

Don Sutton, the winning pitcher, won the game's MVP trophy, while the Yankee Stadium refurbishing job proved more costly for the Americans than it did the Nationals.

July 11, 1978

San Diego Stadium

Steve Garvey wrote another chapter to his career by collecting his second MVP honor in five seasons and by leading the National League to a 7-3 comeback win over the American League at San Diego Stadium.

Garvey was playing with a gash under his chin that required 22 stitches to close it just three days before the big interleague contest. Garvey sustained the injury while playing a Dodger-Astro doubleheader.

His club was down to the Americans, 3-1, in the third inning, following N.L. starter Vida Blue's erratic pitching performance. Blue, the first pitcher ever to start All-Star games for both leagues, was nowhere near as sharp as his competitor, Jim Palmer of the Baltimore Orioles. And Palmer was pitching after supposedly taking cortisone injections in his ailing left shoulder. Blue entered the contest with a 12-4 record for the San Francisco Giants, and was directly responsible for the Giants' surprise emergence in the National League West. Manager Tommy Lasorda took all of this into consideration before naming Blue his starter. Palmer, 10-7, was effective throughout most of the season, despite his personality conflict with manager Earl Weaver.

Rod Carew, the perennial batting champion, wasted no time against Blue in the first by lacing a triple to left, and scoring on George Brett's booming double to left center. Brett took third on Jim Rice's groundout to second. Richie Zisk walked to place runners at first and third before Carlton Fisk stepped up to the plate. Fisk lofted a fly ball to shallow right, which second baseman Joe Morgan speared after making a running grab at the ball. Meanwhile, Brett tagged and scored from third, while Zisk was thrown out trying to steal second.

Jim Palmer remained perfect through his first two innings, and his performance heightened the chances of an American League victory.

Then Carew did his stuff again in the second, smashing his second triple of the game off Blue to extend the A.L.'s lead to 3-0, scoring on George Brett's sacrifice fly. Carew thus became the first batter of any distinction to slam two triples in the same All-Star game.

The A.L. lead suddenly dwindled when Palmer ran into trouble in the third. Leadoff man Larry Bowa of the Phillies banged a single to right

The 1978 All-Star Game

American League	AB	R	H	PO	A	E
Carew (Twins) 1b	4	2	2	6	1	0
Brett (Royals) 3b	3	1	2	0	2	0
Gossage (Yankees) p	0	0	0	0	0	0
Rice (Red Sox) lf	4	0	0	2	0	0
Lemon (White Sox) lf	0	0	0	0	0	1
Zisk (Rangers) rf	2	0	1	0	0	0
Evans (Red Sox) rf	1	0	0	3	0	0
Fisk (White Sox) c	2	0	0	4	1	0
Sundberg (Rangers) c	0	0	0	2	0	0
Thompson (Tigers) ph	1	0	0	0	0	0
Lynn (Red Sox) cf	4	0	1	3	0	0
Money (Brewers) 2b	2	0	0	1	1	0
White (Royals) 2b	1	0	0	1	2	0
Porter (Royals) ph	1	0	0	0	0	0
Patek (Royals) ss	3	0	1	1	1	0
Palmer (Orioles) p	1	0	0	1	0	0
Keough (A's) p	0	0	0	0	0	0
Howell (Blue Jays) ph	1	0	0	0	0	0
Sorenson (Brewers) p	0	0	0	0	1	0
Hisle (Brewers) ph	1	0	1	0	0	0
Kern (Indians) p	0	0	0	0	0	0
Guidry (Yankees) p	0	0	0	0	0	0
Nettles (Yankees) 3b	0	0	0	0	1	0
Totals	31	3	8	24	10	1
National League	AB	R	H	PO	A	E
Rose (Reds) 3b	4	0	1	1	0	0
Lopes (Dodgers) pr–2b	1	0	1	0	1	0
Morgan (Reds) 2b	3	1	0	2	1	0
Clark (Giants) rf	1	0	0	0	0	0
Foster (Reds) cf	2	1	0	2	0	0
Luzinski (Phillies) lf	2	0	1	0	0	0
Fingers (Padres) p	1	0	0	0	1	0
Stargell (Pirates) ph	1	0	0	0	0	0
Sutter (Cubs) p	0	0	0	0	0	0
Niekro (Braves) p	0	0	0	0	0	0
Garvey (Dodgers) 1b	3	1	2	7	1	0
Simmons (Cardinals) c	3	0	1	4	1	0
Concepcion (Reds) ss	0	1	0	2	0	0
Monday (Dodgers) rf	2	0	0	1	0	0
Rogers (Expos) p	0	0	0	0	0	0
Winfield (Padres) lf	2	1	1	1	0	0
Bowa (Phillies) ss	3	1	2	2	4	0
Boone (Phillies) c	1	1	1	3	1	0
Pocoroba (Braves) c	0	0	0	0	0	0
Blue (Giants) p	0	0	0	0	1	0
Smith (Dodgers) ph–rf	3	0	0	1	0	0
Cey (Dodgers) 3b	1	0	0	1	0	0
Totals	33	7	10	27	11	0

```
American League......................... 2 0 1 0 0 0 0 0 0 - 3
National League ......................... 0 0 3 0 0 0 0 4 x - 7
```

DP—Americans 1. LOB—Americans 4, Nationals 7. 2B—Brett, Rose. 3B—Carew (2), Garvey. RBIs—Brett (2), Luzinski, Garvey (2), Fisk, Boone (2), Lopes. SAC FLIES—Fisk, Brett. SB—Bowa, Brett. WP—Rogers. PB—Sundberg.

American League	IP	H	R	ER	BB	SO
Palmer	2⅔	3	3	3	4	4
Keough	⅓	1	0	0	0	0
Sorenson	3	1	0	0	0	0
Kern	⅔	1	0	0	0	0
Guidry	⅓	0	0	0	0	0
Gossage (L)	1	4	4	4	1	1
National League	IP	H	R	ER	BB	SO
Blue	3	5	3	3	1	2
Rogers	2	2	0	0	0	2
Fingers	2	1	0	0	0	1
Sutter (W)	1⅔	0	0	0	0	2
Niekro	⅓	0	0	0	0	0

Umpires—Pryor (N.L.), plate; Chylak (A.L.), first base; Tata (N.L.), second base; Deegan (A.L.), third base; Runge (N.L.), left field; McCoy (A.L.), right field. Time—2:37. Attendance—51,549.

---

center. Bowa then stole second while pinch-hitter Reggie Smith, batting for Blue, struck out. Bowa moved to third on Pete Rose's groundout to first. Then Palmer went through a bit of wildness—walking Joe Morgan and George Foster to load up the bases. A third base on balls to Greg Luzinski drove across the first N.L. run, and Steve Garvey's first single of the evening chased both Morgan and Foster home to knot the score at 3-3.

After that the game belonged to Garvey. The American and National hurlers were locked in a pitching duel until the eighth, at which time Garvey collected his second hit—a line drive triple high against the wall in right center off Rich Gossage of the Yankees. Garvey scored when Gossage uncorked a wild pitch, thus changing the tide for the Americans once again.

The score was 4-3, but Gossage surrendered three more runs before the night was out. A walk by Dave Concepcion, Dave Winfield's single to left, Bob Boone's single, combined with Chet Lemon's booted grounder advancing Winfield to second, scored Concepcion and Winfield. The fourth and final run of the inning came when Boone, taking second on Ron Cey's ground out, was driven home by Davey Lopes' single to right.

By this time, the Americans were unable to recover and push across any additional runs of their own in the bottom of the ninth, going down 1-2-3 to defeat.

Garvey's two hits upped his batting average to .500 (8 for 16) in four All-Star contests. His contributions rounded out the N.L.'s 10 to 8 slugging attack against the losing Americans.

Besides Garvey, manager Tommy Lasorda was blessed with some clutch pitching by Blue's successors: Steve Rogers, Rollie Fingers, Bruce Sutter, and Phil Niekro, all tossing a blanket of zeroes on the scoreboard over the final six innings to clinch the victory.

However, the real story was Garvey, who for a while thought he might miss the San Diego connection. He had been forced out of the second game of a Dodger-Astro doubleheader when teammate Bob Welch's pickoff throw went wild and struck Garvey on the chin. The blow caused a gash, requiring stitches and knocking Garvey out of action and listing him questionable for the All-Star affair. But, the trouper that he is, Garvey decided to play the game and wore a large protective bandage on his chin as a precaution.

When asked by reporters whether the injury interfered with his play, Garvey replied, "I don't hit with my chin."

Even if he did, Garvey would always be "a hit" with any crowd.

July 17, 1979

Kingdome

Known mostly for his offensive contributions, Pittsburgh's Dave Parker showed fans at Seattle's Kingdome that he also possessed fine defensive skills with two important outfield plays to lead his National League team to a 7–6 win over the American League, before a Kingdome crowd of 58,905.

The game promised to be a home run derby, since the Kingdome was like a shooting gallery; hitters shattered it to pieces with homers in all directions. In the Seattle Mariners' first 54 home games, players had belted 131 homers, almost 25 more than hit in any other major league park.

This was a cause for concern for both starting pitchers, Nolan Ryan (12–3) of the California Angels, and Steve Carlton of the Philadelphia Phillies. At least Carlton could finesse opposing hitters with an array of off-speed and change-ups, while Ryan's most effective pitch was his fastball. His curve was sporadic, but, when it was on, he was unhittable.

At the Kingdome, Ryan showed how erratic he could be as the National League got to him early, striking the fireballing right-hander in the very first inning for two quick runs. After Ryan struck out the first two men he faced — Davey Lopes and Dave Parker — Steve Garvey, last year's MVP, drew a walk. Garvey later raced home on Mike Schmidt's triple to right center field. Schmidt was also driven home on George Foster's double down the right field line. Ryan was apparently fooling nobody.

Fortunately for him the scoring ended there, and the Americans responded in their half of the inning with an uprising of their own. Steve Carlton was tagged for three runs, starting with George Brett's walk, Don Baylor's double down the third base line (Baylor went 2-for-4 that evening), and Fred Lynn's two-run homer, driving Baylor home to take the lead 3–2.

The N.L. came roaring back to tie the score in the second when Bob Boone, Lou Brock, and Davey Lopes all singled to fill the bases. Boone scored on Dave Parker's sacrifice fly to center. The N.L. took the lead in the fourth when Mike Schmidt doubled, his second extra base hit of the game, and eventually trotted home on Dave Winfield's groundout.

The game remained a constant seesaw battle and one of the finest

The 1979 All-Star Game

National League	AB	R	H	PO	A	E
Lopes (Dodgers) 2b	3	0	1	4	1	0
Morgan (Reds) ph–2b	1	1	0	1	1	0
Parker (Pirates) rf	3	0	1	0	2	0
Garvey (Dodgers) 1b	2	1	0	5	0	0
Perry (Padres) p	0	0	0	0	0	0
Sambito (Astros) p	0	0	0	0	0	0
Reynolds (Astros) ss	2	0	0	0	1	0
Schmidt (Phillies) 3b	3	2	2	1	1	1
Cey (Dodgers) 3b	1	0	0	2	1	0
Parrish (Expos) 3b	0	0	0	0	0	0
Foster (Reds) lf	1	0	1	0	0	0
Matthews (Braves) lf	2	0	0	2	0	0
Mazzilli (Mets) ph–cf	1	1	1	0	0	0
Winfield (Padres) cf–lf	5	1	1	3	0	0
Boone (Phillies) c	2	1	1	0	0	0
Carter (Expos) c	2	0	1	6	1	0
Bowa (Phillies) ss	2	0	0	1	3	0
LaCoss (Reds) p	0	0	0	0	0	0
Hernandez (Cardinals) ph	1	0	0	0	0	0
Sutter (Cubs) p	0	0	0	0	1	0
Carlton (Phillies) p	0	0	0	0	0	0
Brock (Cardinals) ph	1	0	1	0	0	0
Andujar (Astros) p	0	0	0	0	0	0
Clark (Giants) ph	1	0	0	0	0	0
Rogers (Expos) p	0	0	0	0	0	0
Rose (Phillies) ph–1b	2	0	0	2	0	0
Totals	35	7	10	27	12	1

American League	AB	R	H	PO	A	E
Smalley (Twins) ss	3	0	0	2	2	0
Grich (Angels) 2b	1	0	0	2	0	0
Brett (Royals) 3b	3	1	0	1	2	0
Nettles (Yankees) 3b	1	0	1	1	2	0
Baylor (Angels) lf	4	2	2	1	0	0
Kern (Rangers) p	0	0	0	0	0	0
Guidry (Yankees) p	0	0	0	0	0	0
Singleton (Orioles) ph	1	0	0	0	0	0
Rice (Red Sox) rf–lf	5	0	1	3	0	0
Lynn (Red Sox) cf	1	1	1	0	0	0
Lemon (White Sox) cf	2	1	0	2	0	0
Yastrzemski (Red Sox) 1b	3	0	2	5	1	0
Burleson (Red Sox) pr–ss	2	1	0	0	1	0
Porter (Royals) c	3	0	1	2	0	0
Downing (Angels) c	1	0	1	3	0	0
White (Royals) 2b	2	0	0	2	2	0
Bochte (Mariners) ph–1b	1	0	1	2	0	0
Ryan (Angels) p	0	0	0	0	0	0
Cooper (Brewers) ph	0	0	0	0	0	0
Stanley (Red Sox) p	0	0	0	1	0	0
Kemp (Tigers) ph	1	0	0	0	0	0

American League	AB	R	H	PO	A	E
Clear (Angels) p	0	0	0	0	0	0
Jackson (Yankees) ph-rf	1	0	0	0	0	0
Totals	35	6	10	27	10	0

National League .... 2 1 1 0 0 1 0 1 1 – 7
American League......................... 3 0 2 0 0 1 0 0 0 – 6

DP – Americans 2. LOB – Nationals 8, Americans 9. 2B – Foster, Baylor, Schmidt, Winfield, Porter, Rice. 3B – Schmidt. HR – Lynn, Mazzilli. RBIs – Schmidt, Foster, Baylor, Lynn (2), Parker, Winfield, Yastrzemski, Carter, Bochte, Mazzilli (2). SAC HIT – Bochte. SAC FLY – Parker. WP – Andujar. HBP – By Andujar (Lemon). Balk – Kern.

National League	IP	H	R	ER	BB	SO
Carlton	1	2	3	3	1	0
Andujar	2	2	2	1	1	0
Rogers	2	0	0	0	0	2
Perry	0	3	1	1	0	0
Sambito	2/3	0	0	0	1	0
LaCoss	1 1/3	1	0	0	0	0
Sutter (W)	2	2	0	0	2	3
American League	IP	H	R	ER	BB	SO
Ryan	2	5	3	3	1	2
Stanley	2	1	1	1	0	0
Clear	2	2	1	1	1	0
Kern (L)	2 2/3	2	2	2	3	3
Guidry	1/3	0	0	1	1	0

Umpires – Maloney (A.L.), plate; Weyer (N.L.), first base; Bremigan (A.L.), second base; W. Williams (N.L.), third base; Cooney (A.L.), left field; Rennert (N.L.), right field. Time – 3:11. Attendance – 58,905.

---

offensive shows baseball fans had seen in a long time. In the bottom of the third, the Americans scratched back with two runs to regain the lead 5–4. Baylor singled, and took second on Juaquin Andujar's wild pitch. Andujar was the new N.L. pitcher, succeeding Carlton. Baylor moved to third on Jim Rice's groundout to short. Chet Lemon was hit by a pitch, and Carl Yastrzemski drove a single up the middle to score Baylor, with Lemon stopping at second. Darrell Porter's grounder to third, which Schmidt threw wildly to first, scored Lemon with the go-ahead run.

With three frames left, there was still room for more scoring. The fourth and fifth innings were easy 1–2–3 contests for both sides, but in the top of the sixth Dave Winfield rocketed a double to right and scored on Gary Carter's single to left to tie the game for the second time, 5–5.

But the Americans recaptured their part of the lion's share in the bottom of the sixth against San Diego's celebrated 40-year-old spitballer, Gaylord Perry. No matter what Perry threw, the American batters hit it. Carl Yastrzemski led off with a ground single to right, but Yaz was taken out when manager Bob Lemon sent Rick Burleson in to run for him. Burleson advanced to third on Darrell Porter's ringing double to right center, setting the stage for pinch-hitter Bruce Bochte. Bochte, batting for Chet Lemon, was the only Mariner named to the All-Star team and received a standing ovation from the hometown faithful before stepping in the batter's box. Bochte didn't let his fans down either by bouncing a single over shortstop Larry Bowa's head to score Burleson, and sending the pro–American throng into a frenzy. Maybe the Americans would finally prove victorious!

Such was not the case. N.L. skipper Tommy Lasorda also had some aces up his sleeve. He yanked Perry and brought in Astro ace Joe Sambito. Sambito teamed up with Mike LaCoss in that inning to pull his team out of a jam, leaving the bases loaded, to end the inning.

Jim Kern, the bearded Texas Rangers' relief ace, came in to blank the Nationals in the seventh, until he experienced some wildness himself. Kern was charged with two runs as the A.L. lost its lead and the game in the eighth and ninth innings. Still ahead 6–5, Lee Mazilli, the left-handed batting Met outfielder, cranked a "wrong field" homer off Kern into the left field bleachers to tie the game at 6–6. Mazilli's blast was only the second homer of the 1979 season that Kern had given up in 86 innings.

But Dave Parker shined for the N.L. when he made two sparkling defensive plays in back-to-back innings. In the seventh Jim Rice, 1 for 9 in All-Star competition, popped a lazy fly that dropped fair inside the right field line. Parker, who lost the ball in the lights, recovered and rifled an accurate throw to get Rice out at third.

In the eighth, Parker came through again, this time with the A.L. threatening to score off N.L. star reliever Bruce Sutter. Sutter surrendered a ground single to Brian Downing, leading off the inning, with Bochte sacrificing Downing to second. Reggie Jackson intentionally walked, and Bobby Grich struck out swinging. Parker's play of the game came on Graig Nettles' burning single to right field. Downing tried scoring from second, only to be cut down at the plate by Parker's accurate throw to catcher Gary Carter.

After the three hour and 11 minute contest was over, Bruce Sutter was proclaimed the winning pitcher; he joined Don Drysdale as the only pitcher to collect back-to-back All-Star victories. Drysdale had won two years in a row, in 1967 at Anaheim and in 1968 at Houston.

Parker also won something—the MVP award and respect.

July 8, 1980

Dodger Stadium

The 51st annual All-Star game at scenic Dodger Stadium was a pretty drab affair compared to the 1979 Kingdome slugfest. The most entertaining feature all evening was the stadium's new DiamondVision messageboard, flashing video images of players and game statistics, and a fire that broke out on a hill overlooking the back entrance to the facility.

Meanwhile, the game itself was dull by comparison, unless pitching duels prove exciting. Because that's what this game was dominated by: pitching, pitching, pitching, and more pitching.

James Rodney Richard, 10-4 with a 1.96 earned run average, and Baltimore's Steve Stone, 12-3 and winner of 21 out of his last 25 decisions, locked up in a heated battle through the first three innings. Richard was prepared to go three full innings, but his manager, Bill Virdon, had asked N.L. skipper Chuck Tanner to limit Richard to two because of back, arm and shoulder ailments that had forced him to leave nine of his 16 starts.

Los Angeles reliable, Bob Welch, replaced Richard in the third, and pitched impressively during his three-inning stint, striking out four and surrendering the Americans' first run of the contest in the fifth. Both runs came on a leadoff single by Rod Carew of the Angels, followed by Fred Lynn's towering homer into the right field pavillion seats. Lynn's homer — his third in All-Star play — tied him with a handful of players who had also belted three: Rocky Colavito, Harmon Killebrew, Ralph Kiner, Willie Mays, and Johnny Bench. But this proved to be the Americans' only scoring opportunity, as Welch settled down and the National League battled back to a 4-2 victory at the hands of Dodger defector Tommy John.

After Stone, manager Earl Weaver followed with John, now a member of the New York Yankees. But John was not the John of old. He offered up three runs, all earned, on four hits in two and a third innings. At first, John was in complete control, retiring the first five batters he faced. Then, the roof simply caved in. Ken Griffey greeted him in the fifth with a towering homer over the 395-foot marker in center, drawing the Nationals within one, 2-1.

Consecutive singles by Ray Knight, Phil Garner, and George Hendrick tied the game at 2-2 in the sixth, bringing about John's exit in favor of White

The 1980 All-Star Game

American League	AB	R	H	PO	A	E
Randolph (Yankees) 2b	4	0	2	0	3	2
Stieb (Blue Jays) p	0	0	0	0	0	0
Trammell (Tigers) ss	0	0	0	0	0	0
Carew (Angels) 1b	2	1	2	4	0	0
Cooper (Brewers) 1b	1	0	0	6	0	0
Lynn (Red Sox) cf	3	1	1	2	0	0
Bumbry (Orioles) cf	1	0	0	2	0	0
Jackson (Yankees) rf	2	0	1	0	0	0
Landreaux (Twins) rf	1	0	0	1	0	0
Oglivie (Brewers) lf	2	0	0	1	0	0
Oliver (Rangers) lf	1	0	0	0	0	0
Gossage (Yankees) p	0	0	0	0	0	0
Fisk (Red Sox) c	2	0	0	5	0	0
Porter (Royals) c	1	0	0	0	1	0
Henderson (A's) lf	1	0	0	0	0	0
Nettles (Yankees) 3b	2	0	0	0	1	0
Bell (Rangers) 3b	2	0	0	0	2	0
Dent (Yankees) ss	2	0	1	0	1	0
John (Yankees) p	1	0	0	0	1	0
Farmer (White Sox) p	0	0	0	0	0	0
Grich (Angels) 2b	0	0	0	0	1	0
Stone (Orioles) p	1	0	0	0	0	0
Yount (Brewers) ss	2	0	0	3	2	0
Parrish (Tigers) c	1	0	0	0	0	0
Totals	32	2	7	24	12	2

National League	AB	R	H	PO	A	E
Lopes (Dodgers) 2b	1	0	0	0	2	0
Garner (Pirates) 2b	2	1	1	1	3	0
Smith (Dodgers) cf	2	0	0	0	0	0
Hendrick (Cardinals) cf	2	0	1	0	0	0
Sutter (Cubs) p	0	0	0	0	0	0
Parker (Pirates) rf	2	0	0	0	0	0
Winfield (Padres) rf	2	0	0	2	0	0
Garvey (Dodgers) 1b	2	0	0	7	0	0
Hernandez (Cardinals) 1b	2	0	2	5	0	0
Bench (Reds) c	1	0	0	5	0	0
Stearns (Mets) c	1	0	0	5	0	0
Rose (Phillies) ph	1	0	0	0	0	0
Bibby (Pirates) p	0	0	0	0	0	0
Murphy (Braves) cf	1	0	0	0	0	0
Kingman (Mets) lf	1	0	0	0	0	0
Griffey (Reds) lf	3	1	2	0	0	0
Reitz (Cardinals) 3b	2	0	0	1	0	0
Reuss (Dodgers) p	0	0	0	0	0	0
Concepcion (Reds) ss	1	1	0	0	2	0
Russell (Dodgers) ss	2	0	0	0	2	0
Carter (Expos) c	1	0	0	1	0	0
Richard (Astros) p	0	0	0	0	0	0

National League	AB	R	H	PO	A	E
Welch (Dodgers) p	1	0	0	0	1	0
Knight (Reds) 3b	1	1	1	0	1	0
Totals	31	4	7	27	11	0

```
American League.......................  0  0  0  0  2  0  0  0  0 - 2
National League .......................  0  0  0  0  1  2  1  0  x - 4
```

DP—Americans 1, Nationals 1. LOB—Americans 7, Nationals 5. 2B—Carew. HR—Lynn, Griffey. RBIs—Lynn (2), Hendrick, Winfield, Griffey. SB—Carew, Knight. PB—Porter.

American League	IP	H	R	ER	BB	SO
Stone	3	0	0	0	0	3
John (L)	2⅔	4	3	3	0	1
Farmer	⅔	1	0	0	0	0
Stieb	1	1	1	0	2	0
Gossage	1	1	0	0	0	0

National League	IP	H	R	ER	BB	SO
Richard	2	1	0	0	2	3
Welch	3	5	2	2	1	4
Reuss (W)	1	0	0	0	0	3
Bibby	1	1	0	0	0	0
Sutter (Save)	2	0	0	0	1	1

Umpires—Kibler (N.L.), plate; Barnett (A.L.), first base; Colosi (N.L.), second base; McKean (A.L.), third base; Dale (N.L.), left field; Garcia (A.L.), right field. Time—2:33. Attendance—56,088.

Sox relief star Ed Farmer. Farmer promptly surrendered an easy ground ball out to Dave Winfield, which second-sacker Willie Randolph bobbled, allowing Garner to score from third easily with the tie-breaking run.

But Ken Griffey, unanimously named the game's MVP, smacked Toronto right-hander Dave Stieb's first offering into center for a base hit, thus setting the stage for the N.L.'s final tally. A groundout by Dave Concepcion, a wild pitch by Stieb, and a passed ball by Darrell Porter brought Concepcion home with the fourth run of the game and some breathing room for the Nationals.

Tanner went with Bruce Sutter, the N.L.'s winning pitcher in 1978 and 1979, to close out the game with the two hitless innings of relief. Sutter, unscored upon in five and two-thirds innings in All-Star play, clinched the victory by striking out Detroit catcher Lance Parrish in the bottom of the ninth.

Sutter picked up the save, and Jerry Reuss, who relieved Welch as the second Dodger pitcher of the game, earned the victory. The loss went to Tommy John, and was the final blow to American League players' morale.

August 9, 1981

Municipal Stadium

A strike-shortened season jeopardized the status of baseball's All-Star contest for the first time since World War II brought about the cancellation of the event in 1945.

Unlike that year, this year's contest materialized with satisfying results for fans on both sides. A record crowd of 72,086 – the largest to attend any midsummer classic – jammed into Cleveland's Municipal Stadium to watch a powerful display of offense, including four home runs, and some sloppy pitching, due in part to the strike's eight-week layoff, as the National League defeated the American League 5-4.

A record total of 56 men were used in the game, and the National League set a record by using 29 of the 30 players on their roster. The American League established one for the books by using eight pitchers, and, between the two teams, a total of 15 pitchers were used, setting another record.

Some other numbers popped up with the Nationals' 10th straight win. It was their 18th in the last 19 games, all on the account of two homers by Montreal's Gary Carter, voted the game's MVP, and one homer each by teammates Dave Parker and Mike Schmidt.

Vice President George Bush threw out the first ball to Derrick Williams, a 13-year-old junior high school student, who caught it in the glove of his favorite player, Frank White of the Royals. Also attending the contest were Bowie Kuhn, the league commissioner, and comedian Bob Hope, a partial shareholder in the Cleveland organization.

But for everyone in attendance, tonight was not a pitcher's night. It was designed for the hitters. The game pitted two stellar pitching aces on the mound, Fernando Valenzuela of the Dodgers and Jack Morris of the Tigers. Valenzuela pitched only one inning, allowing just two hits. It was agreed before the game that no pitcher would go more than two innings, due to the extended layoff.

Valenzuela's replacement wasn't so fortunate. Tom Seaver came in to pitch the second, but left after surrendering the A.L.'s first run on three hits. Baltimore's Ken Singleton belted a solo homer to stake the Americans to an early 1-0 advantage.

The 1981 All-Star Game

National League	AB	R	H	PO	A	E
Rose (Phillies) 1b	3	0	1	5	0	0
Hooton (Dodgers) p	0	0	0	0	0	0
Ruthven (Phillies) p	0	0	0	0	0	0
Guerrero (Dodgers) ph	1	0	0	0	0	0
Blue (Giants) p	0	0	0	0	0	0
Madlock (Pirates) 3b	1	0	0	0	0	1
Concepcion (Reds) ss	3	0	0	0	0	0
Smith (Cardinals) ss	0	0	0	1	0	0
Parker (Pirates) rf	3	1	1	1	0	0
Easler (Pirates) rf	1	1	0	0	0	0
Schmidt (Phillies) 3b	4	1	2	0	2	1
Ryan (Astros) p	0	0	0	0	0	0
Garner (Pirates) 2b	0	0	0	0	0	0
Foster (Reds) lf	2	0	0	0	0	0
Baker (Dodgers) lf	2	0	1	2	0	0
Raines (Expos) lf	0	0	0	1	0	0
Dawson (Expos) cf	4	0	1	4	0	0
Carter (Expos) c	3	2	2	5	1	0
Benedict (Braves) c	1	0	0	3	0	0
Lopes (Dodgers) 2b	0	0	0	1	0	0
Trillo (Phillies) 2b	2	0	0	1	1	0
Buckner (Cubs) ph	1	0	0	0	0	0
Sutter (Cubs) p	0	0	0	0	0	0
Valenzuela (Dodgers) p	0	0	0	0	1	0
Youngblood (Mets) ph	0	0	0	0	1	0
Seaver (Reds) p	0	0	0	0	2	0
Knepper (Giants) p	0	0	0	0	1	0
Kennedy (Cardinals) ph	1	0	0	0	0	0
Garvey (Dodgers) 1b	2	0	1	3	1	0
Totals	34	5	9	27	10	2

American League	AB	R	H	PO	A	E
Carew (Angels) 1b	3	0	1	12	0	0
Murray (Orioles) 1b	2	0	0	2	1	0
Randolph (Yankees) 2b	3	0	1	0	5	0
Simmons (Brewers) ph	1	0	1	0	0	0
White (Royals) 2b	1	0	0	1	0	0
Brett (Royals) 3b	3	0	0	0	1	0
Norris (A's) p	0	0	0	0	0	0
Oliver (Rangers) ph	1	0	0	0	0	0
Davis (Yankees) p	0	0	0	0	0	0
Fingers (Brewers) p	0	0	0	1	0	1
Stieb (Blue Jays) p	1	0	0	1	1	0
Winfield (Yankees) cf	4	0	0	0	1	0
Singleton (Orioles) lf	3	2	2	0	0	0
Burleson (Angels) ss	1	0	0	1	3	0
Jackson (Yankees) rf	1	0	0	0	0	0
Evans (Red Sox) rf	2	1	1	2	0	0
Fisk (White Sox) c	3	1	1	4	0	0
Diaz (Indians) c	1	0	0	2	0	0

American League	AB	R	H	PO	A	E
Dent (Yankees) ss	2	0	2	0	2	0
Lynn (Red Sox) ph	1	0	1	0	0	0
Armas (A's) lf	1	0	0	0	0	0
Morris (Tigers) p	0	0	0	0	0	0
Paciorek (White Sox) ph	1	0	1	0	0	0
Barker (Indians) p	0	0	0	0	0	0
Thomas (Brewers) ph	1	0	0	0	0	0
Forsch (Angels) p	0	0	0	0	0	0
Bell (Rangers) 3b	1	0	0	1	2	0
Totals	37	4	11	27	16	1

```
National League ....................... 0 0 0 0 1 1 1 2 0 - 5
American League....................... 0 1 0 0 0 3 0 0 0 - 4
```

DP — None. LOB — Nationals 7, Americans 9. 2B — Dent, Schmidt, Garvey. HR — Singleton, Carter (2), Parker, Schmidt. RBIs — Parker, Schmidt (2), Carter (2), Simmons, Singleton, Lynn, Bell. SB — Dawson, Smith. SAC FLY — Bell. WP — Blue.

National League	IP	H	R	ER	BB	SO
Valenzuela	1	2	0	0	0	0
Seaver	1	3	1	1	0	1
Knepper	2	1	0	0	2	3
Hooton	1⅔	5	3	3	0	1
Ruthven	⅓	0	0	0	0	0
Blue (W)	1	0	0	0	0	1
Ryan	1	0	0	0	0	1
Sutter (Save)	1	0	0	0	0	1

American League	IP	H	R	ER	BB	SO
Morris	2	2	0	0	1	2
Barker	2	0	0	0	0	1
Forsch	1	1	1	1	0	0
Norris	1	2	1	1	0	1
Davis	1	1	1	1	0	1
Fingers (L)	⅓	2	2	2	2	0
Stieb	1⅓	1	1	0	1	1

Umpires — Haller (A.L.), plate; Vargo (N.L.), first base; DiMuro (A.L.), second base; Engel (N.L.), third base; Kosc (A.L.), left field; Quick (N.L.), right field. Time — 2:59. Attendance — 72,086.

With pitchers still rotating, by the fifth inning these constant switches began taking their toll. Ken Forsch of the Angels, the third A.L. hurler in five innings, came in to work after Len Barker, a Cleveland favorite, had thrown two perfect innings. Forsch was tagged by Gary Carter for a homer to left center to tie the game at one.

One inning later, Mike Norris of the A's took over the pitching chores for the Americans. He retired only one batter before Dave Parker hit a

1-and-2 pitch high beyond the fence in right, regaining the lead for the Nationals, 2–1.

In the bottom of the sixth, Dodger ace Burt Hooton also ran into trouble ... big trouble. The Americans took it out on Hooton for three runs that inning, loading the bases with no outs on singles by Ken Singleton, Dwight Evans, and Carlton Fisk. Bucky Dent knocked home the tying run with a single through the right side, and Buddy Bell made it 3–2 with a line drive base hit to left. Ted Simmons padded the lead to 4–2 with a pinch-hit single to right, and by now the Americans looked like they were in business.

Not to Gary Carter they didn't. In the seventh, Carter clouted Ron Davis' first pitch over the boards in dead center — 400 feet away — for his second homer of the night. Carter's solo shot cut the A.L.'s lead to 4–3.

Mike Schmidt made it another National League come-from-behind win with his two-run shot in the eighth off Brewer relief ace Rollie Fingers. Mike Easler, who walked, scored ahead of Schmidt.

Managers Dallas Green of the Phillies and Jim Frey of the Royals were reasonably satisfied with the game's results, considering the long layoff.

As Frey lamented, "We had plenty of chances to win. But they just kept hitting home runs."

With Carter as the main driving force.

July 13, 1982

Montreal Stadium

It was the first All-Star game held in a foreign country. Montreal was the designated site for the 53rd annual All-Star clash, with Expo favorite Steve Rogers receiving the call from manager Tommy Lasorda to face Dennis Eckersley of the Red Sox.

Rogers, obviously nervous before the hometown throng, quickly fell behind, 1-0, after the first inning. Three singles by Ricky Henderson, George Brett, and Dave Winfield pushed across the A.L.'s first and only run of the contest.

From then on, the National League regained control. A.L. manager Billy Martin was thoroughly embarrassed by the outcome as the Nationals came from behind to win, 4-1. It became a grim evening for Martin as his American League batters struck out 10 times, often with men in scoring position. It was the 19th time in 20 years, and 23rd time in 25 years that the Nationals had beaten the Americans, with the Nationals now holding a 34-18-1 edge in the series.

Dave Concepcion's two-run homer off Eckersley in the second inning wiped out the A.L.'s brief lead, and recaptured it for the Nationals, 2-1.

Eckersley was sharp in the beginning, retiring the first five batters he faced, and Rogers and he went head-to-head until the Nationals blew the game wide open on Concepcion's blast. Dale Murphy, who walked, scored on Concepcion's hit.

The N.L.'s other two runs came in the third and sixth respectively. San Diego Padres' pinch-hitter Ruppert Jones banged a triple off the wall in right, and crossed home on Pete Rose's sacrifice fly. Rose, 41, was playing in his 16th All-Star game. Dan Quisenberry surrendered the final run when Al Oliver led off with a double to left in the sixth, and took third when Henderson misplayed the ball for an error. Two outs later, Gary Carter drove Oliver home with a single to center.

Meanwhile, Martin's team put men on base in eight of the nine innings and blew every scoring opportunity. The A.L.'s greatest scoring threat came in the seventh against Cincinnati's Mario Soto, but none of Martin's men could produce the clutch hit. Martin's other disappointment was Ricky

The 1982 All-Star Game

American League	AB	R	H	PO	A	E
Henderson (A's) lf	4	1	3	3	0	1
Lynn (Angels) cf	2	0	0	0	0	0
Wilson (Royals) cf	2	0	0	1	0	0
Hrbek (Twins) ph	1	0	0	0	0	0
Brett (Royals) 3b	2	0	2	0	0	0
Bell (Rangers) 3b	3	0	0	0	1	1
Jackson (Angels) rf	1	0	0	3	0	0
Winfield (Yankees) rf	2	0	1	0	0	0
Cooper (Brewers) 1b	2	0	1	5	0	0
Murray (Orioles) 1b	1	0	0	4	0	0
Yount (Brewers) ss	3	0	0	0	2	0
Grich (Angels) 2b	1	0	0	2	2	0
Yastrzemski (Red Sox) ph	1	0	0	0	0	0
Quisenberry (Royals) p	0	0	0	0	0	0
McRae (Royals) ph	0	0	0	0	0	0
Fingers (Brewers) p	0	0	0	0	0	0
Fisk (White Sox) c	2	0	0	2	0	0
Parrish (Tigers) c	2	0	1	2	3	0
Eckersley (Red Sox) ph	1	0	0	0	0	0
Thorton (Indians) ph	1	0	0	0	0	0
Clancy (Blue Jays) p	0	0	0	0	0	0
Bannister (Mariners) p	0	0	0	0	0	0
White (Royals) 2b	1	0	0	2	1	0
Oglivie (Brewers) ph	1	0	0	0	0	0
Totals	33	1	8	24	9	2

National League	AB	R	H	PO	A	E
Raines (Expos) lf	1	0	0	0	0	0
Carlton (Phillies) p	0	0	0	0	1	0
Horner (Braves) ph	1	0	0	0	0	0
Soto (Reds) p	0	0	0	0	0	0
Thompson (Cubs) ph	1	0	0	0	0	0
Valenzuela (Dodgers) p	0	0	0	0	0	0
Minton (Giants) p	0	0	0	0	0	0
Howe (Dodgers) p	0	0	0	0	0	0
Hume (Reds) p	0	0	0	0	0	0
Rose (Phillies) 1b	1	0	0	1	4	0
Oliver (Expos) 1b	2	1	2	2	0	0
Dawson (Expos) cf	4	0	1	4	0	0
Schmidt (Phillies) 3b	1	0	0	0	0	0
Knight (Reds) 3b	3	0	0	1	4	0
Carter (Expos) c	3	0	1	7	0	0
Pena (Pirates) c	1	0	0	3	0	0
Stearns (Mets) c	0	0	0	0	0	1
Murphy (Braves) cf	2	1	0	2	0	0
Concepcion (Reds) ss	3	1	1	1	1	0
O. Smith (Cardinals) ss	0	0	0	0	1	0
Trillo (Phillies) 2b	2	0	1	0	1	0
Sax (Dodgers) 2b	1	0	1	2	0	1
Rogers (Expos) p	0	0	0	0	0	0

National League	AB	R	H	PO	A	E
Jones (Padres) ph	1	1	1	0	0	0
Baker (Dodgers) lf	2	0	0	0	0	0
L. Smith (Cardinals) lf	0	0	0	1	0	0
Totals	29	4	8	24	12	1

```
American League..................... 1 0 0 0 0 0 0 0 0 - 1
National League .................... 0 2 1 0 0 1 0 0 x - 4
```

DP—Nationals 1. LOB—Americans 11, Nationals 4. 2B—Oliver, Parrish. 3B—Jones. HR—Concepcion. RBIs—Jackson, Rose, Concepcion (2). SB—Raines, Pena, Henderson. SAC FLY—Jackson, Rose. WP—Rogers.

American League	IP	H	R	ER	BB	SO
Eckersley (L)	3	2	3	3	2	1
Clancy	1	0	0	0	0	0
Bannister	1	1	0	0	0	0
Quisenberry	2	3	1	1	0	1
Fingers	1	2	0	0	0	0
National League	IP	H	R	ER	BB	SO
Rogers (W)	3	4	1	1	0	2
Carlton	2	1	0	0	2	4
Soto	2	3	0	0	0	4
Valenzuela	⅔	0	0	0	2	0
Minton	⅔	0	0	0	1	0
Howe	⅓	0	0	0	0	0
Hume (Save)	⅓	0	0	0	0	0

Umpires—Harvey (N.L.), plate; Springstead (A.L.), first base; McSherry (N.L.), second base; McKeon (A.L.), third base; Montague (N.L.), left field; Reilly (A.L.), right field. Time—2:53. Attendance—59,057.

Henderson. With 84 stolen bases in 88 games on the season, Henderson only stole one that night, while the National League team swiped two.

As it stood, Martin's staff of hurlers couldn't do enough to hold off the National League offense. Eckersley, Jim Clancy, Floyd Bannister, Dan Quisenberry, and Rollie Fingers were just not ample support to bring home a victory.

Eckersley absorbed the loss, while his counterpart Steve Rogers was credited with the victory. Rogers was succeeded by six pitchers who combined to pitch shutout ball the last six innings, including: Steve Carlton, Mario Soto, Fernando Valenzuela, Greg Minton, Steve Howe, and Tom Hume, who picked up the save.

The win was not only the Nationals' eleventh straight, but manager Tommy Lasorda's second in as many tries.

For Martin, he had to wait until next time.

July 6, 1983

Comiskey Park

The spectacle every baseball fan had waited for finally arrived, the 50th Anniversary All-Star game at Comiskey Park, where the first midsummer classic was staged in 1933.

Prior to the contest, the streets of Chicago were lined with golden anniversary festivities. The day before, Comiskey Park became the site of an Old-Timers All-Star game which reunited many former big league stars, and afterward a special banquet was thrown in their honor. Scalpers were out hawking $25 tickets (the top priced tickets) for as much as $200, and commemorative souvenirs were already on sale throughout the city. By 5 p.m. the next day, the *real* All-Stars took batting practice at Comiskey before the head-to-head competition began.

N.L. manager Whitey Herzog, who met with reporters the day before the game, sympathized with the American League which had lost 11 straight games and 19 out of 20. As he said, "It would be good for baseball if we lose Wednesday night. But I sure as heck as not going to throw the game. Chub Feeney will be mad at me for saying this. But who cares? I'm an old American Leaguer myself (Herzog formerly managed the Kansas City Royals), and I don't care who wins."

Herzog got his wish.

The Americans finally rose to the occasion and buried their opponents, 13–3, in a game which saw the first All-Star grand slam ever and a number of All-Star records broken.

The hero for the Americans was California Angels' center fielder Fred Lynn, whose slam was part of a seven-run third inning which put his team ahead to stay. When Lynn smacked his big blow, he thrust his right hand into the air as if to signify that the National League domination was over.

By this point, both starting pitchers were gone. Toronto's Dave Stieb (10–7) kept the Nationals in check, while Mario Soto of Cincinnati (9–7) was the victim of shaky defense. Two throwing errors by Dodger second baseman Steve Sax accounted for the first two runs, which, for Soto's sake, were unearned. Meanwhile, Stieb hurled three strong innings. He gave up no runs, one hit, and struck out four. The only run he allowed was also unearned. It

The 1983 All-Star Game

National League	AB	R	H	PO	A	E
Sax (Dodgers) 2b	3	1	1	2	0	1
Hubbard (Braves) 2b	1	0	1	0	0	0
Raines (Expos) lf	3	0	0	2	0	0
Madlock (Pirates) 3b	1	0	0	0	0	0
Dawson (Expos) cf	3	0	0	3	0	0
Dravecky (Padres) p	0	0	0	0	1	0
Perez (Braves) p	0	0	0	0	0	0
Orosco (Mets) p	0	0	0	0	0	0
Bench (Reds) ph	1	0	0	0	0	0
Smith (Cubs) p	0	0	0	1	0	0
Oliver (Expos) 1b	2	1	1	2	1	0
Evans (Giants) 1b	1	0	0	2	1	0
Murphy (Braves) rf	3	0	1	0	0	0
Guerrero (Dodgers) 3b–lf	1	0	0	0	0	1
Schmidt (Phillies) 3b	3	0	0	0	0	1
Benedict (Braves) c	1	0	1	5	0	0
Carter (Expos) c	2	0	0	3	0	0
Durham (Cubs) rf	2	0	0	0	0	0
O. Smith (Cardinals) ss	2	1	1	0	0	0
McGee (Cardinals) cf	2	0	1	2	0	0
Soto (Reds) p	1	0	0	2	0	0
Hammaker (Giants) p	0	0	0	0	0	0
Dawley (Astros) p	0	0	0	0	0	0
Thon (Astros) ss	3	0	1	0	0	0
Totals	35	3	8	24	3	3

American League	AB	R	H	PO	A	E
Carew (Angels) 1b	3	2	2	3	0	1
Murray (Orioles) 1b	2	0	0	4	0	0
Yount (Brewers) ss	2	1	0	0	1	0
Ripken (Orioles) ss	0	0	0	1	0	0
Lynn (Angels) cf	3	1	1	1	0	0
Wilson (Royals) cf	1	0	1	2	0	0
Rice (Red Sox) lf	4	1	2	1	0	0
Oglivie (Brewers) rf	1	0	0	0	0	0
Young (Mariners) p	0	0	0	0	0	0
Quisenberry (Royals) p	0	0	0	0	0	0
Brett (Royals) 3b	4	2	2	1	5	0
Simmons (Brewers) c	2	0	0	4	0	0
Parrish (Tigers) c	2	0	0	1	0	0
Cooper (Brewers) ph	1	1	1	0	0	0
Boone (Angels) c	0	0	0	1	0	0
Winfield (Yankees) rf	3	2	3	3	0	0
Kittle (White Sox) lf–rf	2	1	1	1	0	0
Trillo (Indians) 2b	3	1	1	3	1	0
Whitaker (Tigers) 2b	1	1	1	1	0	0
Stieb (Blue Jays) p	0	0	0	0	2	1
DeCinces (Angels) ph	1	0	0	0	0	0
Honeycutt (Rangers) p	0	0	0	0	0	0
Ward (Twins) ph	1	0	0	0	0	0

American League	AB	R	H	PO	A	E
Stanley (Red Sox) p	0	0	0	0	1	0
Yastrzemski (Red Sox) ph	1	0	0	0	0	0
Henderson (A's) lf	1	0	0	0	0	0
Totals	38	13	15	27	10	2

National League .... 1 0 0 1 1 0 0 0 0 – 3
American League........................ 1 1 7 0 0 0 2 2 x – 13

DP — Americans, 2. LOB — Nationals 6, Americans 9. 2B — Winfield, Oliver, Wilson, Brett. 3B — Brett, Whitaker. HR — Rice, Lynn. RBIs — Sax, Murphy, Carew, Lynn (4), Wilson, Rice, Brett, Winfield, Whitaker (2), Henderson. SB — Sax, Raines. SAC HIT — Stieb. SAC FLY — Brett, Yount, Whitaker. PB — Benedict.

National League	IP	H	R	ER	BB	SO
Soto (L)	2	2	2	0	2	2
Hammaker	⅔	6	7	7	1	0
Dawley	1 ⅓	1	0	0	0	1
Dravecky	2	1	0	0	0	2
Perez	⅔	3	2	2	1	1
Orosco	⅓	0	0	0	0	1
L. Smith	1	2	2	1	0	1

American League	IP	H	R	ER	BB	SO
Stieb (W)	3	0	1	0	1	4
Honeycutt	2	5	2	2	0	0
Stanley	2	2	0	0	0	0
Young	1	0	0	0	0	0
Quisenberry	1	1	0	0	0	1

Umpires — Maloney (A.L.), plate; Wendelstedt (N.L.), first base; Henry (A.L.), second base; Quick (N.L.), third base; Shulock (A.L.), left field; Pallone (N.L.), right field. Time — 3:05. Attendance — 43,801.

---

came on a throwing error he made after fielding a ground ball back to the mound hit by Steve Sax.

But the real victim of this 54th meeting between leagues was N.L. hurler Atlee Hammaker of San Francisco, who replaced Soto in the third. As a starter, Hammaker entered the contest with a 9–4 record, 83 strikeouts and a 1.70 ERA. That was during the regular season. In his first All-Star game appearance, which lasted two and two-thirds innings, Hammaker surrendered six hits and seven runs; most of those runs came on Lynn's slam and a solo home run by Boston's Jim Rice. The other runs were pushed across on a triple by George Brett and singles by Dave Winfield, Manny Trillo, and Rod Carew, his second of the game. Carew, who entered the game hitting .406, turned in a two-for-four performance. He was the game's all-time vote-getter with 1,901,334 votes.

With the Americans leading 9–1 after three innings, they added four more runs, two in the eighth and ninth, hanging on to embarrass the Nationals for the first time since 1971. Four other American League hurlers were used by A.L. manager Harvey Kuenn to hold down the Nationals. They included Rick Honeycutt of Texas, Bob Stanley of Boston, Matt Young of Seattle, and Dan Quisenberry of Kansas City. The victory went to Dave Stieb, while Mario Soto took the loss. The game also marked the first All-Star victory for manager Harvey Kuenn, who was named an All-Star several times himself during his playing career.

Among the All-Star records broken or tied were:

- Seven extra-base hits, tying a record established in 1934 by the American League.
- Most runs scored in a game by one team, exceeding the record set in a 12–0 American League win in 1946.
- Seven runs in one inning broke the record of six, set by the A.L. in 1934.
- Six hits allowed by National League pitcher Atlee Hammaker in the third inning broke the record of five hits allowed in one inning by one pitcher, held previously by the Dodgers' Burt Hooton.

After the game, there was quite a contrast in moods in both clubhouses. The Americans were wild and boisterous; the Nationals were solemn and sedate. Their clubhouse resembled a morgue.

Most of the attention in the Americans' clubhouse centered around Fred Lynn, because of his historic home run. When asked if the All-Star game meant more to him than a regular season game, he replied, "I get a little more pumped up for this game. I swing harder, not by design, but just because I'm a little more pumped up."

On the other hand, when reporters asked Atlee Hammaker to explain the reason for his poor performance, he just wanted to forget it. "To put it bluntly," he said, "it's probably the worst exhibition of pitching you'll ever see. And I couldn't have picked a worse spot for it, either — my first All-Star game and in front of all those people. I have no excuses. I was too terrible to alibi."

Even manager Whitey Herzog gave no excuses for his team's loss. His only comment was, "It was just a good old-fashioned butt-kicking."

And a timely win for the American League at the same park where they recorded their first victory.

July 10, 1984

Candlestick Park

With the American League out to win their second interleague contest in a row, the scene switched to wind-troubled Candlestick Park. The only wish the National League made was that the unpredictable gusty winds at Candlestick would not greatly affect the outcome of the game. For once the Nationals got their wish, as power pitching limited the Americans to eight hits in a 3–1 loss before a sold-out crowd of 57,756 fans.

The game was highlighted by a record-breaking six consecutive strikeouts, combined by flawless efforts on the part of Dodger screwball artist Fernando Valenzuela and Mets' rookie right-hander Dwight Gooden. It also featured a nine-inning high of 21 strikeouts, establishing a new All-Star game mark.

The six strikeouts by Valenzuela and Gooden eclipsed the previous record of five consecutive strikeouts held by Carl Hubbell, set in 1934. However, Hubbell still remains prominent in the record books as the only pitcher to strike out five batters in a row; it took two pitchers to break his mark.

Besides masterful pitching performances, the Nationals put on a little power display of their own. Solo home runs by Montreal catcher Gary Carter and Atlanta center fielder Dale Murphy propelled the Nationals to victory.

"You saw three homers and 21 strikeouts," American League manager Joe Altobelli said in defeat. "What more could you want?" Well, an American League victory for American League fans, for one thing. But this seemed out of reach from the very beginning.

The Nationals charged out of the game instantly to avenge the 13–3 blowout loss of a year ago. They capitalized on two costly errors in the bottom of the first to seize a 1–0 lead. Steve Garvey singled to right with two outs and took second when California Angel right fielder Reggie Jackson, known more for his power-hitting than his defense, bobbled the ball for an error.

Dale Murphy followed with a line single to left that was fielded cleanly by Dave Winfield, who came up throwing as Garvey rounded third. The ball reached home simultaneously with Garvey, who knocked the ball out of Detroit Tiger catcher Lance Parrish's mit for an error, scoring the first National League run.

The 1984 All-Star Game

National League	AB	R	H	PO	A	E
Gwynn (Padres) lf	3	0	1	0	0	0
Raines (Expos) lf	1	0	0	4	0	0
Sandberg (Cubs) 2b	4	0	1	0	0	0
Garvey (Padres) 1b	3	1	1	5	1	0
Hernandez (Mets) 1b	1	0	0	1	0	0
Murphy (Braves) cf	3	1	2	0	0	0
Schmidt (Phillies) 3b	3	0	0	0	4	0
Wallach (Expos) 3b	1	0	0	0	0	0
Strawberry (Mets) rf	2	0	1	0	0	0
Washington (Braves) rf	2	0	1	1	0	0
Carter (Expos) c	2	1	1	9	0	0
Davis (Cubs) c	1	0	0	1	0	0
Gossage (Padres) p	0	0	0	0	0	0
O. Smith (Cardinals) ss	3	0	0	3	0	0
Lea (Expos) p	0	0	0	0	1	0
C. Davis (Giants) ph	1	0	0	0	0	0
Valenzuela (Dodgers) p	0	0	0	0	0	0
Mumphrey (Astros) ph	1	0	0	0	0	0
Gooden (Mets) p	0	0	0	1	0	0
Brenly (Giants) ph	1	0	0	0	0	0
Soto (Reds) p	0	0	0	0	0	0
Pena (Pirates) c	0	0	0	2	0	0
Totals	32	3	8	27	6	0
American League	AB	R	H	PO	A	E
Whitaker (Tigers) 2b	3	0	2	0	5	0
Garcia (Blue Jays) 2b	1	0	0	1	0	0
Carew (Angels) 1b	2	0	0	5	0	0
Murray (Orioles) 1b	2	0	1	3	0	0
Ripken (Orioles) ss	3	0	0	0	0	0
Griffin (Blue Jays) ss	0	0	0	0	1	0
Mattingly (Yankees) ph	1	0	0	0	0	0
Winfield (Yankees) lf–rf	4	0	1	2	1	0
Jackson (Angels) rf	2	0	0	0	0	1
Henderson (A's) lf–cf	2	0	0	0	0	0
Brett (Royals) 3b	3	1	1	3	0	0
Caudill (A's) p	0	0	0	0	0	0
Hernandez (Tigers) p	0	0	0	0	0	0
Parrish (Tigers) c	2	0	0	3	1	1
Sundberg (Brewers) c	1	0	0	6	0	0
Lemon (Tigers) cf	2	0	1	0	0	0
Rice (Red Sox) lf	1	0	0	1	0	0
Stieb (Blue Jays) p	0	0	0	0	0	0
Thorton (Indians) ph	1	0	1	0	0	0
Morris (Tigers) p	0	0	0	0	1	0
A. Davis (Mariners) ph	1	0	0	0	0	0
Dotson (White Sox) p	0	0	0	0	0	0
Bell (Rangers) 3b	1	0	0	0	1	0
Totals	32	1	7	24	10	2

American League......................... 0 1 0 0 0 0 0 0 0 - 1
National League .... 1 1 0 0 0 0 0 1 0 - 3

DP—Nationals, 1. LOB—Americans 4, Nationals 7. 2B—Whitaker, Murray, Washington, Winfield. HR—Brett, Carter, Murphy. RBIs—Murphy, Carter, Brett. SB—Sandberg, Strawberry, Gwynn, O. Smith.

American League	IP	H	R	ER	BB	SO
Stieb (L)	2	3	2	1	0	2
Morris	2	2	0	0	1	2
Dotson	2	2	0	0	1	2
Caudill	1	0	0	0	0	3
W. Hernandez	1	1	1	1	0	1
National League	IP	H	R	ER	BB	SO
Lea (W)	2	3	1	1	0	2
Valenzuela	2	2	0	0	0	3
Gooden	2	1	0	0	0	3
Soto	2	0	0	0	0	1
Gossage (Save)	1	1	0	0	0	2

Umpires—Weyer (N.L.), plate; Clark (A.L.), first base; Rennert (N.L.), second base; Merrill (A.L.), third base; Brocklander (N.L.), left field; Roe (A.L.), right field. Time—2:29. Attendance—57,756.

The only scoring drive of the Americans followed when George Brett hammered a 405-foot blast to straightaway center field to tie the game at one apiece.

The Nationals came back in the bottom of the second inning when Gary Carter homered off American League starter Dave Stieb of Toronto. The home run snapped a 1–1 tie and virtually earned Carter MVP honors after the game.

Dale Murphy put the icing on the cake, so to speak, in the bottom of the eighth with a round-tripper of his own to give the Nationals a 3–1 lead and the victory.

Between the third and eighth inning, though, the scoring on both sides came to a sudden halt as the twilight hours of the game seemed to take their toll. Victims of a 5:30 p.m. (Pacific Coast time) start, the shadows around home plate played a definite factor in recording 21 strikeouts until the stadium lights took their full effect.

Shadows or not, the National League proved one thing: For once Candlestick Park turned out to be a blessing in their favor.

July 16, 1985

Metrodome

What promised to be an impressive display of home run power on both sides turned into a one-sided shellacking as the Nationals drubbed the Americans, 6-1, at the Metrodome, before a seemingly pro–American League sell-out crowd of 54,960 fans.

The Metrodome, known throughout the American League as the "Homerdome" for its friendly confines, actually hampered the American League team's attack more than it did the National League's. While the Americans' lineup was comprised mostly of power hitters, the Nationals' lineup seemed better suited for the artificial surface. They not only had athletes who could hit for distance, but who also could hit for average, hit the long ball, run, and throw.

In other words, the Americans again seemed overmatched as the Nationals racked up their 13th victory of the last 14 midsummer classics (21st of the past 23 and 32nd of the past 40). All N.L. manager Dick Williams had to do was fill out the lineup card and his players did the rest. A.L. skipper Sparky Anderson only wished he was as lucky.

The trampoline-like springiness of the Metrodome's artificial playing surface kept the ball bouncing in the National League's favor from the very start, even though the Americans jumped out to an early 1-0 lead in the bottom of the first inning. The lone run came on a run-scoring single by Royals third-sacker George Brett.

The Nationals roared right back in the top of the second inning to tie the game at 1-1. Then, in the third inning, the funny bounces of the Metrodome's SuperTurf carpet became the Americans' undoing. Against Detroit starter Jack Morris, Cardinals second baseman Tommy Herr popped a hit in front of Yankees right fielder Dave Winfield, who, at 6'6", had to practically climb a ladder to keep the ball from bouncing over his head and hold Herr to a double. Moments later, after Herr scored on a single by Padres first baseman Steve Garvey, Atlanta's Dale Murphy looped a fly ball into short center field which Yankees center fielder Ricky Henderson caught over-the-shoulder on the first hop to hold Murphy to a less-than-routine double, the N.L.'s second of the inning.

The 1985 All-Star Game

National League	AB	R	H	PO	A	E
Gwynn (Padres) lf	1	0	0	1	0	0
Crus (Astros) lf	1	0	0	2	0	0
Raines (Expos) lf	0	1	0	0	0	0
Herr (Cardinals) 2b	3	1	1	0	1	0
Ryan (Astros) p	1	0	0	0	0	0
Pena (Pirates) c	1	0	0	4	1	0
Garvey (Padres) 1b	3	0	1	5	0	0
Clark (Cardinals) 1b	1	0	0	4	0	0
Murphy (Braves) cf	3	0	1	1	0	0
McGee (Cardinals) cf	2	0	1	1	0	0
Strawberry (Mets) rf	1	2	1	3	0	0
Parker (Reds) rf	2	0	0	0	1	0
Nettles (Padres) 3b	2	0	0	0	1	0
Wallach (Expos) 3b	2	1	1	1	1	0
Kennedy (Padres) c	2	0	1	0	0	1
Virgil (Phillies) c	1	0	1	3	0	0
Valenzuela (Dodgers) p	0	0	0	0	0	0
Rose (Reds) ph	1	0	0	0	0	0
Reardon (Expos) p	0	0	0	0	1	0
Wilson (Mets) ph	1	0	0	0	0	0
Gossage (Padres) p	0	0	0	0	0	0
O. Smith (Cardinals) ss	4	0	0	1	3	0
Hoyt (Padres) p	1	0	0	0	0	0
Templeton (Padres) ph	1	0	1	0	0	0
Sandberg (Cubs) 2b	1	1	0	0	3	0
Totals	35	6	9	26	12	1

American League	AB	R	H	PO	A	E
Henderson (Yankees) cf	3	1	1	1	0	0
Molitor (Brewers) 3b–cf	1	0	0	0	0	0
Whitaker (Tigers) 2b	2	0	0	1	1	0
Garcia (Blue Jays) 2b	2	0	1	0	3	0
Brett (Royals) 3b	1	0	0	2	1	0
Bradley (Mariners) cf	1	0	0	1	0	0
Petry (Tigers) p	0	0	0	0	0	0
Hernandez (Tigers) p	0	0	0	0	0	0
Murray (Orioles) 1b	3	0	0	5	2	0
Brunansky (Twins) rf	1	0	0	0	0	0
Ripken (Orioles) ss	3	0	1	2	1	0
Trammell (Tigers) ss	1	0	0	0	0	0
Winfield (Yankees) rf	3	0	1	0	0	0
Moore (Angels) p	0	0	0	0	1	0
Boggs (Red Sox) 3b	0	0	0	0	0	0
Rice (Red Sox) lf	3	0	0	1	0	0
Fisk (White Sox) c	2	0	0	2	0	0
Whitt (Blue Jays) c	0	0	0	2	0	0
Ward (Rangers) ph	1	0	0	0	0	0
Gedman (Red Sox) c	1	0	0	4	0	0
Morris (Tigers) p	0	0	0	1	0	0
Key (Blue Jays) p	0	0	0	0	0	0

American League	AB	R	H	PO	A	E
Baines (White Sox) ph	1	0	1	0	0	0
Blyleven (Indians) p	0	0	0	1	2	0
Cooper (Brewers) ph	0	0	0	0	0	0
Stieb (Blue Jays) p	0	0	0	0	0	0
Mattingly (Yankees) 1b	1	0	0	4	0	0
Totals	30	1	5	27	11	0

National League .... 0 1 1 0 2 0 0 0 2 – 6
American League......................... 1 0 0 0 0 0 0 0 0 – 1

DP – Nationals 1. LOB – Nationals 10, Americans 7. 2B – Herr, Murphy, Wallach, McGee. RBIs – Garvey, McGee (2), Kennedy, Virgil (2), Brett. SB – Henderson, Strawberry, Winfield, Cruz, Garcia. SAC FLY – Brett. HBP – BY Blyleven (Strawberry). WP – Valenzuela.

National League	IP	H	R	ER	BB	SO
Hoyt (W)	3	2	1	0	0	0
Ryan	3	2	0	0	2	2
Valenzuela	1	0	0	0	1	1
Reardon	1	1	0	0	0	1
Gossage	1	0	0	0	1	2

American League	IP	H	R	ER	BB	SO
Morris (L)	2⅔	5	2	2	1	1
Key	⅓	0	0	0	0	0
Blyleven	2	3	2	2	1	1
Stieb	1	0	0	0	1	2
Moore	2	0	0	0	0	1
Petry	⅓	0	2	2	3	1
Hernandez	⅔	1	0	0	1	2

Umpires – McCoy (A.L.), plate; Kibler (N.L.), first base; Brenigan (A.L.), second base; C. Williams (N.L.), third base; Coble (A.L.), left field; Marsh (N.L.), right field. Time – 2:54. Attendance – 54,960.

The Nationals pushed across some insurance runs in the fifth when Philadelphia catcher Ozzie Virgil broke his bat on a curveball thrown by Cleveland's Bert Blyleven. Virgil still managed to punch the ball to left for a two-run single, and padded the N.L.'s lead to 4-1.

Finally, in the ninth, the lights mercifully went out at the Metrodome and the Americans' chances for a late-inning comeback were put to rest, when Detroit's Dan Petry walked the bases loaded. St. Louis' Willie McGee then stepped up to the plate and clobbered the ball to right center field, bouncing into the seats for a ground-rule double. McGee's artificial turf-bounce double scored the N.L.'s final two runs, and, more importantly, gave his team a 6-1 victory in the process.

Which is more than the Americans could say having the home-field advantage did for them this year.

July 15, 1986

Astrodome

The last time the A.L. team visited the Houston Astrodome in 1968, it was a game they'd like to forget. Don Drysdale and five other N.L. pitchers shut down the Americans' offense, 1-0, recording 12 strikeouts in the process.

Call it poetic justice maybe, but the A.L.'s return visit 18 years later came out differently; they settled an old score as they hung on to a 3-2 victory over the Nationals. Better yet, it marked the Americans' first win in a National League park since 1962 (the last victory came at Wrigley Field, in game two).

No doubt about it, the Americans wanted this game badly. So did Boston Red Sox hurler Roger Clemens, 15-2 at the All-Star break, who retired the side during his three innings of work. For his efforts, Clemens, who struck out two and kept the Nationals hitless, was later named the game's MVP.

Noting his performance, Kansas City's Dick Howser, the winning manager, said, "Clemens was excellent; he was decisive."

Decisive indeed.

A close runner-up for this same award had to be Detroit Tigers second baseman Lou Whitaker. Whitaker, batting eighth in the lineup and noted for some power, put the Americans ahead to stay when he belted a two-run home run in the top of the second. Scoring ahead of Whitaker was New York Yankees outfielder Dave Winfield, who, weeks before the game, was harrassed in the media by team owner George Steinbrenner for his lack of leadership on the field. Winfield showed he was a leader when he doubled off another Bronx star, New York Mets fireballer Dwight Gooden, the victim of the A.L's scoring binge, much to the chagrin of team manager Whitey Herzog, winless in All-Star competition.

Gooden tried matching Clemens pitch for pitch, but he seemed to struggle a bit in the early innings, just enough to give the Americans all they needed to build momentum towards a rare victory.

The A.L. scored once more in the top of the seventh, making it 3-0. Hard-throwing Mike Scott of the Houston Astros took the mound, taking

1986 All-Star Game

American League	AB	R	H	PO	A	E
Puckett (Twins) lf	3	0	1	5	0	0
Henderson (Yankees) lf	3	0	0	2	0	0
Moseby (Blue Jays) lf	0	0	0	0	0	0
Boggs (Red Sox) 3b	3	0	1	0	1	0
Jacoby (Indians) 3b	1	0	0	1	1	0
Parrish (Tigers) c	3	0	0	4	0	0
Rice (Red Sox) ph	1	0	0	0	0	0
Gedman (Red Sox) c	0	0	0	1	1	0
Joyner (Angels) 1b	1	0	0	3	1	0
Mattingly (Yankees) 1b	3	0	0	7	0	0
Ripken (Orioles) ss	4	0	0	0	1	0
T. Fernandez (Blue Jays) ss	0	0	0	0	0	0
Winfield (Yankees) rf	1	1	1	0	0	0
Barfield (Blue Jays) rf	3	0	0	2	0	0
Whitaker (Tigers) 2b	2	1	1	0	3	0
White (Royals) 2b	2	1	1	1	1	0
Clemens (Red Sox) p	1	0	0	1	0	0
Higuera (Brewers) p	1	0	0	0	0	0
Baines (White Sox) ph	1	0	0	0	0	0
Hough (Rangers) p	0	0	0	0	0	0
Righetti (Yankees) p	0	0	0	0	0	0
Aase (Orioles) p	0	0	0	0	0	0
Totals	33	3	5	27	9	0

National League	AB	R	H	PO	A	E
Gwynn (Padres) lf	3	0	0	1	0	0
Sax (Dodgers) 2b	1	0	1	0	1	0
Sandberg (Cubs) 2b	3	0	0	0	2	1
Scott (Astros) p	0	0	0	0	0	0
S. Fernandez (Mets) p	0	0	0	0	0	0
G. Davis (Astros) ph	1	0	0	0	0	0
Krukow (Giants) p	0	0	0	0	1	0
K. Hernandez (Mets) 1b	4	0	0	5	0	0
Carter (Mets) c	3	0	0	9	0	0
J. Davis (Cubs) c	1	0	1	0	3	0
Pena (Pirates) pr	0	0	0	0	0	0
Strawberry (Mets) rf	2	0	1	1	0	0
Parker (Reds) rf	2	0	1	0	0	0
Schmidt (Phillies) 3b	1	0	0	0	0	0
Brown (Giants) 3b	2	1	1	1	0	0
Murphy (Braves) cf	2	0	0	2	0	0
C. Davis (Giants) cf	1	0	0	0	0	0
O. Smith (Cardinals) ss	1	0	0	3	2	0
Brooks (Expos) ss	2	1	0	1	0	0
Gooden (Mets) p	0	0	0	0	0	0
Bass (Astros) ph	1	0	0	0	0	0
Valenzuela (Dodgers) p	0	0	0	0	0	0
Raines (Expos) lf	2	0	0	1	0	0
Totals	32	2	5	24	9	1

American League........................ 0 2 0 0 0 0 1 0 0 – 8
National League .... 0 0 0 0 0 0 1 0 1 – 2

DP – Americans 5, Nationals 4. 2B – Winfield, Brown, Sax. HR – Whitaker, White. RBIs – Whitaker (2), White, Brown, Sax. SB – Puckett, Moseby, Sax. WP – Hough. PB – Gedman. Balks – Gooden, Hough.

American League	IP	H	R	ER	BB	SO
Clemens (W)	3	0	0	0	0	2
Higuera	3	1	0	0	1	2
Hough	1⅓	2	2	1	0	3
Righetti	⅔	2	0	0	0	0
Aase (Save)	⅔	0	0	0	0	0
National League	IP	H	R	ER	BB	SO
Gooden (L)	3	3	2	2	0	2
Valenzuela	3	1	0	0	0	5
Scott	1	1	1	1	0	2
S. Fernandez	1	0	0	0	2	3
Krukow	1	0	0	0	0	0

Umpires – Froemming (N.L.) plate, Palerno (A.L.) first, Runge (N.L.) second, Reed (A.L.) third, Gregg (N.L.) left field, McClelland (A.L.) right field. Time – 2:28. Attendance – 45,774.

---

over for Los Angeles Dodgers right-hander Fernando Valenzuela, who struck out five in a row during three innings of work. Valenzuela's short work of the Americans tied him with Carl Hubbell, who first set the record for five consecutive strikeouts in 1934. Fernando's victims: Don Mattingly, Cal Ripken, Jesse Barfield, Lou Whitaker and pitcher Ed Higuera.

Scott's performance paled in significance, however. Serving up a fastball over the plate, Kansas City Royals second baseman Frank White promptly yanked the ball into the stands for a solo home run.

The Nationals made a late inning bid in the bottom of the ninth to come back, aided by a Steve Sax double and narrowed the score, 3–2. But any chance of a N.L. come-from-behind victory was dashed when Baltimore Orioles bullpen ace Don Aase recorded the final out.

After the game, Clemens, who grew up in nearby Houston, where he pitched high school ball before going to the University of Texas, still seemed starstruck by all the attention and his performance. "Coming home and pitching like this in an All-Star game is a dream come true," he said.

Not so, Roger. It was more like a dream that the Americans finally beat the Nationals in their own ball park.

Appendix I
Team Statistics

Team Batting — 1930s

1933: NL — .235, AL — .290; *1934:* AL — .359, NL — .222; *1935:* NL — .129, AL — .250; *1936:* NL — .219, AL — .290; *1937:* NL — .317, AL — .371; *1938:* AL — .206, NL — .242; and *1939:* NL — .206, AL — .194.

Team Batting — 1940s

1940: AL — .103, NL — .241; *1941:* NL — .286, AL — .194; *1942:* AL — .200, NL — .194; *1943:* NL — .270, AL — .276; *1944:* AL — .188, NL — .364; *1945:* (No Game, World War II); *1946:* NL — .097, AL — .389; *1947:* AL — .235, NL — .156; *1948:* NL — .229, AL — .207; and *1949:* AL — .317, NL — .324.

Team Batting — 1950s

1950: NL — .192, AL — .163; *1951:* NL — .308, AL — .286; *1952:* AL — .278, NL — .167; *1953:* AL — .161, NL — .313; *1954:* NL — .350, AL — .436; *1955:* AL — .227, NL — .289; *1956:* NL — .306, AL — .297, *1957:* AL — .270, NL — .265; *1958:* NL — .313, AL — .290; *1959 (Game 1):* AL — .222, NL — .300; and *1959 (Game 2):* AL — .182, NL — .194.

Team Batting — 1960s

1960 (Game 1): NL — .316, AL — .176; *1960 (Game 2):* NL — .294, AL — .242; *1961 (Game 1):* AL — .105, NL — .297; *1961 (Game 2):* NL — .156, AL — .133; *1962 (Game 1):* NL — .242, AL — .138; *1962 (Game 2):* AL — .270, NL — .286; *1963:* NL — .176, AL — .324; *1964:* AL — .257, NL — .235; *1965:* NL — .306, AL — .235; *1966:* AL — .171, NL — .182; *1967:* NL — .176, AL — .163; *1968:* AL — .100, NL — .185; and *1969:* NL — .275; AL — .182.

Team Batting — 1970s

1970: AL — .273, NL — .233; *1971:* NL — .161, AL — .241; *1972:* AL — .182, NL — .242; *1973:* NL — .294, AL — .156; *1974:* AL — .133, NL — .303; *1975:* NL — .351, AL — .278; *1976:* AL — .172, NL — .303; *1977:* NL — .273, AL — .229; *1978:* AL — .258, NL — .313; and *1979:* NL — .286, AL — .286.

Team Batting — 1980s

1980: AL — .219, NL — .226; *1981:* NL — .257, AL — .297; *1982:* AL — .242, NL — .276; *1983:* NL — .229, AL — .395; *1984:* AL — .218, NL — .250; and *1985:* NL — .257, AL — .166.

Team Slugging — 1930s

1933: NL — .412, AL — .387; *1934:* AL — .359, NL — .222; *1935:* NL — .194, AL — .469; *1936:* AL — .344, NL — .452; *1937:* NL — .317, AL — .371; *1938:* AL — .265, NL — .303; and *1939:* NL — .235, AL — .290.

Team Slugging — 1940s

1940: AL — .138, NL — .345; *1941:* NL — .543, AL — .306; *1942:* AL — .400, NL — .290; *1943:* NL — .432, AL — .448; *1944:* AL — .188, NL — .485; *1945* (No Game, World War II); *1946:* NL — .097, AL — .694; *1947:* AL — .294, NL — .250; *1948:* NL — .314, AL — .310; and *1949:* AL — .439, NL — .541.

Team Slugging — 1950s

1950: NL — .365, AL — .245; *1951:* NL — .641, AL — .600; *1952:* AL — .389, NL — .556; *1953:* AL — .161, NL — .344; *1954:* NL — .575, AL — .744; *1955:* AL — .318, NL — .378; *1956:* NL — .528, AL — .459; *1957:* AL — .324, NL — .382; *1958:* NL — .133, AL — .290; *1959 (Game 1):* AL — .333, NL — .533; and *1959 (Game 2):* AL — .455, NL — .419.

Team Slugging — 1960s

1960 (Game 1): NL — .605, AL — .265; *1960 (Game 2):* NL — .647, AL — .273; *1961 (Game 1):* AL — .211, NL — .486; *1961 (Game 2):* NL — .568, AL — .486; *1962 (Game 1):* NL — .273, AL — .207; *1962 (Game 2):* AL — .568, NL — .486; *1963:* NL — .176, AL — .353; *1964:* AL — .343, NL — .529; *1965:* NL — .556, AL — .441; *1966:* AL — .229, NL — .212; *1967:* NL — .314, AL — .245; *1968:* AL — .200, NL — .231; and *1969:* NL — .550, AL — .394.

Team Slugging — 1970s

1970: AL — .364, NL — .302; *1971:* NL — .452, AL — .552; *1972:* AL — .333, NL — .333; *1973:* NL — .618, AL — .281; *1974:* AL — .167, NL — .545; *1975:* NL — .541, AL — .361; *1976:* AL — .276, NL — .606; *1977:* NL — .636, AL — .343; *1978:* AL — .419, NL — .406; and *1979:* NL — .514, AL — .457.

Team Slugging — 1980s

1980: AL — .344, NL — .323; *1981:* NL — .657, AL — .405; *1982:* AL — .273, NL — .483; *1983:* NL — .257, AL — .737; *1984:* AL — .406, NL — .468; and *1985:* NL — .371, AL — .166.

Appendix II
Individual Records

Batting — Lifetime

Most Games: Aaron (24), Mays (24), Musial (24), Williams, T. (18), and Robinson, B. (18).

Most Consecutive Games: Mays (17), Aaron (17), and Williams, T. (10).

Highest Batting Average (20 + at-bats): Gehringer (.500) and Herman, W. (.433).

Highest Slugging Percentage (20 + at-bats): Garvey (.955) and Killebrew (.654).

Most At-Bats: Mays (75) and Williams, T. (46).

Most Runs: Mays (20) and Williams, T. (10).

Most Hits: Mays (23), Williams, T. (14), and Fox, N. (14).

Most Extra Base Hits: Musial (8), Mays (8), and Williams, T. (7).

Most Total Bases: Musial (40), Mays (40), and Williams, T. (30).

Most Singles: Mays (15) and Fox, N. (14).

Most Doubles: Simmons; Cronin; Gordon, J.; Oliva; Kluszewski; Banks, E.; Oliver, A.; and Winfield, all tied at (3).

Most Triples: Mays (3) and Robinson, B. (3).

Most Home Runs: Musial (6), Williams, T. (4), and Lynn, F. (4).

Most RBIs: Williams, T. (12) and Musial (10).

Most Bases on Balls: Williams, T. (11), Musial (7), and Mays (7).

Most Strikeouts: Mantle (17) and Mays (14).

Most Stolen Bases: Mays (6).

Batting — Game

Most Official At-Bats: Jones, W. (7) — 1950 (14 innings).

Most Runs: Williams, T. (4) — 1946.

Most Hits: Medwick (4) — 1937; Williams, T. (4) — 1946; and Yastrzemski (4) — 1970 (12 innings).

Most Total Bases: Williams, T. (10) — 1946; Vaughan (9) — 1941; and Rosen (9) — 1954.

Most Singles: Boyer, K. (3) — 1956; Henderson, R. (3) — 1982; and many other players all tied at (3).

Most Doubles: Simmons (2) – 1934; Medwick (2) – 1937; Kluszewski (2) – 1956; and Banks (2) – 1959; and Simmons (2) – 1934.

Most Triples: Carew (2) – 1978.

Most Home Runs: Vaughan (2) – 1941 (consecutive); McCovey (2) – 1969 (consecutive); Carter (2) – 1981 (consecutive); Williams, T. (2) – 1946; and Rosen (2) – 1954 (consecutive).

Most RBIs: Williams, T. (5) – 1946; Rosen (5) – 1954; Lynn (4) – 1983; and Vaughan (4) – 1941.

Most Bases on Balls: Gehringer (3) – 1934 and Cavarretta (3) – 1944.

Most Strikeouts: Clemente (4) – 1967 (15 innings); Oliva (3) – 1967 (15 innings); Gehrig (3) – 1934; Johnson, R. (3) – 1935; Gordon (3) – 1942; Keltner (3) – 1943; Hegan (3) – 1950; Mantle (3) – 1956; Hack (3) – 1939; Roseboro (3) – 1961; McCovey (3) – 1968; and Bench (3) – 1970.

Most Stolen Bases: Mays (2) – 1963.

Most Caught Stealing: Oliva (2) – 1967.

Most Hit by Pitch: (1) by many players.

Most Grounded into Double Plays: Richardson (2) – 1963.

Pitching – Lifetime

Most Games: Bunning (8); Drysdale (8); Marichal (8); Seaver (8); and Wynn, E. (7).

Most Consecutive Games: Blackwell (6) and Wynn, E. (6).

Most Games Started: Gomez (5); Roberts (5); and Drysdale (5).

Most Games Finished: Gossage (4); Harder (4); Blackwell (3); and Sutter (3).

Most Saves: Sutter (2).

Most Games Won: Gomez (3); Blue, V. (2); Friend, B. (2); Marichal (2); Drysdale (2); and Sutter (2).

Most Games Lost: Cooper (2); Passeau (2); Ford (2); Tiant (2); and Hunter (2).

Lowest Earned Run Average: Harder (0.00) – 13 innings and Marichal (0.50) – 18 innings.

Most Innings: Drysdale (19) and Gomez (18).

Most Runs: Ford (13) and Roberts (10).

Most Hits: Ford (19); Roberts (17); and Spahn (17).

Most Home Runs: Blue (4) and Hunter, C. (4).

Most Bases on Balls: Palmer, J. (7); Warneke (6); Hubbell (6); and Roberts (6).

Most Wild Pitches: Blackwell (2); Roberts (2); Marichal (2); Brewer (2); and Stieb (2).

Pitching — Game

Most Runs: Hammaker (7) — 1983; Consuegra (5) — 1954; Ford (5) — 1955; Odom (5) — 1969; and Palmer, J. (5) — 1977.

Most Earned Runs: Hammaker (7) — 1983; Conseugra (5) — 1954; and Palmer, J. (5) — 1977.

Most Hits: Bridges (7) — 1937; Warneke (6) — 1933; Passeau (6) — 1941; and Hammaker (6) — 1983.

Most Hits in an Inning: Hammaker (6) — 1983 (3rd inning); Hughson (5) — 1944 (5th inning); Consuegra (5) — 1954 (4th inning); and Odom (5) — 1969 (3rd inning).

Most Bases on Balls: Hallahan (5) — 1933 and Palmer, J. (4) — 1978.

Most Bases on Balls in an Inning: Wynn (3) — 1959 (5th inning); Palmer, J. (3) — 1978 (3rd inning); Messersmith (3) — 1974 (3rd inning); and Kern (3) — 1979 (9th inning).

Most Strikeouts: Hubbell (6) — 1934; Vandermeer (6) — 1943; Jansen (6) — 1950; Jenkins (6) — 1967; Pierce (5) — 1956; and Radatz (5) — 1963, 1964.

Most Strikeouts, Consecutive: Gooden and Valenzuela (6) — 1984; Valenzuela (5) — 1986; and Hubbell (5) — 1934.

Most Strikeouts, Consecutive Innings: Gooden and Valenzuela (6) — 1984; Valenzuela (5) — 1986; and Hubbell (6) — 1934.

Appendix III
Most Valuable Players

1962 (Game 1): Wills
1962 (Game 2): Wagner, L.
1963: Mays
1964: Callison
1965: Marichal
1966: Robinson, B.
1967: Perez, T.
1968: Mays
1969: McCovey
1970: Yastrzemski
1971: Robinson, F.
1972: Morgan
1973: Bonds
1974: Garvey
1975: Madlock and Matlack (co-winners)
1976: Foster
1977: Sutton
1978: Garvey
1979: Parker
1980: Griffey
1981: Carter
1982: Concepcion
1983: Lynn
1984: Carter
1985: Hoyt
1986: Clemens

Index

A

Aaron, Hank 77, 86, 89, 91, 92, 93, 96, 132, 144, 147, 150, 157, 160
Aase, Don 197
Adcock, Joe 100
Allen, Johnny 23
Allen, Richie 123, 129, 131
Alley, Gene 129
Alou, Felipe 111
Alston, Walt 71, 74, 81, 82, 85, 99, 100, 103, 120, 128, 131, 160
Altman, George 106, 116
Altobelli, Joe 189
Anderson, Sparky 144, 150, 164, 173, 192
Andujar, Juaquin 173
Antonelli, Johnny 74, 81, 92
Aparicio, Luis 91
Appling, Luke 16, 29, 48
Ashburn, Richie 49, 51, 61, 63, 67
Averill, Earl 2, 7, 10, 17
Avila, Bobby 64, 71, 73

B

Bailey, Ed 84, 117
Baker, Del 32
Banks, Ernie 82, 85, 88, 91, 96, 98
Bannister, Floyd 184
Barfield, Jesse 197
Barker, Len 180
Battey, Earl 111, 117
Bauer, Hank 69, 131
Baylor, Don 171, 173
Bell, Buddy 181
Bell, Gus 69, 74, 82, 84, 85
Bench, Johnny 136, 138, 144, 150, 156, 158, 161, 175
Benton, Al 33

Berger, Wally 8
Berra, Yogi 2, 61, 69, 74, 75, 84, 88, 93, 95, 96, 154
Bickford, Vern 56
Blackwell, Ewell 44, 46, 48, 59, 63
Blanton, Cy 19
Blass, Steve 147
Blue, Vida 144, 158, 167, 170
Blyleven, Bert 150, 153, 194
Bochte, Bruce 174
Bonds, Bobby 150, 152, 153
Boone, Bob 169, 171
Boone, Ray 73
Borowy, Hank 39, 41
Boudreau, Lou 29, 33, 35, 51, 53, 56, 82
Bowa, Larry 167, 169, 174
Boyer, Ken 79, 81, 91, 92, 100, 102, 122
Branca, Ralph 46, 51
Brecheen, Harry 46, 48
Brett, George 30, 167, 171, 182, 187, 191, 192
Brett, Ken 156
Brewer, Jim 150, 152
Brewer, Tom 81
Bridges, Tommy 19, 24
Brissie, Lou 56
Brock, Lou 171
Brown, Mace 23
Buhl, Bob 98
Bunning, Jim 82, 84, 91, 108, 113, 119, 122, 128
Burleson, Rick 174
Bush, George 178

C

Callison, Johnny 120, 122
Campanella, Roy 69
Campaneris, Bert 166
Carew, Rod 144, 147, 149, 164, 167, 175, 187

Carlton, Steve 136, 171, 173, 184
Carrasquel, Chico 77
Carter, Gary 173, 174, 178, 180, 181, 182, 189, 191
Case, George 36
Cavarretta, Phil 39, 41
Cedeno, Cesar 147, 150, 161
Cepeda, Orlando 92, 108, 111, 120
Cerv, Bob 86
Cey, Ron 154, 157, 169
Chance, Dean 122, 129, 131
Chandler, A.B. "Happy" 60
Chandler, Spud 33, 46
Clancy, Jim 184
Clemens, Roger 195, 197
Clemente, Roberto 104, 107, 111, 126, 129, 143, 146
Cochrane, Mickey 11, 14
Colavito, Rocky 89, 92, 95, 108, 111, 116, 125, 175
Colbert, Nate 149
Coleman, Joe 49, 52
Concepcion, Dave 161, 169, 177, 182
Conley, Gene 74, 77, 78
Consuegra, Sandy 138
Cooper, Mort 33, 36, 38
Cooper, Walker 41, 46
Crandall, Del 91, 96
Cronin, Joe 7, 8, 10, 13, 23, 27, 29, 46
Crowder, Alvin 7
Cuellar, Mike 131
Culp, Ray 138
Cunningham, Joe 92

Dietz, Dick 143
Dillinger, Pat 56
DiMaggio, Dom 42, 52
DiMaggio, Joe 14, 16, 17, 19, 24, 26, 29, 30, 32, 33, 48, 49, 51, 53, 56, 64, 82, 195
DiMaggio, Vince 38
Doby, Larry 59, 71, 74
Doerr, Bobby 36, 38, 39, 41, 42, 48, 82
Donovan, Dick 106
Downing, Brian 174
Downing, Al 131
Dressen, Charlie 67
Drysdale, Don 2, 89, 91, 92, 93, 95, 113, 114, 122, 125, 131, 133, 174
Duren, Ryne 92
Durocher, Leo 16, 23, 33, 35, 51, 64, 78
Dyer, Eddie 46, 48
Dykes, Jimmie 7

E

Easler, Mike 181
Eckersley, Dennis 182, 184
Elliott, Bob 61, 63
Ellis, Dock 144
Elston, Don 92
Ennis, Del 75
Erskine, Carl 74
Estrada, Chuck 98
Evans, Dwight 181
Evers, Hoot 51

D

Daley, Bud 92
Danning, Hank 29, 30
Dark, Alvin 61, 119, 160
Davillo, Vic 123
Davis, Curt 16
Davis, Ron 181
Davis, Tommy 117, 119
Davis, Willie 152
Dean, Dizzy 2, 11, 14, 16, 17, 19
Demaree, Frank 14, 20
Dent, Bucky 181
Derringer, Paul 24, 27, 32
Dickey, Bill 10, 11, 17, 18, 24, 45
Dickson, Murray 69
Dierker, Larry 136

F

Face, Roy 91, 92, 95
Fain, Ferris 61, 69
Farmer, Ed 177
Farrell, Dick 122, 125
Feeney, Chub 185
Feller, Bob 24, 26, 29, 32, 42, 44
Fette, Lou 24
Fidrych, Mark 161, 164
Fingers, Rollie 153, 156, 170, 181, 184
Fisk, Carlton 149, 167, 181
Flood, Curt 133
Foiles, Hank 85
Ford, Whitey 73, 74, 75, 77, 79, 89, 92, 100, 103, 104

Fornieles, Mike 106
Forsch, Ken 180
Fosse, Ray 140, 142
Foster, George 161, 163, 164, 169, 171
Fox, Nellie 71, 74, 75, 81, 85, 86, 88, 89, 91, 93
Foxx, Jimmie 8, 11, 13, 29
Freehan, Bill 136, 147
Fregosi, Jim 120, 133
French, Larry 27
Frey, Jim 181
Frey, Lonnie 24
Frick, Ford 2, 48
Friend, Bob 79, 88, 96, 99
Frisch, Frankie 7, 8, 11

G

Galan, Augie 14, 39
Garcia, Mike 67, 69
Garner, Phil 175
Garver, Ned 61
Garvey, Steve 2, 154, 156, 157, 158, 160, 161, 164, 167, 169, 170, 171, 189, 192
Gehrig, Lou 7, 8, 11, 13, 16, 17, 19, 20
Gehringer, Charley 5, 7, 8, 13, 16, 19, 113
Gibson, Bob 131, 136, 142, 143, 147
Gilliam, Jim 95
Giusti, Dave 150
Gomez, Lefty 5, 7, 10, 11, 19, 23
Gooden, Dwight 189, 195
Goodman, Ivan 24
Gordon, Joe 24, 32, 39, 44, 56
Goslin, Leon 16
Gossage, Rich 158, 166, 169
Grant, Jim 123
Gray, Ted 57, 59
Green, Dallas 181
Greenberg, Hank 24
Grich, Bobby 174
Griffey, Ken 161, 175, 177
Grim, Bob 85
Grimm, Charley 14, 16, 42
Grissom, Lee 19
Groat, Dick 91–2, 111, 117
Grove, Lefty 14, 16, 23

H

Hack, Stan 38
Haddix, Harvey 75
Hafey, Chick 7
Hallahan, Bill 5
Hammaker, Atlee 187, 188
Haney, Fred 89, 95
Harder, Mel 10, 11, 19
Harrelson, Bud 142, 143
Harridge, Will 33
Harris, Bucky 49, 51
Hartnett, Gabby 7, 14, 24, 26
Hemsley, Rollie 11, 13
Henderson, Rickey 182, 184, 192
Hendrick, George 175
Henrich, Tommy 33, 82
Henry, Bill 100
Herbert, Ray 116
Herman, Billy 14, 27, 30, 36, 38
Herr, Tommy 192
Herzog, Whitey 185, 188, 195
Heydler, John 5
Hickman, Jim 140, 143
Higbe, Kirby 44
Higgins, Michael 14
Higuera, Ed 197
Hodges, Gil 56, 61, 63, 82, 85, 140, 143
Holtzman, Ken 150
Honeycutt, Rick 188
Hooton, Burt 181, 188
Hope, Bob 178
Horton, Willie 143
Houk, Ralph 119
Houtteman, Art 59
Howard, Elston 108, 120
Howard, Frank 136
Howe, Steve 184
Howser, Dick 107, 195
Hubbell, Carl 2, 7, 8, 10, 14, 17, 29, 36, 59, 110, 131, 189, 197
Hughson, Tex 38, 41, 42, 138
Hume, Tom 184
Humphrey, Hubert H. 128
Hunt, Ron 126
Hunter, Catfish 129, 131, 132, 143, 150, 156, 158, 160, 161
Hutchinson, Freddie 61, 63

J

Jackson, Larry 100, 117, 119
Jackson, Reggie 2, 77, 111, 144, 146, 174, 189
Jansen, Larry 59
Jenkins, Ferguson 129, 131, 144
Jensen, Jackie 86, 88
John, Tommy 175, 177
Johnson, Bob 41
Jones, Randy 161
Jones, Ruppert 182
Jones, "Toothpick Sam" 95
Joost, Eddie 53, 56

K

Kaat, Jim 126
Kaline, Al 77, 85, 89, 91, 98, 129
Kasko, Eddie 108
Kazak, Eddie 53, 55
Kell, George 49, 53, 59, 63, 84
Keller, Charley 42, 44
Keltner, Ken 36, 39, 51
Kennedy, John F. 111
Kern, Jim 174
Killebrew, Harmon 92, 106, 125, 129, 144, 146, 175
Kiner, Ralph 56, 59, 60, 61, 63, 175
Kissinger, Henry 160
Kluszewski, Ted 69, 73, 74, 77, 81
Knight, Ray 175
Knowles, Darrel 138
Koosman, Jerry 136
Koufax, Sandy 108, 125, 126
Kramer, Jack 42, 44
Kubek, Tony 106, 108
Kuenn, Harvey 67, 75, 84, 91, 96, 188
Kuhn, Bowie 2, 178
Kurowski, Whitey 41

L

Laabs, Chet 36
Labine, Clem 85
Laker, Norm 102
Landis, Kenesaw 1, 33
Lane, F.C. 1

Lasorda, Tommy 167, 170, 174, 182, 184
Lavelle, Gary 164
Law, Vern 98, 100, 103
Lee, Bill 24
Lemon, Bob 49, 59, 61, 64, 66, 71, 174
Lemon, Chet 169, 173, 174
Leonard, Emil (Dutch) 38
Lewis, Buddy 48
Logan, Johnny 77
Lolich, Mickey 146, 147
Lollar, Sherm 91
Lombardi, Ernie 23, 24
Lopat, Eddie 61, 63
Lopata, Stan 77
Lopes, Davey 169, 171
Lopez, Al 75, 77, 96, 100, 102, 103, 123, 125
Lowery, Peanuts 42
Luzinski, Greg 164, 169
Lyle, Sparky 153, 166
Lynn, Fred 164, 175, 185, 188

M

McAuliffe, Dick 125
McBride, Ken 116, 117
McCarthy, Joe 2, 14, 17, 23, 24, 26, 27, 33, 36, 38
McCarver, Tim 126
McCormick, Frank 24, 29
McCormick, Mike 96, 106
McCovey, Willie 126, 136, 138, 139, 143
McDaniel, Lindy 100
McDougald, Gil 85, 86, 88, 92
McDowell, Sam 138, 143
McGee, Willie 194
McGlothin, Jim 131, 132
McGraw, John 2, 7
Mack, Connie 2, 7
Mack, Ray 29
McKechnie, Bill 27, 32
McLain, Denny 126, 136, 138, 139
McMillan, Roy 79
McNally, Dave 138, 149
McQuinn, George 41, 51
Madlock, Bill 158, 160
Maglie, Sal 63
Mahaffey, Art 114
Maloney, Jim 123
Malzone, Frank 82, 88, 93, 117

Mantle, Mickey 69, 74, 75, 81, 84, 86, 88, 96, 108, 129, 158
Manush, Heinie 8
Marichal, Juan 122, 123, 128, 131
Marion, Marty 41
Maris, Roger 96, 108
Marshall, Mike 154
Martin, Billy 164, 182, 184
Martin, Pepper 7
Masterson, Walt 49, 51
Mathews, Eddie 67, 85, 89, 96, 100, 108
Matlack, Jon 156, 160
Mattingly, Don 197
Mauch, Gene 125
May, Lee 149
Mays, Willie 73, 77, 79, 84, 85, 86, 88, 89, 92, 96, 98, 99, 100, 103, 108, 113, 117, 119, 120, 123, 125, 129, 133, 160, 175
Mazeroski, Bill 86, 91, 98
Mazilli, Lee 174
Medwick, Joe 10, 11, 14, 19
Mele, Sam 126
Messersmith, Andy 154, 156, 157
Michaels, Cass 53, 59
Miller, Eddie 30
Miller, Stu 104, 108, 110
Minoso, Minnie 64, 69, 73, 82, 85, 102
Minton, Greg 184
Mitchell, Dale 56
Mize, Johnny 19, 20, 39, 46, 55, 69
Monbouquette, Bill 96, 99
Moon, Wally 2
Moran, Billy 113, 116
Morgan, Joe 143, 147, 149, 150, 161, 164, 167, 169
Morris, Jack 178, 192
Mossi, Don 82, 85
Mullin, Pat 51
Muncrief, Bob 41
Munger, George 46
Mungo, Van Lingle 10, 19
Murcer, Bobby 144
Murphy, Dale 182, 189, 191, 192
Murtaugh, Danny 104, 147, 149
Musial, Stan 38, 39, 41, 51, 55, 60, 61, 63, 64, 73, 75, 77, 78, 81, 85, 86, 88, 92, 98, 100, 102, 113, 119

N

Narleski, Ray 88
Nettles, Graig 174
Newcombe, Don 55, 56, 59, 61, 63
Newhouser, Hal 38, 39, 41, 42, 44, 46, 48, 49
Nicholson, Bill 39, 41
Niekro, Phil 136, 170
Nixon, Richard M. 86, 139, 140
Norris, Mike 180
Nuxhall, Joe 77

O

O'Dell, Billy 86, 88, 95
Odom, John 136, 138
Oliva, Tony 129, 133
Oliver, Al 158, 182
Osteen, Claude 143, 150, 152
Otis, Amos 140, 143
O'Toole, Jim 117
Ott, Mel 14, 23, 27, 29
Owen, Mickey 33

P

Pafko, Andy 59, 60
Paige, Satchel 67, 69
Palmer, Jim 140, 147, 164, 167, 169
Pappas, Milt 123, 125
Parker, Dave 164, 171, 174, 178, 180
Parnell, Mel 53, 55
Parrish, Lance 177, 189
Pascual, Camilo 111, 122
Passeau, Claude 30, 32, 33, 42, 44
Pearson, Albie 117
Pennock, Herb 32
Pepitone, Joe 119
Perez, Tony 129
Perry, Gaylord 128, 142, 147, 156, 174
Perry, Jim 142, 143
Pesky, Johnny 42
Peters, Gary 131
Petry, Dan 194
Pierce, Billy 67, 75, 79, 84, 85, 92
Pinson, Vada 92
Podres, Johnny 100, 114

Pollet, Howie 42, 56
Porter, Darrell 173, 174, 177
Power, Vic 91
Purkey, Bob 108, 113

Q

Quisenberry, Dan 182, 184, 188

R

Radatz, Dick 119, 120, 122
Radcliff, Raymond 14
Raffensberger, Ken 41
Randolph, Willie 166, 177
Raschi, Vic 49, 51, 52, 57, 64
Reese, Pee Wee 48, 53, 69
Reuss, Jerry 158, 177
Reynolds, Allie 67, 69
Rice, Jim 167, 173, 174, 187
Richard, James Rodney 175
Richards, Paul 106, 107, 108
Richardson, Bobby 117
Richert, Pete 125, 126, 128
Rigney, Bill 114
Ripkin, Cal 197
Roberts, Robin 57, 61, 63, 67, 73, 74, 75
Robinson, Brooks 120, 126, 129, 142, 143
Robinson, Eddie 53, 64
Robinson, Frank 93, 129, 146
Robinson, Jackie 53, 55, 56, 57, 64
Rogers, Steve 170, 182, 184
Rojas, Cookie 149
Rolfe, Red 17, 19, 24
Rollins, Rich 113
Roosevelt, Franklin D. 2, 3, 17, 33
Rosar, Buddy 44
Rose, Pete 140, 150, 161, 163, 169, 182
Roseboro, Johnny 108, 116
Rosen, Al 71, 73, 74, 136
Rowe, Preacher 61
Rowe, Schoolboy 32
Ruffing, Red 10, 24
Runnels, Pete 92, 114
Rush, Bob 64
Russell, Bill 152
Ruth, Babe 2, 5, 7, 147, 158

Ryan, Connie 41
Ryan, Nolan 152, 164, 171

S

Sain, Johnny 46, 48, 51
Sambito, Joe 174
Sanford, Jack 84
Sanguillen, Manny 149
Santo, Ron 119, 123, 126
Sauer, Hank 64, 66
Sawyer, Eddie 61, 63
Sax, Steve 185, 187, 197
Schmidt, Mike 171, 173, 178, 181
Schmitz, Johnny 51
Schoendienst, Red 39, 57, 60, 77, 85, 133, 136
Schumacher, Hal 11
Schwall, Don 108
Scott, George 166
Scott, Mike 195, 197
Seaver, Tom 131, 140, 150, 164, 178
Selkirk, George 24
Seminick, Andy 55
Sewell, Rip 2, 41, 42, 44, 45
Shea, Frank 46, 48
Short, Chris 122, 131
Shotten, Burt 57, 60, 64
Siebert, Sonny 128
Sievers, Roy 108
Simmons, Al 7, 8
Simmons, Curt 64, 67, 82, 84, 85
Simmons, Ted 181
Singer, Bill 136, 150
Singleton, Ken 181
Skinner, Bob 88, 96
Skowron, Bill 84, 96
Slaughter, Enos 39, 51, 57, 60, 67, 69, 70
Smith, Mayo 136, 138
Smith, Reggie 157, 158, 169
Snider, Duke 60, 69, 73
Soto, Mario 182, 184, 185, 187, 188
Southworth, Billy 36, 39, 56
Spahn, Warren 46, 53, 67, 79, 81, 88, 106, 108
Speier, Chris 149
Spence, Stan 44, 48
Stanley, Bob 188
Stargell, Willie 123, 144
Staub, Rusty 161

212   *Index*

Steinbrenner, George 195
Stengel, Casey 57, 61, 64, 66, 67, 71, 73, 82, 85, 86, 91, 92, 93, 111, 128
Stenhouse, Dave 114
Stephens, Vern 39, 44
Stieb, Dave 177, 185, 188, 191
Stone, Dean 74
Stone, Steve 175
Stoneman, Bill 149
Stottlemyre, Mel 128, 136
Sullivan, Frank 75, 77, 78
Sutter, Bruce 170, 174, 177
Sutton, Don 147, 150, 152, 158, 164, 166

T

Tanana, Frank 161, 164
Tebbetts, Birdie 51, 53
Temple, Johnny 79, 81, 93
Terry, Bill 8, 10, 13, 17, 23
Terry, Paul 7
Thomas, Frank 86
Tiant, Luis 133, 156
Tobin, Jim 41
Torre, Joe 123
Traynor, Pie 7
Triandos, Gil 91
Trillo, Manny 187
Trucks, Virgil 56
Turley, Bob 86, 88
Twitchell, Ed 150

V

Valenzuela, Fernando 178, 189, 197
Vander Meer, Johnny 23, 36, 59
Vaughan, Arky 13, 20, 24, 27, 30, 136
Vernon, Mickey 51, 75
Versalles, Zoilo 123
Virdon, Bill 175
Virgil, Ozzie 194
Vosmik, Joe 13

W

Wagner, Leon 113–14, 116–17

Wakefield, Dick 36
Walker, Bill 11
Walker, Dixie 39, 41
Walker, Jerry 93, 95
Walters, Bucky 27, 32, 39, 41
Waner, Paul 7
Ward, Arch 1
Warneke, Lonnie 5, 10, 16
Washington, Claudell 158
Weaver, Earl 140, 144, 147, 175
Welch, Bob 170, 175, 177
Wertz, Vic 63, 84
West, Max 27
West, Sammy 19
Whitaker, Lou 195, 197
White, Bill 92, 106, 108, 119
White, Frank 178, 197
Wilhelm, Hoyt 92, 104
Williams, Billy 122, 125, 143, 149
Williams, Derrick 178
Williams, Dick 133, 153, 156, 157, 192
Williams, Stan 100
Williams, Ted 2, 19, 30, 32, 33, 39, 42, 44, 45, 49, 55, 60, 70, 75, 81, 82, 84, 88, 91, 92, 98, 102, 120, 128, 136, 158
Wills, Maury 108, 111, 126, 128
Wilson, Jim 79, 81
Winfield, Dave 169, 171, 173, 177, 182, 187, 189, 192, 195
Wise, Rick 150
Wood, Wilbur 149
Wyatt, John 122
Wyatt, Whitlow 27, 32
Wynegar, Butch 166
Wynn, Early 75, 82, 84, 88, 89, 93
Wynn, Jimmy 154, 157, 158, 160

Y

Yastrzemski, Carl 138, 142, 144, 158, 174
Yawkey, Tom 32
York, Rudy 23, 33, 36, 39
Young, Matt 188

Z

Zisk, Richie 164, 166, 167